FOREWORD

SINCE THE INCEPTION of the Formula 1 world championship in 1950, Autosport has been there to witness the greatest drives by the sport's best drivers.

From Juan Manuel Fangio to Jim Clark, through Ayrton Senna to Lewis Hamilton – their fantastic exploits behind the wheel have been brought to life in our pages.

Now we have gathered together the finest performances of the most legendary drivers in one book. The cars have evolved massively since Fangio locked horns with Alberto Ascari and his contemporaries in the fifties, but the passion and excitement – not to mention the technological challenge – remains as fervent as ever.

These selected races demonstrate the finest achievements of 25 post-war greats. These are the races in which they demonstrated their driving genius by either overcoming adversity or simply being in a class apart from their rivals.

The reports also showcase the writing skills of our finest correspondents through the generations; from Autosport founder Gregor Grant, to the poetic Pete Lyons, via the lavish Nigel Roebuck to Mark Hughes's current analytical brilliance.

The original copy has been reproduced, but the design of the reports has been adjusted for production reasons. The photography comes from LAT's fabulous archive and perfectly encapsulates the drama, glamour and bravery of these time-honoured heroes.

So indulge yourself in the best our fantastic sport has to offer.

ANDREW VAN DER BURGT
Editor, Autosport

NEW MICHELIN Energy Saver.
The tyre that saves fuel* mile after mile.
1/2

CONTENTS

MIKE HAWTHORN | 1953 FRENCH GP |
The RACE of the CENTURY
Only two seasons before he had been racing in a pre-war Riley at Goodwood. Now Mike Hawthorn was a works Ferrari driver going wheel to wheel with the world champions – and beating them
BY GREGOR GRANT

Fangio Still Fabulous!

NON-STOP CLARK AT SPA

SHELL
SHELL
Graham Hill's GREATEST

AYRTON WALKS ON WATER
John Player Special

LEWIS HAMILTON | 2008 BRITISH GP |
Hamilton STANDS TALL
After two no-scores and a media backlash, the McLaren man desperately needed a top result. He did much more than that, silencing his critics with one of the greatest wet-weather drives
BY MARK HUGHES
Santander
Abbey
Santander
vodafone

Hamilton STANDS TALL

After two no-scores and a media backlash, the McLaren man desperately needed a top result. He did much more than that, silencing his critics with one of the greatest wet-weather drives

BY MARK HUGHES

LEWIS HAMILTON | 2008 BRITISH GP | JULY 6 McLAREN MP4-23

QUALIFYING

McLAREN'S AERO UPGRADES, including a four-plane front wing, meshed perfectly with its aggressive use of the tyres on a day that Ferrari struck trouble, and Heikki Kovalainen took maximum advantage to secure his first pole position.

"The car just feels fantastic at the moment and it got better throughout each session," he reported after going 0.5 seconds clear of anyone else.

Lewis Hamilton did not manage to extract the car's potential here. After throwing away his first Q3 run with a gravelly off on the exit of Priory, he got crossed up out of Abbey on his final run and was much more circumspect through the scene of his previous off. He also dropped 0.4sec to Heikki between Stowe and the exit of Bridge, more than a heavier fuel load could account for. All of this left him fourth.

Mark Webber slotted his Red Bull into second – his first front-row start with the team. This was no light-fuel glory run either, Webber being fuelled just one lap lighter than Kovalainen.

The apparent root of Ferrari's problem was its familiar trait of not getting its front tyres to work quickly enough. Through Copse and Maggotts/Becketts it was generally unresponsive and understeery, and the more the team tried to dial this out, the more the car suffered power oversteer through the slow turns. The car also seemed more sensitive to the crosswinds than did the McLaren. Kimi Räikkönen was able to qualify only third, with Felipe Massa down in ninth after not getting out in time for a second Q3 run. This was because of a delay fitting his right-rear wheel, due to a faulty fixing on the wheel gun. The Ferraris had the same fuel load as Hamilton's McLaren.

Robert Kubica failed to set a lap in Q3. Under braking for Stowe on his first flyer, the BMW locked up and slewed sideways. Suspecting that he had a puncture, he trailed back to the pits, but no tyre problem was found. A fault in the differential was suspected and he didn't get back out, leaving him 10th and making Nick Heidfeld the team's leading representative with fifth-fastest time. He'd trailed Kubica by only two-hundredths in Q2 and was very relieved that he seemed to have overcome his season-long struggle to bring his tyres promptly up to temperature.

Renault's Fernando Alonso was in sixth place, just a few hundredths slower than Heidfeld, albeit with a couple of laps' less fuel. Fernando was in aggressive form throughout practice, hustling the R28. Team-mate Nelson Piquet scraped into Q3, a couple of tenths off Alonso, then proceeded to qualify a solid seventh, this time 0.4sec away, half of that with fuel load.

Toro Rosso was building on its recent progress and Sebastian Vettel did a great job to qualify for Q3, where he was loaded up with a heavy fuel load. His eighth place there was flattered by the travails of Massa and Kubica, but it was still an excellent effort. Team-mate Sébastien Bourdais – very quick in wet practice – was never as happy as Vettel with his balance in the dry and lined up 13th, 0.4sec off Vettel in Q2.

Red Bull's David Coulthard lined up 11th for his final British GP.

The Toyotas were not as competitive on the bumpy Silverstone as at the billiard-smooth Magny-Cours, the difference in track characteristics seemingly a major factor. Jarno Trulli opted to set up the car in the expectation of a wet race, leaving him 14th, two places behind team-mate Timo Glock.

But at least Toyota was in better form than Williams or Honda. Only Kazuki Nakajima made it out of Q1, qualifying 15th. Nico Rosberg's car was suffering terrible handling out of the slower corners and he was stuck back in 18th behind the

Mark Webber's Red Bull and Heikki Kovalainen's McLaren are to the fore, but hidden in the pack, waiting to pounce, is Hamilton (above); a new set of inters for Hamilton proves crucial (below)

Hondas, both Rubens Barrichello (16th) and Jenson Button (17th) complaining of front tyres that were not coming up to temperature.

Adrian Sutil and Giancarlo Fisichella brought up the rear in the revised Force Indias, just a tenth or so adrift of the Hondas and Williams.

RACE

There are technical reasons that go some way towards explaining how Lewis Hamilton pulled off such a stunning wet-weather victory and why his winning margin was over a minute. They are to do with tyre choice and performance, wrong calls by Ferrari, etc. But they don't account for everything. The gap between them and what transpired is only explained by the human factor – and a drive of such virtuosity that it will in time be spoken of in the same breath as Barcelona '96 or Donington '93. Hamilton produced a mesmerising performance, locked in a groove that left his rivals spinning all around him.

Lewis's second stint was sensational. His first was merely exceptional. Heavy rain earlier in the day had left the circuit glistening and treacherous. The rain had stopped for now, but was widely expected to return even before the first stops. Thus everyone started the race on inters. Extreme wets would have been better in the early laps, but it was expected the inters would soon clear enough water to bring them into their ideal range.

Hamilton took the lap to the dummy grid at a near crawl, trying to pick out where the standing water was. From the grid to Maggotts/Becketts it was only patchily wet, but thereafter it got worse,

and from Abbey to Woodcote it was very wet and super-slippery; Räikkönen had a wild oversteering moment exiting Abbey – and the race hadn't even started. Off the dummy grid, Hamilton experimented with his starting technique. The voice of race engineer Phil Prew crackled over the radio. He'd watched the start from the live data on his screen, monitored the revs and wheelspin, and suggested an alteration for the start proper. "No," replied Lewis calmly, "the start was good."

He proved as much when the lights went out. Mellow, low revs bring the engine gently on the cam without alerting the rear tyres, and in an instant he was slicing up the inside of Webber's front-row Red Bull and sitting it out with Heikki into Copse, the rest somewhere in the enormous ball of spray. For a moment it looked like Lewis had grabbed the lead but by his own admission he backed off too early. Kovalainen hung on gamely around the outside, the longer but faster way around and, as they came to funnel-in on the exit, Heikki was determined not to lift. Hamilton's front-left actually rubbed Kovalainen's right-rear, both McLarens twitching raggedly on oversteer with Lewis ducking out of the spray ball to run alongside at over 160mph, getting back into line behind as Maggotts/Becketts loomed out of the gloom. This was magnificent, gloves-off duelling.

Räikkönen had a good view of the wayward silver cars from a few metres back, with Webber getting as close as he could to the Ferrari exiting Becketts, trying to get a run on it as they entered Hangar Straight. In the blinding spray, Webber got his right-rear onto the white line of Chapel and in an instant the Red Bull was spinning through 180 degrees. There followed a terrifying couple of seconds as he faced the oncoming 16 cars, hoping that they could see him through the spray. They all avoided him, some probably without even realising it. He restarted last and proceeded to slice through the lower half of the field, vying with the leaders as fastest man on the track. But the mistake had cost him dearly, losing over 20sec right there and ultimately a lot more. He would finish 10th.

Massa was another first-lap spinner, entering Abbey chicane in seventh place and leaving it backwards, restarting ahead only of Webber. It was to be the first of five spins for the man who entered this race as world championship leader. Behind the Massa incident, David Coulthard nudged his

Hamilton takes the lead from team-mate Kovalainen (below); Robert Kubica will make his first mistake of the year (above)

Red Bull into the sister Toro Rosso of Sebastian Vettel and in perfect formation they beached themselves in the gravel trap – an inauspicious final home race for DC.

The two McLarens screamed across the line ahead of Räikkönen, Heidfeld's BMW, the battling Renaults of Piquet and Alonso, then Jarno Trulli's Toyota harried intensely by Kubica's BMW. Drivers were sawing at their wheels, cars at all sorts of angles through the slower turns, wheels side by side in the spray. Alonso passed both Piquet and Heidfeld on the second lap to go fourth, his tyres seeming to come on song faster than theirs as he was briefly the quickest man on the track.

As the McLarens completed their second lap, Hamilton got a better exit out of Luffield and moved inside of Kovalainen, their profiles overlapping as they raced through the Woodcote kink towards the pit straight. Not many cars had been over the piece of Tarmac Lewis found himself on and the standing water there flicked him into a big twitch. Realising he'd almost taken himself and his team-mate out right there, he tucked meekly back in.

But it was clear that Heikki was holding up Lewis and on lap five the leader stayed hard over to the left as they approached Stowe, making it clear that Lewis could have the place. He needed no second invitation, sliced ahead and pulled away at 0.5sec per lap.

It might have been interpreted as team play, with Heikki assigned the job of holding Räikkönen at bay while Hamilton escaped, but it was nothing of the sort; Heikki was struggling. After nine laps he was struggling even more, his rear tyres giving up the ghost after repeated slow-corner oversteer.

"It was clear that Heikki was giving his rears a harder time than Lewis was in the wet," reported McLaren's Martin Whitmarsh afterwards, "whereas in the dry earlier in the weekend Lewis was taking more out of his fronts than Heikki."

Hamilton's high-momentum technique in the wet meant there was less acceleration to do on the exits, less drama – though that was a relative term. He had plenty to keep him occupied. The demands of the track in this state were mentally taxing enough but Hamilton faced an extra challenge:

'Umbrellas were coming out all around... The rain had arrived, falling from clouds black and ugly enough to totally discredit Ferrari's weather forecasters'

his visor was repeatedly misting up.

"No matter what I did, the right-hand side just kept fogging over. I was having to lift it between turns one and two and clean the inside, then put it down for Maggotts/Becketts, then open it and clean it again before Stowe. I was doing that every lap."

Lewis was very aware, too, of the need not to hurt his tyres, one of the lessons of China last year having been learned. "I think I did a better job than ever of managing the tyres," he said.

There was a lot to be thinking about and he would soon need some extra discipline, too, for a quick Kovalainen spin at the treacherous Abbey chicane on lap nine allowed Räikkönen to pass for second. From there, the Ferrari man began to hunt down Hamilton, his 6sec lead being totally wiped out over the next 10 laps. "I think we were set up better than them [McLaren] for the dry," said Räikkönen afterwards, "because as the track dried we improved quicker than him."

The track drying was a relative term, for they were still around 13sec off a dry-weather time and there was no question of whether to stay on inters as the first stops loomed. The only question was whether to leave the existing inters on or fit new ones. If you were a McLaren or Ferrari strategist your answer would depend upon what your weather forecasters were telling you: McLaren's were telling it that a rain cloud was on its way imminently; Ferrari's were saying there was going to be only a brief, light shower.

Kovalainen was the first of the leaders to pit, at the end of lap 19. A new set of inters were fitted and he was on his way. Two laps later Hamilton and Räikkönen pitted as one. The Ferrari crew left Kimi's existing set of tyres on and refuelled him for 7.5sec. McLaren got their man onto new rubber and fuelled him for around 1sec longer. It allowed them to exit still in front of the Ferrari. From this moment on, Ferrari's race was doomed – something that was being strongly suggested even as they completed their out-laps – umbrellas were coming out all around the circuit. The rain had arrived, falling from clouds black and ugly enough to totally discredit Ferrari's weather forecasters.

Felipe Massa treads carefully over the super-slick surface. The Ferrari man will spin, spin, spin, spin and spin again. Phew

KONI
50 years of Formula 1
This year, KONI will celebrate half a century of Formula 1 expertise. Since 1958 we have experience in developing technologies for winners. Like our latest shock absorber invention, FSDactive, helping Vodafone McLaren Mercedes to the top ranks of the competition and your car to improved performance all the way. Don't you think it's time to switch tracks?
KONI
VODAFONE McLAREN MERCEDES
OFFICIAL SUPPLIER
www.koni.com
50 years F1
ITT
Engineered for life

Sébastien Bourdais' Toro Rosso sends up a spray of water (above); a jubilant Hamilton sprays the champers (right)

On a drying track worn inters are significantly faster than new ones, the worn tread blocks putting significantly more rubber surface area on the road. On a wet track, however, the worn grooves of used intermediates don't clear much water and make them much slower. And this track was suddenly very wet. Remarkably, it barely seemed to make any difference to Hamilton's speed, his new rubber and superb feel, and the excellent balance of the McLaren, allowing him to continue at about the same pace he'd been going before his stop.

Räikkönen, on his worn rubber, was losing 5/6sec per lap initially, even more as the tyres then lost temperature, too. From being hot on Hamilton's tail as they'd pitted, he was 21sec behind just five laps later. "We made a mistake with the tyre choice," said Räikkönen. "Otherwise we had a chance to win the race."

The rain increased dramatically on the 24th lap. Kovalainen, on his fresh rubber, was now all over the back of the Ferrari and being badly held up. So much so that Heidfeld, also on fresh inters, was soon right with them. As the gripless Kimi ran out wide at Luffield 2 on the 26th lap, so Heikki was able to nip inside. But he was slow exiting on his compromised line and Heidfeld was able to pass the Ferrari and the McLaren in one move! Nick was second, but almost half a minute behind the remarkable Hamilton.

Given the huge chunks of time Räikkönen was losing, it was difficult to understand why Ferrari did not bring him in for new rubber. He was surrendering up to 8sec per lap to Hamilton and could have paid for the extra pitstop in around four laps on new tyres. Instead they just hoped – in vain – that the rain would ease. Renault, in much the same situation with Alonso, elected to correct their error of having left him on his existing tyres at his first stop and stopped him again just six laps later. This dropped him out of immediate contention but would pay back ultimately. This left Piquet – who had changed to fresh tyres at his first stop – in fifth and chasing down Räikkönen, but being caught by Kubica, who would pass him.

'The extremes would be probably 10sec faster, so even if you had to come back in to chang e them, you'd pay for your stop within about three laps'

Once he had been passed by Heidfeld's BMW, Kovalainen was left behind at a great rate. His rear tyres had given up again. Only the fact that Kimi was behind him and struggling even more, and thereby protecting him, allowed him to stay out.

Ferrari tried to patch up their torn strategy by running Räikkönen just as long as it took to get him into the window where they could fuel him to the end. He made the stop at the end of the 30th lap, half-distance. Four laps later Kovalainen did the same, rejoining just ahead of Räikkönen and behind seventh-placed Alonso.

A lap after Heikki's stop, the rain intensified. The track was awash. Cars started flying off the road, not least leader Hamilton at Abbey. With his misted visor he had become disoriented, and had to cut across the grass rather than spin. He still had a lead of 25sec over Heidfeld and so carried on. Kubica, now a distant third, repeated Hamilton's error – and escape – on the same lap.

As this was happening, Barrichello, his Honda fuelled heavy and running in 10th, had an off at Club and almost hit the barriers. He realised his inters were just too worn for this level of rain. He made the call over the radio: "Get the extreme wets ready". It was an inspired shout – and totally his. "I just realised that extremes would be probably 10sec faster in those conditions, so even if you then had to come back in to change them back, you'd pay for your stop within about three laps."

He still had plenty of fuel on board as he came in for his extremes – which was just as well. There was a problem with the Honda rig and they couldn't get any fuel in. This delayed not only Rubens but also Button, who was queued right behind him

and waiting for his own extreme wets.

Hamilton pitted a lap later and there was some speculation that he too might be fitted with extremes. "We considered it," said Whitmarsh, "but in the position we were, the low-risk option was the flexibility of inters." As Lewis was making his in-lap, he was being caught hand over fist by the lapped Barrichello, who simply drove around the McLaren at Stowe as if it were standing still.

Lewis began lapping on his fresh inters in the 1m44-46s region, way quicker than anyone else on inters. But it was around 3sec slower than Barrichello who, with his huge grip advantage, soon had himself up to second, albeit knowing he had another stop to make for the fuel. Button had lost a great opportunity of a similar performance by getting caught out by standing water at Bridge shortly after his stop.

A lap later Kubica suffered a similar fate at Abbey – and thereby lost third place and the chance of retaking the lead of the championship. It was his first significant mistake of the season.

Heidfeld remained Mr Consistent in third place, later to regain second when Barrichello made his third stop on lap 46 for fuel and a switch back to inters now that the rain had eased off once more. Rubens dropped only one place, though, such had been the margin his extreme wets had bought him over the battling Trulli (yet to make his second stop), Alonso and Kovalainen. Räikkönen had fallen from this group with a couple of spins, which when added to Massa's excursions, brought the total number of Ferrari rotations to eight!

Kovalainen passed Alonso for fifth on the 46th lap, but spun it away again a couple of laps later, Fernando and Räikkönen flashing by Heikki as he rejoined. Shortly after they were all lapped by Hamilton. The team had been requesting he slow down. But Lewis was in a groove all his own. "If I go any slower I'll lose concentration," he told them. So they just stood back and watched, enjoying the show with 90,000 delirious fans.

Trulli finally made his second stop, leaving Alonso fourth but under big pressure from Kimi and Heikki. Räikkönen was all over the Renault and finally found a way by entering Stowe, leaving Fernando, whose inters were past it, to try to fend off the McLaren. Alonso defended superbly and it was only when Kovalainen ran wide into Brooklands that it inadvertently allowed the Finn to find a way through into Luffield with just two laps to go. Kazuki Nakajima's Williams was next in line to attack the floundering Renault, but he was denied a chance to do so by being passed into Vale for seventh on the last lap by Trulli.

This frantic late action was all conducted a lap behind the dominant Hamilton. Heidfeld followed across the line 68sec later, with a delighted Rubens third, the last unlapped runner. Considering the disastrous strategy calls and spins, Räikkönen was lucky to take fourth. He also set his sixth straight fastest lap, one shy of Alberto Ascari's 1950s record.

Hamilton arrived here under pressure. He left as the joint championship leader. But his greatest achievement was the most dazzling display of driving genius we've seen for years. ■

RESULTS

60 LAPS (191.604 MILES)

1	Lewis HAMILTON	McLaren MP4-23	1h39m09.440s
2	Nick HEIDFELD	BMW F1.08	1h40m17.517s
3	Rubens BARRICHELLO	Honda RA108	1h40m31.713s
4	Kimi RAIKKONEN	Ferrari F2008	59 laps
5	Heikki KOVALAINEN	McLaren MP4-23	59 laps
6	Fernando ALONSO	Renault R28	59 laps

WINNING SPEED 115.926mph

FASTEST LAP RAIKKONEN, 1m32.150s (124.797mph)

POLE POSITION KOVALAINEN, 1m21.049s (141.890mph)

LAP LEADERS KOVALAINEN 1-4; HAMILTON 5-21, 23-60; HEIDFELD 22

MIKE HAWTHORN | 1953 FRENCH GP | JULY 5
FERRARI 500

The RACE of the CENTURY

Only two seasons before he had been racing in a pre-war Riley at Goodwood. Now Mike Hawthorn was a works Ferrari driver going wheel to wheel with the world champions – and beating them

BY GREGOR GRANT

MIKE HAWTHORN SAVED the day for Scuderia Ferrari after being involved for more than half the distance of 60 laps of the new Gueux circuit at Reims in a fantastic battle with Juan Manuel Fangio (Maserati). On 10 separate occasions their cars came past the pits dead level; the Argentinian did all he knew to snatch victory, but Hawthorn drove an inspired race, and finished one second ahead.

José Froilán González (Maserati) led the race for 28 laps but had to stop for fuel when he had 24 secs in hand from Alberto Ascari (Ferrari). Despite his pit-stop, the 'Prairie Bull' came through to take third place, almost catching Fangio on the line.

The crowd were so excited that Hawthorn was mobbed when he came in to receive his victor's laurels. It was a proud moment when *God Save the Queen* was played for the third British driver to win a *Grand Prix de l'ACF* – the late Sir Henry Segrave (Sunbeam) won in 1923 and W Williams (Bugatti) in 1928 and 1929.

RACE

Owing to the disqualification of the Maglioli/Carini 4.5 Ferrari in the Twelve Hours sports car race, there were rumours that Scuderia Ferrari had packed up and gone home in high dudgeon. Then came stories of an intention to start, but only for a sufficient number of laps to fulfil their contract. As it happened, all four cars were unloaded and there was no more talk of any trouble.

Reg Parnell's name mysteriously appeared in the programme with a Connaught, and he was also credited in the local papers with doing several practice laps on the Friday evening. He was certainly a real Invisible Man – so invisible in fact that he wasn't in Reims at all. The two fuel-injection Connaughts were driven by Roy Salvadori and B Bira. The other British entries were Bob Gerard (Cooper-Bristol), Ken Wharton (Cooper-Bristol), Stirling Moss (Cooper-Alta), Peter Collins (HWM), Lance Macklin (HWM), and a third HWM driven by Giraud-Cabantous.

The start itself was unbelievable. So soon as Charles Faroux unfurled his flag, there were hoots and hisses from a section of the crowd which was not too pleased with the sports car-race disqualification. However, Faroux is too old a stager to be affected overmuch, and he carried on as if nothing were the matter.

Down went the flag and González rocketed from the third row to draw away from Fangio and Bonetto as the field of 24 cars shrieked past the tribunes and under the new Dunlop Bridge en route for the reconstructed Gueux section. They were out of sight until onlookers could pick up the flashes of red as the cars rushed down Garenne Straight towards the Thillois right-hander. Sure enough, it was González in front, leading by a couple of seconds from a tight bunch consisting of Ascari, Villoresi, Fangio, Hawthorn, Bonetto, Marimón and Farina, with Bira also in the picture; Maserati, Ferrari, Ferrari, Maserati, Ferrari, Maserati, Maserati, Ferrari and Connaught – they went past in a solid mass of red, relieved by Marimón's

100
DUNLOP

A bemused Fangio tours in. All season he had been trying to give Maserati its first world championship GP victory. It was Alberto Ascari who usually denied him, but on this occasion it had been a young Brit...

blue-and-yellow car and Bira's green one.

Lap two and González had 4secs over his pursuers. Then began a titanic struggle for second featuring Villoresi, Ascari and Hawthorn, with Farina and Fangio just behind. Bonetto dropped back after overdoing things at Thillois. Harry Schell put a rod through the side of his Gordini; this left Trintignant, Mières and Behra to carry the flag for 'The Sorcerer'. Salvadori's engine cut out, and he retired after two laps when in 13th place, but Bira was going like a train in the other Connaught.

There was no stopping González. Preferring to run with half-full tanks and come in to refuel about half-distance, the Argentinian was setting about piling on the biggest possible lead. On lap four, Villoresi, Hawthorn and Ascari went through wheel to wheel, 5secs behind González. Farina still headed Fangio, whose protege Marimón was keeping on the tail of the master, and drawing away from Trintignant. De Graffenried (Maserati) was leading Bonetto and Bira, whilst Moss was battling with Behra and Mières. The last-named went out with a broken back axle.

With González out in front, the fierce struggle behind never let up for a moment. The Maserati did the first five laps at an average speed of over 112mph. Fangio began to close on Farina, whilst Ascari, Hawthorn and Villoresi continually chopped and changed their places – less than half a second separating all three. After eight laps, the first seven cars lapped the tail-enders, and on lap nine Macklin's HWM stopped at the pits with clutch failure. Moss appeared to be having trouble changing gear, and began to drop back; he was beginning to be overhauled by Gerard and Wharton.

After 10 laps, the leader was 7secs ahead, and the top 10 positions were as follows:

1, González (Maserati), 27mins 32.8secs, 181.814km/h. (112.98mph); 2, Hawthorn (Ferrari); 3, Ascari (Ferrari); 4, Villoresi (Ferrari); 5, Farina (Ferrari); 6, Fangio (Maserati); 7, Marimón (Maserati); 8, Trintignant (Gordini); 9, de Graffenried (Maserati); 10, Bonetto (Maserati)

Four laps later came another blow to Gordini. Trintignant coasted in and retired with transmission bothers, leaving Jean Behra as sole survivor – in 11th place. González kept increasing his lead, and at 20 laps had 18secs advantage, with the four Ferraris still battling behind. However, Fangio thought it about time that he should get amongst the circus act, and swept past Farina under the Dunlop Bridge, only to be retaken into Thillois.

Lap 24 saw a most extraordinary sight. After González went through, the entire group of Ascari, Villoresi, Hawthorn, Fangio, Farina and Marimón – all trying to pass each other – hurtled by the tribunes. Even the Maserati and Ferrari pit staffs were shaken, and one felt sorry for the respective team managers attempting to convey positions to the drivers. Fangio then went to town, and whistled past Farina, Villoresi and Ascari in that order, to sit on Hawthorn's tail. González signalled he was coming in to refuel, and Fangio acknowledged a mysterious legend on the board with a wave of his hand. On lap 29, the leader came in, and was away in about 28secs, dropping to sixth place. On the same lap, Villoresi did everything wrong at Thillois, and Farina gave the revolver's sign.

One lap later, Fangio, Ascari and Hawthorn started a tremendous dogfight for the lead. Fangio held it for a couple of tours, then Hawthorn for three more. On lap 35 they went past the pits absolutely wheel-to-wheel, and Farina had managed to edge ahead of Ascari. González was pressing Marimón, and Villoresi had dropped to seventh place. Further back came Bonetto, de Graffenried, Behra, Louis Chiron (OSCA), Rosier (Ferrari) and Gerard (Cooper-Bristol). Moss was still circulating, but Wharton had given up after a lengthy pit-stop, after covering 17 tours. Peter Collins (HWM), Yves Giraud-Cabantous (HWM) and Johnny Claes (Connaught) were also still in the race, but Bayol's OSCA had been retired after 18 laps and Bira's Connaught, with a broken differential, after 28.

'Ascari, Villoresi, Fangio, Hawthorn, Farina and Marimón hurtled by. Even the Maserati and Ferrari pit staffs were shaken'

The crowd had eyes for nothing else other than the superb Ferrari-Maserati argument. On lap 38, Hawthorn had nearly 2secs over Fangio, whilst the incredible González had not only overtaken Marimón and Farina but had shrieked past an astonished Ascari. The lap record was taking a battering: Ascari did 2mins 42.5secs on his 16th lap; four tours later, Fangio knocked off the odd half-second; four more, and Farina had whittled it down to 2mins 41.6secs. Next time round, Fangio cut half a second off for an 186.531km/h average.

Marimón, in sixth place, came into his pit with a burst oil-cooler chucking out lubricant all over the place. Whilst this car was being fixed, Bonetto

WHAT HAPPENED NEXT...

Fangio finally ended Ferrari's long unbeaten run, at a thrilling Italian Grand Prix, another race decided at the last corner of the last lap. This was also the concluding GP of the interim 2-litre 'Formula 2' era.

...who is mobbed by his mechanics and the crowd after an epic victory. Five years later Hawthorn would become the first British world champion. And just months after that he would be killed in a road crash

coasted in to retire. Chiron stopped on the circuit, and was reported to be pushing his blue OSCA.

The battle at the front continued unabated. Farina swept past González, but was repassed at Garenne, with Ascari trying desperately to force his way through. Fangio and Hawthorn kept up their epic ding-dong, and the crowd all round the circuit were almost berserk with excitement. The Argentinian was bringing all his vast experience into play, but could make no impression on that cool, green-clad figure in the Ferrari. Everyone seemed to sense that Fangio had met another master of motor racing. This was certainly Hawthorn's hour, and Enzo Ferrari must have blessed the day he signed up the 'Farnham Flyer'.

Mere words cannot describe the closing laps. Never before has such a desperate struggle been waged on a Grand Prix circuit. Ascari, with his reputation at stake, went all out to get ahead of González, but José Froilán would have none of it. Farina was still there, but Villoresi had dropped back considerably. Behra's Gordini was wuffling round on five cylinders; Chiron was loudly cheered for managing to push-start his ailing OSCA which toured round sounding like a 125cc two-stroke; Bob Gerard (Cooper-Bristol) was easily first of the remaining green machines.

In the Ferrari pit Ugolini was definitely foxed by González's earlier refuelling stop. The puzzle for the 'Prancing Horse' was — could Fangio carry on non-stop? All four Ferraris could go the distance, but the Maserati's tank capacity was not revealed. Possibly Fangio's comparatively slow opening laps were due to the weight of fuel he was carrying.

With five laps to go, Fangio came past a wheel-width ahead of Hawthorn, but they went round chopping and changing. Four left to go, and Fangio weaved as Hawthorn tried to pass. Mike took to the grass momentarily in front of the new timing box, recovered and was level as the cars disappeared under the Dunlop Bridge. González was holding Ascari, and Farina had dropped back a trifle.

The excitement was indescribable. Everyone was on his (or her) feet, and in the tribunes scores of field glasses were levelled towards Thillois.

"C'est Hawthorn — Non, c'est Fangio!" howled the PA announcer. Up in the Press tribune the Argentinian commentator was practically in a state of collapse. After all, he'd been jabbering non-stop for over two hours, and could scarcely obtain any breathing space.

Three more laps. Again the cars were dead-level past the timing box, as were those of González and Ascari. Hard-headed journalists, veterans of dozens of *grandes épreuves*, threw nonchalance to the winds and became madly excited onlookers. One gentleman went so far as to tear up his notes, stand on his hat and finally fall over his desk.

Faroux unfurled his flag. Two laps to go. Surely this couldn't go on? Over in the timing box, the photo finish equipment was ready — and it looked certain to be needed.

The last lap: for the 10th time the leaders dead-heated over the line, and González led Ascari by about a centimetre. Farina panted on behind, whilst Villoresi was practically exhausted.

None will ever forget that finish. At Thillois, Hawthorn edged ahead, and the Ferrari held its slender lead down the straight, with Fangio crouching in his car to try to get every ounce of speed out of the Maserati. But Hawthorn's getaway at Thillois gave him that little bit of advantage... Down went the flag, with the Ferrari about 40 yards in front.

But before everyone could collapse completely, there was another terrific thrill. Making a last-minute bid, González left Ascari standing out of Thillois and tore down the straight at such a pace that he all but caught Fangio on the line. In this 'Race of the Century', only 7.6secs separated the first five cars.

Maseratis so nearly toppled the Ferraris, but with second and third places — and the lap record — they can afford to feel confident of the future.

Mike Hawthorn emerged from this race as a real champion. He alone kept Ferrari from defeat. Obviously it was a case of every man for himself, and *'Le Papillon'* took his chance and proved to the racing world that he ranks with the best post-war drivers. ■

RESULTS

60 LAPS (311.195 MILES)

1	Mike HAWTHORN	Ferrari 500	2h44m18.60s
2	Juan FANGIO	Maserati A6GCM	2h44m19.60s
3	Froilán GONZALEZ	Maserati A6GCM	2h44m20.00s
4	Alberto ASCARI	Ferrari 500	2h44m23.20s
5	Giuseppe FARINA	Ferrari 500	2h45m26.20s

WINNING SPEED 113.637mph

FASTEST LAP FANGIO and ASCARI, 2m41.10s (115.901mph)

POLE POSITION FANGIO, 2m41.20s (115.829mph)

LAP LEADERS GONZALEZ 1-29; FANGIO 30-31, 35-36, 39-41, 45-47, 49-53, 55-56; HAWTHORN 32-34, 37-38, 42-44, 48, 54, 57-60

46

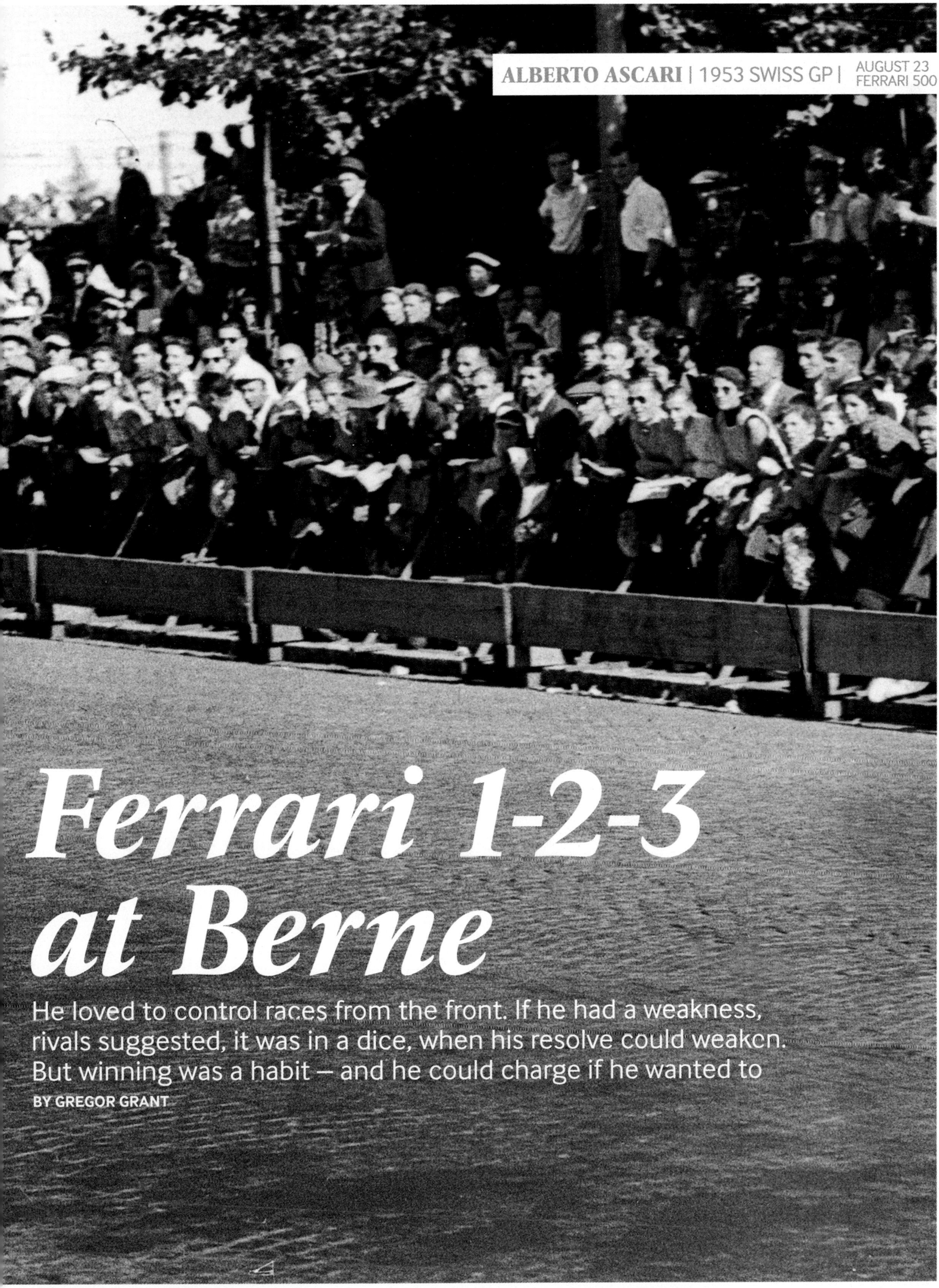

Ferrari 1-2-3 at Berne

He loved to control races from the front. If he had a weakness, rivals suggested, it was in a dice, when his resolve could weaken. But winning was a habit – and he could charge if he wanted to

BY GREGOR GRANT

ALBERTO ASCARI MADE certain of his second successive world title by winning the 13th Swiss Grand Prix, on the fine Bremgarten circuit last Sunday. He led for the first 40 laps of the 65-lap *grande épreuve*, lost 87.5 seconds for a plug change, but retook the lead from Farina 14 laps later, and went on to win more or less as he pleased. Fangio (Maserati) made a strong bid, but lost third gear and then changed cars with Bonetto at 10 laps. On his 29th lap the Argentinian dropped a valve and retired after producing a record smoke-screen. Ken Wharton drove a superb race to finish seventh with his Cooper-Bristol, although many bhp down on the powerful Italian cars. During his run, Ascari lapped in 2m 41.3s — nearly 101mph.

PRACTICE

There is every indication that a very large crowd will watch the *Grosser Preis der Schweiz* on the fast Berne circuit. Accommodation is almost impossible to find, for the attraction of seeing the world's fast road-racing motorcycle and car men is almost irresistible, and draws folk from every part of Europe.

Juan Manuel Fangio (Maserati) makes the best time in the first practice period with 2m 40.1s (163.698km/h), 0.6secs better than Alberto Ascari (Ferrari). Ken Wharton (Cooper-Bristol) is easily the best of the British contingent with 2m 51.5s (152.816km/h). Fred Wacker's Gordini crashes and the American is taken to hospital with superficial injuries.

Friday's practice is mostly in the wet. Mike Hawthorn's 2m 48.1s is 0.1sec faster than Ascari, and 3.4secs better than Fangio. Wharton is again top of the green cars with 3m 2.6s.

RACE

Expectations of a big crowd have certainly been realised. Over 75,000 people line this beautiful circuit in the Bremgarten forest. High speeds are anticipated for the GP, but folk who keep their eyes on both bikes and cars find it difficult to believe that the unsupercharged 2-litre cars will go much quicker than the fantastic 500cc 'fours' of Geoff Duke and Co.

As usual, the front row is an all-red affair, but the second rank has the blue Gordini of Trintignant, and the blue-and-yellow Maser of Marimón. Paul Frère has taken over Duncan Hamilton's HWM, but Bira's Connaught fails to materialise.

Fangio makes a wonderful start, followed by Ascari and Marimón. Farina's engine falters, but the German GP winner gets away without stalling. Last away is Scherrer in the third HWM.

Round they come on lap one, and it is Ascari in the lead by a car's length from Fangio, ahead of Hawthorn, Marimón, Villoresi, Bonetto, Farina, de Graffenried, Trintignant, Wharton and Macklin. Jacques Swaters crashes at the hairpin and is taken to hospital. Rosier also runs out of road, near Glasbrunnen Rampe, but walks back to the paddock.

Next time round and Ascari has pulled out a couple of seconds over Fangio, and the order is unchanged. Paul Frère's HWM goes out with engine maladies — a big-end bolt fractures — and a lap later Macklin has a 30secs pit-stop.

Already the race is sorting itself out into groups: the first consists of Ascari, Fangio, Hawthorn, Marimón, Farina, Bonetto and Farina; group two is Trintignant, de Graffenried, Lang and Wharton; then come the rest, headed by Behra and Landi.

Ascari is getting away from Fangio at the rate of a second per lap. Farina indulges in a spot of fist-shaking at Bonetto, and both close up trying to pass Villoresi. By lap five, the first six cars have lapped Scherrer's HWM and Peter Hirt's ex-Fischer Ferrari 'four'. Wharton is shadowing de Graffenried's Maserati, but Lang is making no impression on Trintignant. Landi's older-type Maserati 'six' is plainly outpaced.

Relentlessly Ascari piles on the seconds. Then Fangio loses his third gear and drops back considerably. Farina scuttles past Bonetto, Villoresi and Hawthorn to take third, and he is visibly closing on Fangio. But on lap 10 the Argentinian comes into the pits followed by team-mate Bonetto, and they switch cars.

Ascari leads Farina by 23.5secs, and one tour later Fangio comes in to have his nearside-front wheel changed — obviously a spot of kerb-clouting somewhere. This drops the Maserati to 10th, leaving Marimón to keep the 'Trident' in the picture.

Villoresi and Hawthorn go round in close company, and further back Lang cannot shake off Wharton, whose Cooper-Bristol is heading de Graffenried's Maserati.

With 15 laps gone, Ascari has lapped de Graffenried and will soon do the same to Wharton and Lang.

The position at 20 laps is:

1, Ascari (Ferrari), 55m 26.3s
2, Farina (Ferrari), 56m 1.7s
3, Hawthorn (Ferrari), 56m 24.2s
4, Villoresi (Ferrari,) 56m 37.5s
5, Marimón (Maserati), 56m 45.3s
6, Bonetto (Maserati); 7, Fangio (Maserati);
8, Trintignant (Gordini); 9, Wharton (Cooper);
10, de Graffenried (Maserati)

Villoresi has something jamming his steering and loses 83secs at the pits, dropping to sixth place. Ascari passes through behind Fangio, who is a lap in arrears.

On lap 25 both Villoresi and Wharton touch the fence at the hairpin but continue. Scherrer's HWM stops near the same place with ignition trouble and the Swiss begins to push his car to the pits. Trintignant laps his team-mate Behra.

Hawthorn and Marimón are having a superb

Juan Fangio makes the best start in his Maserati, but Ascari will be in the lead before the end of the opening lap

Ferrari's Luigi Villoresi gives chase to Felice Bonetto's Maserati, the car in which Fangio had started the race (below); Lance Macklin's HWM passes Jacques Swaters' crashed Ferrari (bottom)

WHAT HAPPENED NEXT...

Ascari shocked Ferrari by signing for Lancia. The latter's complex car would not be ready, however, until the closing stages of 1954. It might then have taken the fight to Mercedes in 1955 had not Ascari been killed testing a Ferrari sports car at Monza.

ding-dong behind Farina, while Fangio is doing everything he knows to make up for his lost time. Emerging from the hairpin, the Argentinian revs his motor sky-high and coming through to the tribunes there is an ominous clatter and his car begins laying a record smokescreen. So thick is the smoke that following drivers have to throttle down. Thus exits Juan Manuel at 30 laps.

At this stage Ascari leads by almost a minute from Farina, at 157.740km/h. Scherrer arrives exhausted at the pits and mechanics start changing the magneto.

Marimón is giving Hawthorn a battle, and the blue-and-yellow car sweeps ahead on lap 33, just as Villoresi signals to his pit for water. That prang at the hairpin must have started a radiator leak. Macklin calls in at the pits with a smoking exhaust, and remains there for a long time, finally retiring with an even more smoking exhaust when he tries to restart.

Marimón's effort in passing Hawthorn gives him the best lap so far of 2m 45.7s (158.165km/h). Previous fastest was Farina with 2m 47.2s. Villoresi loses nearly a minute filling up with water. Behind, Lang and Wharton are locked in combat, the pre-war Mercedes-Benz star not being able to make an inch on the British driver whose car must be at least 30bhp down on the 'works' Maserati.

'To the obvious annoyance of his team-mates, Ascari goes even faster… Farina is palpably annoyed and tells the winner so'

Ascari sails on his untroubled way — that is until the 39th lap, when the world champion goes through with an ominous misfire. Immediately, out comes the Prancing Horse's 'Faster!' signal for Farina and, as Ascari stops for new plugs, team-mate Giuseppe steps on the loud pedal to such effect that he gets down to 2m 43.1s (160.687km/h).

Ascari is stationary for 1m 27s, and he starts off again in fourth place behind the still-duelling Marimón and Hawthorn, who are about 45 secs behind Farina.

The sun is troubling drivers as they whistle down past the tribunes. It is useless to use tinted goggles, as they would be unable to see in the dark, wooded sections of the circuit. Trintignant, in sixth place, is closing up fast on Bonetto, but just as the Frenchman is about to overtake the Italian, the Gordini *bête noire* appears and exit 'Trint' with back-axle failure. Wharton refuels in the excellent time of 19secs, and Villoresi has radiator cement added to try to stop the water leak.

On the 45th lap Hawthorn edges past Marimón who, two laps later, executes a *tête à queue* when something happens to his transmission, ending a really first-class drive. Meanwhile Ascari is catching up fast on both Farina and Hawthorn.

Scherrer's HWM rejoins the race after several attempts to start the engine, and moves off many laps in arrears. De Graffenried retires with ignition trouble on his Maserati.

At 50 laps, Farina leads Hawthorn by just 15.2secs, with Ascari 10.3secs behind the 'Farnham Flyer'; Bonetto, in fourth place, is fully a lap behind. From the Ferrari pit out comes the 'Hold Positions' signal, comprising light blue-and-yellow Prancing Horse flags held horizontally. This surely means that Farina is going to be allowed to win.

However, to the obvious annoyance of his team-mates, Ascari goes even faster than before, hurtles past Hawthorn on lap 52, and two laps later regains the lead, setting up the fastest lap of the day with 2m 41.3s (162.480km/h).

Villoresi, intended to catch Lang, tries his best but has to call in again for more water. Wharton is firmly in seventh place, but with no hope of overtaking Villoresi.

Thereafter Ascari goes on to win as he pleases. Farina is palpably annoyed and tells the winner so. Up goes the Italian flag on the pole in front of the tribune, and the world champion is photographed for the umpteenth time wearing a vast laurel wreath.

The 13th Grand Prix of Switzerland is over. Thousands of cars thread their way in the solid stream of traffic to Berne. Scores of small boys go on a hunt for discarded programmes, paper hats, empty bottles and all possible variety of 'loot'.

The anticipated Maserati-Ferrari battle rather fizzled out when Fangio had trouble, and it is obvious that Officine Maserati will be in serious trouble for drivers next season, if, as rumoured, Fangio and González are joining up with Mercedes-Benz.

One would like to see Wharton in a faster car. We all know what he can do with BRM and, given the chance, can be rated as amongst the best half-dozen drivers of today. ■

RESULTS

65 LAPS (294.033 MILES)

1	Alberto ASCARI	Ferrari 500	3h01m34.40s
2	Giuseppe FARINA	Ferrari 500	3h02m47.33s
3	Mike HAWTHORN	Ferrari 500	3h03m10.36s
4=	Juan FANGIO/ Felice BONETTO	Maserati A6GCM	64 laps
5	Hermann LANG	Maserati A6GCM	62 laps

WINNING SPEED 97.162mph

FASTEST LAP ASCARI, 2m41.30s (100.960mph)

POLE POSITION FANGIO, 2m40.10 (101.717mph)

LAP LEADERS ASCARI 1-40, 54-65; FARINA 41-53

JUAN FANGIO | 1957 GERMAN GP | AUGUST 6
MASERATI 250F

Fangio Still *Fabulous!*

They were the young pretenders. He was 46. They had a huge lead. He was driving harder than ever – staying up a gear, taking risks. Seven lap records later the Old Master had put them in their place

BY STUART SEAGER

VEEDOL
VEEDOL

The chase is over. Fangio's Maserati splits the Ferraris of Peter Collins (7) and Mike Hawthorn (8). Collins fought back at the next corner, but Fangio was leading before the lap was completed

JUAN MANUEL FANGIO confirmed without question his status as World Champion at the Nürburgring last Sunday, when, in a dazzling display of virtuoso driving, he won the German Grand Prix at a race average of 142.9km/h (88.7mph), which exceeds the existing outright lap record for this tortuous 14-mile mountain circuit, set up last year by Fangio himself in a Ferrari at 141.2km/h. In achieving this he broke that lap record no less than 10 times, eventually hurtling round on the 20th of the 22 laps at a speed of 147.3km/h (91.5mph). His feat was the greater, and the excitement during the closing laps the more intense, because Hawthorn and Collins, who finished second and third in their Ferraris, completed the race without a single stop, whereas Fangio had to halt for fuel and new rear tyres at the half-distance after leading, and then had to catch up and pass the two English drivers, doing so in the penultimate lap. The Vanwalls, after their impressive performance at Aintree, found their suspension characteristics unsuited to the very bumpy 'Ring, although Moss finished fifth, behind Musso (Ferrari), with Brooks ninth.

The Formula 2 race, an innovation which was run concurrently with the Formula 1 contest, was won by Edgar Barth (Porsche), with Brian Naylor (Cooper) – new to the circuit and the car – a worthy second, after Salvadori (Cooper) had set up fastest lap at 84.5mph and then retired with suspension trouble.

PRACTICE

After weeks of rainy weather over the whole continent of Europe, the skies cleared about the middle of last week and by the time official practice began on the Friday before the race, a heat wave had set in, and it was soon evident that the pace was going to be as hot as the weather. Full works teams had been entered by Maserati, Ferrari and Vanwall, to be driven by the *crème de la crème* of the world's drivers, and the lap times became shorter and shorter. This was Vanwall's first visit to the Nürburgring, and they soon found that conditions were very different from the playing fields of Aintree – in fact, anyone who has not visited the 'Ring cannot imagine just how formidable a test of car and driver this amazing "natural" circuit is. Built by the Weimar Republic before the war (with the aid of a vast army of otherwise unemployed labour) it swoops and plunges for 14 miles around the Eifel mountains in West Germany, embodying an infinite variety of gradient and corner, hemmed in with hedge and forest, with scarcely a hundred yards of road visible ahead of the driver anywhere along the way, except for the final two-mile straight (albeit steeply undulating) run-in to the concrete plateau of the pit area, with its stands, control tower, huge illuminated scoreboard and kaleidoscope of coloured flags and

Fangio dives into the Karussell aboard chassis 2529. His softer Pirelli tyres forced him to undertake a half-tanks one-stop policy. And a slow pitstop forced him into his greatest drive

hoardings. The surface is far from smooth and suspensions take a fearful beating, not to mention brakes, gearboxes – and drivers.

Vanwalls found that their spring rates and damper settings were not in tune with the bumps and the cars were very difficult to hold down. Intensive work was put in on the Friday night but although things were somewhat better during the Saturday trials, it was pretty certain they were not going to have things all their own way this time. All the same, Moss clocked 9mins 41.2secs, exactly equal to the existing lap record, and Brooks clipped over 5secs off that. However, Schell, Collins, Behra and Hawthorn also beat Moss's time and eyebrows were energetically raised when Fangio turned in a round at 9mins 25.6secs. "Of course, he won't be able to do that in the race," everyone said.

Doubts had also been felt as to the wisdom of incorporating a Formula 2 event in with the "big boys", but these "little chaps" go so fast now that the practice times for F1 and F2 cars overlapped considerably. Salvadori, Naylor and Brabham had been going very well indeed. Tony Marsh did not seem quite so happy (in spite of some sections of the course being as near to a hill climb as he could wish for!) and he had the additional misfortune to strip a crown-wheel in practice, giving him a scramble to put it right in time. The two final Cooper entrants, Dick Gibson and Australian Paul England, seemed a little overawed by the whole undertaking. The opposition lay in the Porsches of Barth, Maglioli and de Beaufort. They were all nominally 550 Spyders, but Barth and Maglioli had also driven in practice one of the new ones with the curious little tail fins, although it did not prove particularly fast.

RACE

As 1.15pm approached the tension mounted and the buzz of speculative conversation was drowned as the first cars emerged from the paddock tunnel to be lined up in front of the pits and then wheeled into their places on the grid. Two minutes to go – engines were started again and the swarms of mechanics and photographers were banished from the grid, leaving a knot of officials standing right in front of the roaring pack. The final boards were held up – 30secs – 20secs – one by one the board-holders ran for cover, leaving the starter holding the German flag aloft in the middle of the track until he too sprinted to the side, dropped the flag and they were away!

The whole front row roared off in line abreast, and Hawthorn only just managed to get his nose ahead to take the lead into the South Turn and head the pack as they returned behind the pits. As the numbers ticked up on the scoreboard we saw that at halfway round the order was Hawthorn, Collins, Fangio, Behra, Moss, Musso and Schell, but Moss dropped back and as the leaders roared past the stands at the end of the first lap it was Hawthorn, Collins, Fangio, Behra, Musso, Schell and Brooks with Moss right on his tail and Lewis-Evans in the third Vanwall just behind. Stirling

The wide pit apron allowed a 4-3-4 grid. Fangio – on pole – Hawthorn, Jean Behra (Maserati) and Collins lead the field away

After second places in France and Britain, Italy's Luigi Musso (above) had to settle for fourth here. The Kansas City Flash, aka Masten Gregory (below), finished 10th

closed up on Brooks at the South Turn and passed him on the stretch behind the pits.

Second time round and the order was still the same, but Fangio was now beginning to turn on the heat, and he came right up behind Collins at the North Turn and took him smartly on the corner. In a similar manner, Schell nipped inside to pass Musso into fifth place. Salvadori was leading the Formula 2 cars, lying 11th overall, and Gibson, right at the tail of the field, pulled into his pit, apparently having excursed off the road and was feeling not too happy about the front suspension.

Hawthorn had completed the standing lap in 9mins 42.5secs, but on the second time round Fangio lowered his own record to 9mins 34.6secs

'Brooks made a twirly sign with an upraised finger… Lewis-Evans, on one of those humped kinks on the climb to the Karussell, had "lost" the Vanwall'

and did the third lap in 9mins 33.4secs, having taken the lead from the two Ferraris, not to lose it again until his pit stop, and was 6secs ahead of Collins, who had now moved just ahead of Hawthorn. Behra and Schell were still fourth and fifth and the Vanwalls came through in line astern, led this time by Lewis-Evans. Masten Gregory, in a Scuderia Centro-Sud Maserati painted in blue and white American stripes, was motoring very well in 10th place and a battle was on between Hans Herrmann in the other C-S Maserati, Roy Salvadori and Edgar Barth, Salvadori just squeezing in front again at the North Turn. Gibson came in again and retired. By this time we had heard that Horace Gould had had the bad luck to suffer crown-wheel failure in his privately entered Maserati on the second lap.

On the fifth lap Fangio clocked 9mins 33secs and on the sixth 9mins 32.5secs as he increased his lead to more than 20secs over the Ferraris that were pursuing him. Hawthorn now had passed Collins again and the order had settled into: Fangio, Hawthorn, Collins, Behra, Schell, Musso, Moss, Lewis-Evans, Brooks. On the eighth lap Fangio was 27secs ahead, having knocked the record down to 9mins 30.8secs. Herrmann was signalling all was not well with the rear end of his car, Barth had temporarily passed Salvadori and Brabham had retired with transmission failure.

On the 10th lap, the first of the Maseratis, Behra's, came in for fuel and a wheel change, dropping from fourth to ninth place in the process; Salvadori had retaken Barth, setting up a fastest F2 lap in 10mins 8.9secs.

Drama came in very large doses on the 11th lap – half-distance. Fangio, with 27.8secs in hand, scrambled into the pits for fuel and tyres, having further reduced the lap record to 9mins 29.5secs. As the blue-overalled mechanics whisked new rear wheels into place, Hawthorn and Collins howled past into the lead – and they were not going to need a stop at all! Fangio roared away in third place, but now over a minute to the bad; Schell came through, then Musso, Moss, Behra, Brooks – but no Lewis-Evans! It was recalled that Brooks on his previous passing had made a twirly sign with an upraised forefinger that could betoken a spin somewhere, and it transpired that Stuart Lewis-Evans, on one of those tricky humped kinks on the fast climb up to the Karussell had "lost" the Vanwall and shot through the hedge backwards – luckily without hurt, although out of the race. Then Roy Salvadori's Cooper limped in with the offside rear wheel leaning drunkenly inwards: the wishbone had fractured and his race was run, Barth now leading the F2 class comfortably. However, Roy's previous lap in 10mins 3.8secs was to stand fastest for the class.

The Nürburgring crowd salutes Fangio's brilliance – and Collins and Hawthorn also seem delighted for the just-crowned World Champion (right)

The Spaniard Paco Godia, in his privately entered Maserati, was also posted as "retired" at this time – never a dull moment!

Next time around it was Schell's turn to call in for fuel and tyres, dropping from fourth to seventh place, whilst Fangio thundered on in pursuit of the two Ferraris, overhauling them at the rate of 8-9 secs per lap! More drama occurred in the Formula 2 battle, for now Maglioli's Porsche had fallen out with engine trouble, letting Brian Naylor through into second place behind Barth. Naylor, who was thoroughly enjoying the wonderful handling of his new acquisition, was driving a very good race – fast, yet without caning the car unnecessarily, as it is so very easy to do on this punishing circuit. Tony Marsh came in soon afterwards to refuel, went out again and two laps later was in once more – also with a broken wishbone. However, it was seen that Salvadori's car could be cannibalised and various unemployed pit crews set frantically to work and took the nearside wishbone off Roy's car and fitted it to Tony's, and the latter was able to join the race three laps later and go on to finish.

Herrmann was the next to fall out. Having pulled up at the pits, a sad pool of oil quickly formed under the back axle and the white Maserati went to the "dead car" park.

On the 17th lap, Fangio lowered the lap record still further, to 9mins 28.5secs, and was now only 25.6secs behind Hawthorn. Mike and Peter in their valiant efforts to hold off the *Weltmeister*, were continually swapping places, yet were never more than a length or so apart and with only five laps to go the excitement was intense. Would the Ferraris manage to hold off the flying Maserati? Could Fangio pull out yet more speed? Yes, he could – and did. On the 18th lap he clocked 9mins 25.3secs and lay 20secs behind. On the 19th it was down to 9mins 23.4secs (13secs behind). And after the 20th lap a roar went up from 90,000 throats when an apoplectic German announcer gave out the incredible lap time of 9mins 17.4secs! As Hawthorn and Collins thundered past the stands, nose to tail, Fangio was about 100 yards behind them; on the back leg of the South Turn, the three cars were equally spaced, and as they entered the North Turn, Fangio was in front of Collins! Before he was halfway round on the penultimate lap, Fangio was in the lead again! Easing up (relatively speaking) he finished the 22nd and final lap to take the flag 3.6secs ahead of Hawthorn, with Collins half a minute behind. The winners were followed in by Musso, Moss, Behra and Schell. As close a finish to a Grand Prix as one could wish for – and the crowd loved it!

Masten Gregory just pipped Tony Brooks into eighth place, 10th was Scarlatti (Maserati) and 11th was Bruce Halford's Maserati, another well-driven private entry. Barth had won the F2 event with the works Porsche and a delighted Brian Naylor took second place, with the Dutch driver de Beaufort (Porsche) third and Tony Marsh fourth. ■

RESULTS

22 LAPS (311.816 MILES)

1	Juan FANGIO	Maserati 250F	3h30m38.30s
2	Mike HAWTHORN	Ferrari 801	3h30m41.90s
3	Peter COLLINS	Ferrari 801	3h31m13.90s
4	Luigi MUSSO	Ferrari 801	3h34m15.90s
5	Stirling MOSS	Vanwall	3h35m15.80s

WINNING SPEED 88.82mph

FASTEST LAP FANGIO, 9m17.40s (91.540mph)

POLE POSITION FANGIO, 9m25.60s (90.213mph)

LAP LEADERS HAWTHORN 1-2, 15-20; FANGIO 3-11, 21-22; COLLINS 12-14

WHAT HAPPENED NEXT...

Having clinched his fifth world championship with this his 24th and final GP victory, Fangio decided to retire. However, keen not to harm the ailing Maserati team, he did not do so until after he had finished fourth in the 1958 French GP on July 6.

JACK BRABHAM | 1960 FRENCH GP | JULY 3
COOPER T53

A FANTASTIC FRENCH GRAND PRIX

The straights of Reims were regarded as perfect Ferrari territory. But the little Cooper of Jack Brabham had the temerity to get among them in the early laps. It couldn't last. But it did

BY GREGOR GRANT

Bumbling, bombastic, bonkers 'Toto' Roche was a catalyst of chaos at Reims for many years

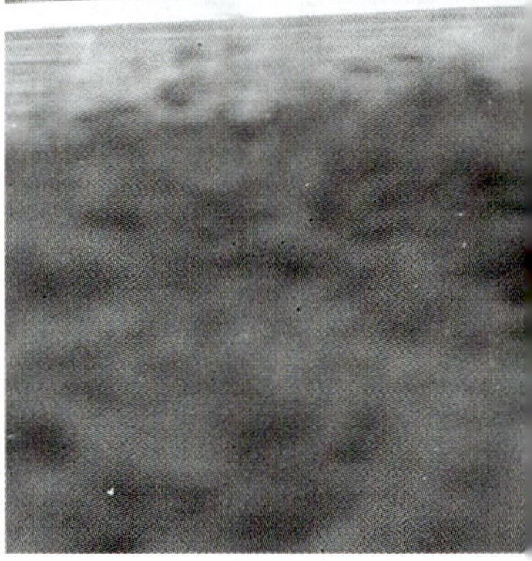

AFTER A RACE which brought back memories of Mike Hawthorn's famous duel with Juan Manuel Fangio in 1953, world champion Jack Brabham won the 46th Grand Prix de l'ACF at Reims last Sunday with the remarkable average speed of 212.113km/h (131.8mph) – nearly 3km/h faster than Stirling Moss's 1959 lap record, and over 7km/h quicker than Brooks's race-winning figures of 205.079km/h.

For 29 laps Brabham had a wheel-to-wheel struggle with the Ferraris of Phil Hill and Wolfgang von Trips, the three cars travelling at over 180mph down the Soissons straight. Hill's transmission broke, and two laps later von Trips's car did likewise, leaving Brabham with a lead of 84secs over second man Olivier Gendebien in the Yeoman Credit Cooper-Climax, who just managed to pip Bruce McLaren after another epic battle. Into fourth place came another Yeoman Cooper in the hands of Henry Taylor, followed by the Lotuses of Jim Clark and Ron Flockhart.

A mix-up at the start caused the elimination of Graham Hill's BRM and Maurice Trintignant's Cooper-Maserati, to say nothing of the eventual retirement of Tony Brooks (Vanwall), damage to Lucien Bianchi's Cooper and delay for Bruce Halford in the third Yeoman machine.

It was a complete and utter victory for British-built cars; of the nine machines still running at the end, seven were from the UK, and the remaining two had Cooper chassis.

Such was the speed at which the race was run that the 50 laps took under the two hours minimum as decreed by the FIA for World Championship Formula 1 events. This raised the problem as to whether or not Championship points would be awarded; apparently the CSI decided that the results would stand!

PRACTICE

Thursday evening's training produced a 2mins 16.8secs, 218.467km/h (135.76mph) by Jack Brabham (Cooper-Climax), unofficial timing giving the car's speed down the Soissons straight as 292km/h (181.45mph). Next in line was Graham Hill (BRM), 2mins 18.4secs, 215.941km/h, then came Phil Hill (Ferrari) with a 2mins 18.7secs lap, 215.474km/h, and Dan Gurney (BRM) and von Trips (Ferrari), each with 2mins 19.4secs – 0.1sec quicker than Innes Ireland's Lotus.

Team Lotus became referred to as Team MacLotus, with their all Scottish line-up of Innes Ireland, Jim Clark and Ron Flockhart. Yeoman Credit's three Cooper-Climaxes were in the hands of Olivier Gendebien, Henry Taylor and Bruce Halford. Gino Munaron replaced Scarlatti in the Cooper-Castellottis, while the Centro-Sud Cooper-Maseratis were down to be driven by Trintignant, Gregory and Burgess. Tony Vandervell's Vanwall did not have the really powerful engine fitted and Brooks was not outstandingly quick with 2mins 28.8secs. Richie Ginther drove a Scarab (2mins 31.4secs), while the third Ferrari was piloted by Willy Mairesse.

For Friday's final session, Gendebien's car had a new Colotti five-speed gearbox, and all three Yeoman Credit drivers improved on their previous times. Brooks was delayed for some time in the Vanwall with a detached magneto earthing wire; even so, the car was not as quick as anticipated, Tony's best lap being 2 mins 23.3secs. Actually no fewer than nine drivers were under 2mins 20secs, and none was better than Brabham's 2mins 16.8secs. Phil Hill improved to 2mins 18.2secs, to give him second-best time. Chuck Daigh's Scarab engine had bearing trouble, so Lance Reventlow was left without a raceworthy machine. He decided

Dan Gurney retires his overheating BRM (below); Bottom: Gino Munaron (30) briefly gets tangled in the race-long battle between Olivier Gendebien (44) and Bruce McLaren (18)

to pack up altogether from the present series and to concentrate on the production of an entirely new rear-engined Scarab which, it is hoped, will be ready for December's Grand Prix of the USA at Riverside, Los Angeles.

RACE

Following Trevor Taylor's victory in the first heat of the Formula Junior event, the 21 Grand Prix machines came out for a reconnaissance tour of the circuit. There were the usual scenes before the depart, with squads of *gendarmes* clearing the course of folk whose jobs were strictly not necessary. British announcer Anthony Marsh had to compete with whirring helicopters, banging maroons and what have you as the cars were assembled under lowering grey skies–most unusual for Reims!

The start was complete chaos. No sooner had the 30secs board been displayed than 'Toto' Roche dropped his flag. Graham Hill couldn't get his BRM into bottom gear owing to a dragging clutch and stalled his engine. He was shunted from behind by Trintignant. Bianchi (Cooper) took immediate avoiding action, careered across the road and bashed the nose of his car against the timing box. Halford did a mighty swerve and seemed to make contact with Brooks's Vanwall. Eventually all took off, with the exception of the unfortunate Hill and Trintignant whose cars were *hors de combat*.

Meanwhile, Phil Hill and Brabham and von Trips sprinted for the lead, leaving huge black marks on the road, clouds of blue smoke and a pungent smell of burnt rubber. Hill's Ferrari was in front as the field vanished under the Dunlop Bridge, and was still there when the cars roared down the Soissons straight. At Thillois, Brabham nipped smartly in front, and as the roaring projectiles sizzled past the tribunes, it was Brabham (Cooper), Hill (Ferrari), von Trips (Ferrari), Gurney (BRM), Ireland (Lotus), Bonnier (BRM), Mairesse (Ferrari), McLaren (Cooper), Flockhart (Lotus). Bringing up the rear were Halford (Cooper) and Bianchi's slightly battered machine.

The lap record didn't survive long, for 'Taffy' von Trips did his second tour in 2mins 19.6secs (214.085km/h). Both Ferraris were pressing Brabham's Cooper like mad, and the trio commenced a tremendous battle, passing and repassing whenever the opportunity presented itself. The drill was to slipstream and look for an opening; past the pits it was frightening to watch, as one would pull out to try to get into the fast bend first. Behind, Ireland and Bonnier were bonnet-to-bonnet, with Gendebien a few yards to the rear. On his fourth lap Hill clocked 2mins 18.8secs (215.319km/h) to edge in front of Brabham, but the Australian immediately regained the lead. Brooks stopped at his pits to complain of fierce vibration after his start-line shunt, whilst Ian Burgess also halted to make some adjustment on his Centro-Sud Cooper with the latest Maserati engine.

Faster and faster went the leaders, and in his sixth lap Hill surged ahead with another record lap in 2mins 18.7secs (215.474km/h). Brabham replied with 2mins 17.8secs (216.881km/h), but still couldn't shake off the American, who, on occasion, was almost wheel-to-wheel with team-mate von Trips. Already the race average was over 130mph. Hill's Ferrari had a sadly bashed front after bouncing off Brabham's rear wheels during the second lap, but it didn't seem to make much difference to his speed. Anyway, Jack was thankful that there was no apparent damage – and for the extra impetus he received out of Thillois!

Now it was Brabham v the Ferraris, Ireland v Bonnier and Gendebien v McLaren. There was absolutely no let-up, and the race was being run at well over the lap record. Lap eight, and the three leaders blared past the tribunes with Phil Hill's Ferrari about a cigarette-paper thickness in front. Next time round and Brabham had seized the advantage; on the 10th tour the race order read:

1, Brabham (Cooper-C), 23m 25.6s
2, Hill (Ferrari), 23m 25.8s
3, von Trips (Ferrari), 23m 27.4s
4, Ireland (Lotus), 23m 42.2s
5, Bonnier (BRM), 23m 42.4s
6, Gendebien (Cooper-C) 23m 45.6s
7, McLaren (Cooper-C), 23m 46.5s
8, Gurney (BRM), 24m. 05.0s
9, Mairesse (Ferrari), 24m 06.2s
10, Gregory (Cooper-M), 24m 29.3s
11, Flockhart (Lotus), 24m 31.3s
12, Taylor (Cooper-C), 24m 33.2s
13, Clark (Lotus), 24m 34.7s

Brooks made two more pit stops to complain about the vibration and dodgy brakes. The Vanwall was finally pushed away – probably to Brooks's relief. Burgess came in again, this time with gearbox troubles, and mechanics started to take off the lid. Henry Taylor scooted in front of Flockhart and set off to go for Gregory's Cooper-Maserati. One also noted the advance of Bianchi who was beginning to catch up on Halford. Jim Clark was having difficulty with his Lotus gear-change.

Still the leaders changed places, with Hill and Brabham batting round as hard as they knew, and von Trips trying to force the issue. Through the fast bend it looked decidedly dicey. Bonnier stopped briefly on lap 12, dropping to 13th place. Next lap, and the leaders had doubled both Halford and Bianchi, Munaron's Ferrari-powered device having already suffered that fate.

Bruce Halford retires his Cooper. Fortunately, his mechanic sees the funny side (left); Graham Hill's BRM was a victim of Roche's antics

Lap 13 it was Hill by about a millimetre; 14 tours and Brabham had once more taken the advantage, only to lose it to Phil on the two ensuing laps. Burgess stopped again, shortly after Bonnier was doubled. Poor Jo – he had scarcely a brake to his name, and when he wasn't going towards Paris out of the Muizon hairpin, he was taking the Reims road at Thillois.

Behind the big tear-up in front, Gendebien, Ireland and McLaren were having quite a party. Sometimes it was difficult to separate them. Taylor was well away from the Lotuses of Clark and Flockhart, who had Gregory mixing it with them. BRM lost Gurney when he came in with chronic overheating on lap 18. Munaron (Cooper-Castelotti) and Mairesse (Ferrari) vanished from the boards, and were next seen pushing their crippled cars from Thillois. Bianchi stopped with final drive trouble, to leave Halford very much on his own. Up came 20 laps with the race order as follows:

1, Brabham, 46m 33.2s
2, von Trips, 46m 34.1s
3, Hill, 46m 35.4s
4, Ireland, 47m 18.6s
5, Gendebien, 47m 18.8s
6, McLaren, 47m. 19.6s

Lap 22 and Flockhart had been doubled by Brabham, von Trips and Hill in quick succession. Bonnier was now in real trouble, with a complete absence of stoppers, and came in on lap 23 to retire. Next tour and both Taylor and Clark had a fine view of Brabham & Co disappearing in the distance. This was Grand Prix racing Mark 1 order; suddenly Brabham pulled out all the stops, took a 3.5secs lead on Phil Hill, when he brought the lap record down to 2mins 17.5secs, 217.354km/h (135.06mph). For two laps he maintained a 4secs advantage, then von Trips replaced Hill in second place, 5secs behind Brabham.

Then came a heavy blow to Scuderia Ferrari. As he swooped down from Thillois, Hill's transmission broke, and he coasted right past his pits to come to rest almost at the Dunlop Bridge. It was now up to von Trips, but on the Soissons straight his crown- wheel and pinion disintegrated. He managed to negotiate the hairpin, but came to rest shortly afterwards and started pushing.

This left Brabham with a 1min 24secs lead over the battling Gendebien, Ireland and McLaren trio, all others having been doubled. Taylor, driving a very fine race, now lay in fifth place, well ahead of Clark and Flockhart. Burgess had reappeared, to be joined by Gregory, but both the Centro-Sud cars were many laps in arrears.

Then, on lap 34, Innes Ireland came slowly into his pit with the front anti-roll bar detached, leaving Gendebien and McLaren with a straight fight for second place – and what a fight it was. Every lap McLaren would overtake the Le Mans winner on the Soissons straight, but Gendebien continually beat the New Zealander on braking, and, using the Colotti five-speed box to the full advantage, was in front by the time the cars went

RESULTS

50 LAPS (257.931 MILES)

1	Jack BRABHAM	Cooper T53	1h57m24.90s
2	Olivier GENDEBIEN	Cooper T51	1h58m13.20s
3	Bruce McLAREN	Cooper T53	1h58m16.80s
4	Henry TAYLOR	Cooper T51	49 laps
5	Jim CLARK	Lotus 18	49 laps
6	Ron FLOCKHART	Lotus 18	49 laps

WINNING SPEED 131.805mph

FASTEST LAP BRABHAM, 2m17.50s (135.062mph)

POLE POSITION BRABHAM, 2m16.80s (135.753mph)

LAP LEADERS BRABHAM 1-3, 5, 7, 9-10, 12, 14, 18-50; Phil HILL 4, 6, 8, 11, 13, 15-17

past the tribunes. Brabham continued to circulate, his engine sounding as rare as ever, the Australian driving like the world champion he is. All eyes were on the Gendebien-McLaren duel going on behind, and each time round it was the same.

On lap 38 Yeoman Credit suffered their first casualty when Halford came in with low oil pressure. He re-emerged, did two slow laps, and finally retired with run engine bearings. Meanwhile, Ireland had restarted, to make Team MacLotus complete again.

With Brabham 'slowed down' to a mere 2mins 23secs or thereabouts lap times, the Gendebien-McLaren contest brought them nearer and nearer to the Australian, without, however, the least hope of catching him. As the race neared its end, the adversaries got amongst the Lotuses which were also having a dice, and Gendebien managed to obtain a second or so during the doubling process.

The last lap, and Brabham was reported at Thillois. The chequered flag was ready — but Roche wasn't. Brabham shot over the finishing line before the flag was waved at all, but saw it in his rear mirrors and knew that the race was over.

It was now a case of waiting to see the outcome of the battle for second place. Down to Thillois swept Gendebien, pursued by McLaren and the Lotuses; Gregory had also become involved, many laps, of course, in arrears. McLaren lost ground trying to overtake the red car, and by the time he reached the hairpin, all chance of catching Gendebien had gone. Into fourth place came Henry Taylor to make it a grand day for Yeoman Credit. The two Lotuses crossed the line together but fifth place was awarded to Clark by a wheel.

Taffy von Trips had been cheered to the echo when he walked past the pits after pushing his car home, signing dozens of autographs on the way. Brabham was mobbed by his supporters, and both Gendebien and McLaren were given a tremendous reception. As all this was going on, the cars were already lining up on the grid for the second 10-lap heat of the Formula Junior race. ■

Mr Motor RACING!

The more powerful Ferraris pounded away but the year-old Lotus responded every time. This was Moss at his most brilliant. The gap between an era's best driver and its next best had never been greater

BY GREGOR GRANT

STIRLING MOSS | 1961 MONACO GP | MAY 14
LOTUS 18

Moss rounds the Station Hairpin (above). Maurice Trintignant's Cooper-Maserati leads the 'Sharknose' Ferraris of Phil Hill, Wolfgang von Trips and Richie Ginther, and the Porsche (2) of Jo Bonnier (right)

THRILLING OVER 120,000 spectators and millions of television viewers, Stirling Moss in Rob Walker's Lotus-Climax fought off three Ferraris and the Porsche team to win the 19th Grand Prix of Monaco at the record-breaking speed of 113.787km/h (70.70mph). His was a miracle drive; Ginther, Phil Hill, Bonnier and von Trips did their lot trying to catch the wiry, white-helmeted figure in the dark blue 1960-type Lotus, who firmly believed that he hadn't a hope of winning the first of the season's *grandes épreuves*. The opposition was most formidable, comprising three of the latest Ferraris, two fuel-injected and one 'carburettor' Porsche, in addition to the 1961 versions of Lotus and Cooper-Climax.

With about 150bhp, as against the reputed 185bhp of Richie Ginther's 120-degrees Ferrari, the masterly Moss held off a race-long pursuit to win from the skilful little American by just 3.7secs. Stirling took the lead on the 14th of the 100 laps, and thereafter kept in front of the howling pack of Ferraris and Bonnier's Porsche. It was a case of Moss fighting on his own. John Surtees put up the best show of all the other British drivers and was rapidly overhauling von Trips (Ferrari) when trouble struck on the 69th lap, and the older-type engine of the Yeoman Credit Cooper seemingly had a tappet break.

Fastest lap of the race was shared by Moss and Ginther, whose 1min 36.3secs was only one-tenth slower than Bruce McLaren's 1960 record with the 2.5-litre Coventry Climax.

World Champion Jack Brabham was never in the picture and retired after 38 laps with overheating problems. His team-mate Bruce McLaren dropped back after running out of petrol at the Gasometer hairpin. Jim Clark's new Lotus was in and out of the pits with carburation and plug bothers. Graham Hill's BRM broke its fuel pump drive and Tony Brooks's sister car had engine troubles after becoming tangled up with the exhaust system of Gurney's Porsche. Bonnier abandoned his Porsche after 60 laps, and Herrmann was delayed with gearbox problems.

Von Trips was classified fourth, although two laps from the end he crashed the Ferrari after the throttle mechanism came apart. Cliff Allison kept his UDT-Laystall Lotus going after the scavenge pump had packed up, but Michael May's Lotus retired with gearbox failure.

It was probably a good thing from Moss's point of view that Ferrari waited till the 73rd lap before Tavoni signalled Ginther to overtake Phil Hill and press the attack home. Hill's car was beginning to suffer from erratic steering and his efforts to catch the flying Moss became more of a physical effort every lap.

PRACTICE

The blue Mediterranean sparkled in the brilliant sunshine when the first training session opened on Thursday. Only Porsche was missing from the line-up, the cars not having arrived in time from Germany. There was a certain amount of dissatisfaction concerning the method of qualifying for the 16 places in the Grand Prix. The 10 actual works entries were assured of places, as were Stirling Moss and Maurice Trintignant. Those required to qualify were the UDT-Laystall Lotuses of Henry Taylor and Cliff Allison, Michael May in Seidel's Lotus, Masten Gregory (Camoradi Cooper-Climax), Lucien Bianchi and Olivier Gendebien (Emerysons), Hans Herrmann (Porsche) and Richie Ginther (Ferrari).

The rub was that the four 'dogfight' places each carried only half the starting money that had been guaranteed to the factory men, Moss and Trintignant. Thus the chosen folk could work on the sum of £1000 per car, whilst the others could not hope to pick up more than £500.

SEFAC Ferrari were determined to have three cars on the grid. Ginther was given the new 120-degrees car; Phil Hill and Taffy von Trips had the older-type engines, but, even so, there were subtle differences in their cars. Team Lotus appeared with the 1961 machines, Ireland's having experimental Dunlop disc brakes.

Jack Brabham had set himself a difficult programme, flying to the USA just after Silverstone, returning in order to practise on Thursday, then off again to Indianapolis for his final qualifying laps, with yet another trip back for Sunday's race.

Jim Clark (Lotus) made best time of all on Thursday, but shortly afterwards dropped it at Ste Devote, bounced off the anti-crash

barriers and finished up on the opposite side of the road with a very bent motor car. The Ferraris were most impressive, and it was fairly obvious that all three would be in the line-up.

Anyway, practice really began in earnest on Friday morning, when many bleary-eyed folk came straight out of the night-boxes to watch. There was little sleep for those who had rooms near the circuit, for Mitter's raucous DKW two-stroke engine was being revved up at 5.30am just outside the Hotel Metropole. The Juniors had the first session, then out came the GP machinery. Ginther made certain of qualifying by returning best time of 1min 39.3secs in the 120-degrees

'Innes found second gear instead of fourth. He crashed inside the tunnel to emerge with an exceedingly bent car'

Ferrari. Phil Hill was half a sec slower, and Graham Hill (BRM) did 1min 40secs – 0.3sec quicker than von Trips. Innes Ireland did 1min 40.5secs with the 'Flying Pencil' Lotus, and John Surtees was fastest of the non-factory people with 1min 41.1secs in the Yeoman Credit Cooper-Climax.

Jo Bonnier drove two Porsches and returned a 1min 41.3secs and the Anglo-Swiss driver Michael May did 1min 42secs with Seidel's Lotus. Hans Herrmann put a third Porsche in the running with 1min 42.4secs. Thus, at the end of the session, the four best for the disputed places were Surtees, May, Herrmann and Cliff Allison (UDT-Laystall Lotus).

Stirling Moss found that the chassis of his alternative car, the Cooper, was about a couple of inches out of true, so decided to drive the Lotus. Without looking in the least as if he was going fast, he returned the best time of Saturday's final training with 1min 39.1secs. Innes Ireland had quite a shunt in the tunnel; apparently the new Lotus has the gear selectors the opposite way round from the 1960 cars, and Innes found second gear instead of fourth. He crashed inside the tunnel to emerge with an exceedingly bent motor car. He was taken to hospital with a broken leg and several bruises.

Team Lotus worked all night to mend Clark's car, but Ireland's machine was completely wrecked. Surtees, endeavouring to better his already good time, had engine bothers, and Reg Parnell kept his fingers crossed hoping that his rivals wouldn't get under 1min 41.1sec. First shock was when Herrmann equalled this, and then May did 1min 42secs. After Ireland's crash, when Moss stopped to make sure that Innes was being looked after properly, there was a hiatus. Masten Gregory had been getting round in 1min 43secs, scrubbing new tyres and also bedding in brake linings. By the time he was given the OK to get moving, training was over, and Camoradi had lost their chance of having a car on the grid.

The organisers stated that Ireland's place would not be given to anyone else, but after studying the regulations they found that they were committed to 16 starters, therefore Cliff Allison was in with the UDT car. Henry Taylor had tried desperately to qualify his Lotus, but a singular lack of hairy horses dropped him down to three-fifths of second under Allison's best. Trintignant did not have to justify his selection, and his best was just a fifth of a second quicker than Taylor. Slowest of all was Brabham, whose Thursday effort of 1min 44secs put him on the back row of the grid. Neither Bianchi nor Gendebien qualified the Emerysons, but Bruce McLaren made sure of a third-row start with 1min 39.8secs with the works Cooper-Climax.

Porsche decided to put Bonnier and Herrmann in the fuel-injected cars and give Gurney the older carburettor machine.

Graham Hill put BRM amongst the possibles with an excellent and apparently unhurried 1min 39.6secs. Tony Brooks did 1min 40.1secs, just two-tenths of a second better than Jo Bonnier.

RACE

There is nothing quite like the Monte Carlo race. As the hour of the depart drew near, thousands of spectators crowded from windows and from every possible vantage point. The harbour was gay with craft dressed for the occasion, and, from the decks of a US frigate, scores of white-clad sailors had their own grandstand.

It can be said that Michael Parkes was mainly responsible for the

Dan Gurney and Tony Brooks exit Portier. They would subsequently tangle. The BRM (16) retired as a result but the Porsche man survived to finish fifth

new anti-crash metal barriers which had replaced the unpopular straw bales and wooden poles. It may be recalled that he escaped unhurt when a wheel came off our Rapier in the Monte Carlo Rally eliminating test and he bounced off the experimental barrier at Ste Devote. The organisers were so impressed that they arranged to erect the barriers all around the circuit.

Brabham arrived from USA looking rather tired (and small wonder), after qualifying his Cooper-Climax at 145.14mph at Indianapolis. He was mobbed by newsmen eager to find out the details. Chapman's men had done a fine job in repairing Clark's Lotus, but all were glum following the news of Innes Ireland's accident.

Director of the Race Louis Chiron closed the circuit in a blue DS19 Citroën and the 16 starters lined up on the Quai d'Albert. The 'count-down' could be heard clearly over the PA, despite the racket kicked up by Eurovision's turbojet helicopter. Engines were revved up, down came the flag, and the 19th Grand Prix of Monaco was on.

Ginther made a magnificent start and rounded the Gasometer turn first, followed by the usual traffic jam. Everyone managed to sort himself out without undue bumping and boring, and as the field howled past the tribunes it was Ginther, Clark, Moss and Brooks. The passage up from Ste Devote to the Casino was a thrilling sight. Round the square opposite to the Hotel de Paris, down the hill past the Tip Top and the crowded terraces of the Hotel Metropole screamed the 16. Tyres squealed under vicious braking for the nasty right-hander at the Mirabeau, then down to the Station Hairpin, out on to the promenade and under the notorious tunnel streamed the field, with the red Ferrari in front. Came the tricky Chicane as the cars regained the seafront, followed by the swerve at the tobacconist's kiosk and the run down Quai d'Albert to start all over again.

Ginther still led, followed 3secs later by Clark, Moss, Brooks, Gurney, Bonnier, Phil Hill, McLaren, Graham Hill, von Trips, Surtees, Brabham, Herrmann, Trintignant, Allison and May in that order. All present and correct, and what a relief.

As the field reappeared for the second time, Ginther was 4secs in front of Moss – and there was no sign of Clark. Then, as the rest swept by, the low green car went slowly into its pits and mechanics lifted the engine cover.

Behind the leading duo a dogfight had developed. Brooks, showing his old fire, led McLaren, the two Hills, von Trips and Surtees, each desperately trying to pass one another. Ginther was driving superbly, but Moss was relentlessly putting on the pressure. Phil Hill moved up over Brooks to attack the two Porsches, as Surtees stormed past von Trips. Jim Clark eventually restarted, but was forced to call in again.

Both Moss and Bonnier were breathing down Ginther's neck, with Phil Hill taking Gurney's measure, and just biding his time. At the tail end Michael May had overtaken Allison and Brabham had moved up over Herrmann. With 10 laps completed the order was:

1, Ginther (Ferrari), 17m 7.8s, 110.157km/h

2, Moss (Lotus), 17m 8.8s

3, Bonnier (Porsche), 17m 11.3s

4, Gurney (Porsche), 17m 19.1s

5, Hill (Ferrari); 6, Brooks (BRM); 7, McLaren (Cooper); 8, Hill (BRM); 9, Surtees (Cooper); 10, von Trips (Ferrari); 11, Brabham (Cooper); 12, Herrmann (Porsche); 13, Trintignant (Cooper); 14, May (Lotus); 15, Allison (Lotus); 16, Clark (Lotus).

Moss was now obviously going to take the initiative. The master was making motor racing look absurdly simple, and he indicated his intention to go in front. Graham Hill's engine spluttered and banged, and after 12 laps he drew into the pits for the first retirement.

On lap 14, Stirling Moss took the lead, and Bonnier followed him through into second place as Ginther gave way. Phil Hill had now taken Gurney, who was also being threatened by von Trips; Surtees was giving McLaren no peace. After 15 laps, Moss led Bonnier by 2secs, and had already doubled Allison. Two laps later, the three red Ferraris were in line ahead in pursuit of Moss and Bonnier.

After 20 laps, Moss led Bonnier by 8secs, Ginther by 9.2secs and Hill by 12.2secs. The race average had gone up to 111.08 km/h, and Ginther had already recorded 1min 39.2secs (114.143km/h). Five laps later, Trintignant had been doubled, and the unfortunate Clark again stopped for attention. Ferrari now gave Hill the sign to take Ginther, for Moss was gradually getting too far away for comfort. Ginther gave way to his team-mate, who thereupon closed right up on Bonnier, whom he overtook on the 27th lap, with Stirling 11.5 secs ahead.

At 30 laps, Allison had been doubled for the second time, and

'Moss was obviously going to take the intiative. The master was making motor racing look absurdly simple'

Herrmann stopped to sort out gearbox problems. Moss led Hill by 9.9secs, with Bonnier less than a second behind the American and 2.5secs in front of von Trips. Surtees was obviously going to take McLaren for sixth, and Brooks was duelling with Gurney's Porsche.

Just as Moss was about to lap Brabham on the 35th tour, the World Champion drew into his pits, and remained there. May, who had been driving really well in his first Formula 1 race, stopped with gearbox troubles, was announced as retired, then later re-emerged, only to abandon for good.

Ginther covered his 32nd and 35th laps in 1min 38.7secs, and 1min 38.4secs respectively. Jack Brabham restarted, did three slow laps, then packed up for good. Moss continued to hold about 10secs advantage, whilst Surtees had taken McLaren's sixth place and begun his pursuit of von Trips. On lap 41, Ginther replaced Bonnier in third place, to close up once again on Phil Hill. The race average had shot up to over 112km/h.

McLaren, trying to regain some of the ground lost to Surtees, recorded a lap in 1min 38.3secs (115.179km/h).

At half distance Ferrari pressure had never relaxed for a moment, but the tantalising Stirling Moss still went on his way. An occasional

Michael May's GP debut in a Lotus 18 was ended by a broken oil pipe

puff of smoke from the rear end worried his supporters a trifle, but was apparently nothing about which to be concerned.

So, with 50 laps of this fiercely disputed contest on the board, the position was:

1, Moss (Lotus), 1h 25m 36.8s, 112.104km/h
2, Hill (Ferrari), 1h 25m 44.6s
3, Ginther (Ferrari), 1h 25m 44.6s
4, Bonnier (Porsche), 1h 25m 47.6s
5, von Trips (Ferrari), 1h 26m 14.7s
6, Surtees (Cooper), 1h 26m 22.2s
7, McLaren (Cooper), 1h 26m 22.2s
8, Gurney (Porsche), 1h 27m 06.3s
9, Brooks (BRM), 1h 27m 07.6s
10, Trintignant; 11, Allison; 12, Clark

On lap 54, Tony Brooks, attempting to overtake Gurney, somehow became tangled up with the Porsche's exhaust system. Possibly he knocked his BRM out of gear, but anyway he must have over-revved momentarily, and the second Owen car was out of the race. Next time round, Stirling Moss had doubled Gurney, and Hill had cut the Lotus's lead to 4secs. Surtees produced a lap in 1min 37secs (116.721km/h) and was now out to take von Trips's fourth place.

Just as the 60th lap was chalked up, Porsche hopes were blasted when Jo Bonnier stopped at the station and started to walk back to his pits. Gurney had, of course, been lapped, whilst Herrmann was circulating way back behind Trintignant and Allison.

Phil Hill made a desperate bid to get to grips with Moss, getting to within 3.8secs of the blue Lotus on the 60th tour. Ginther came up almost level with his team-mate, then dropped behind a few yards – presumably on instructions from Tavoni. It was quite amusing to watch the Ferrari mechanics let Moss go by before quickly flashing the board to their drivers. They were also worried about Surtees, who was continually a threat to von Trips.

The Moss versus the Ferraris duel continued. On the 70th lap, the gap was 4.9secs, and the race average the astonishing one of 112.979km/h. Came a blow to Yeoman Credit when Surtees slowed, and finally packed up near the station with steam issuing from his exhaust pipe. His had been a fine drive, considering that the engine was, more or less, a 1960 'cooker'.

Stirling Moss doubled Bruce McLaren on his 73rd tour, and a couple of laps later the New Zealander had also been overtaken by

Phil Hill's pit board says it all: that man Moss is tantalisingly down the road. The Ferrari pit was frenetic by the finish as the leader calmly reeled off the laps

Moss talks to journalist Bernard Cahier after the race (above). Graham Hill's BRM (18) was the first retirement (below); von Trips crashed his Ferrari (40) but was still classified fourth

WHAT HAPPENED NEXT...

Moss would win again, thanks to another superb drive, this time at the Nürburgring, but Ferrari was the team of the season. The title battle between Phil Hill and von Trips ended in tragedy when the German crashed fatally into the crowd at Monza.

the two Ferraris. Around this time Richie Ginther was given the sign to mount the assault, and Hill moved over to let him through. Hill's car was doing more than its share of weaving, so it looked as though the steering department was not altogether 100 per cent.

With 20 laps to complete something went wrong with the petrol supply on McLaren's Cooper and he stopped at the Gasometer Hairpin. He pushed the car to the pits, and more fuel was taken aboard. Herrmann stopped also, and mechanics fiddled about with the engine, before he restarted. His must have been a peculiar sort of Porsche, for the official handout stated *'Arret de la voiture No. 6 Herrmann – Il repart après s'être ravitaille en eau.'* Whether the car or the driver required water was not quite clear!

As the race went on tension mounted. 'Faster, faster' signalled Ferrari, till finally Ginther had the message 'Give it the lot'. The young Californian responded magnificently and returned a lap in 1min 36.9secs. However, even that wasn't good enough, so he brought it down to 1min 36.3secs on lap 84, to come within 3secs of Moss. The master replied in typical fashion – he equalled Ginther's new time. Von Trips had been in trouble somewhere, for only the three leaders were now on the same lap. McLaren's pit stop had dropped him behind Gurney, whilst Allison was circulating slowly with a smokescreen set up by a defective scavenge pump. Trintignant still raced round non-stop in the Cooper-Maserati, outpaced but not disheartened.

People could scarcely contain themselves during the Moss v Ferrari battle. With precisely 10 laps till the end, the order was:

1, Moss, 2h 29 m 30.8s, 113.588km/h

2, Ginther 4.5s behind

3, Hill 14.6s behind

Ginther tried everything, but Moss's racecraft matched the superior speed of the red car. The American could quite easily have thrown caution to the winds and bet everything on Moss committing an error. However, Mr Motor Racing just doesn't oblige his rivals in that manner, and even if Ginther had managed to get in front, it was doubtful whether or not he could have stayed there.

With Ferrari almost going berserk in their pits, Stirling Moss carried on what had seemed a few days before to be an impossible task. The vast British contingent willed him to win. Lap 99 and the excitement was so intense that one could almost hear the ticking of countless stopwatches.

From the tribunes all eyes were on the exit from the tunnel. Then, a tremendous burst of cheering rent the air as the squat little blue car carrying the number 20 whistled through the Chicane for the last time, swerved past the tobacconist's kiosk, and with Moss's arm upraised in a victory salute, took the chequered flag just 3.6secs in front of the gallant Ginther in the new Ferrari.

Stirling was mobbed at the end, and poor Mrs Moss fell foul of the police trying to get near to her son. It was Stirling Moss night in Monte Carlo, the celebrations going on till daylight. ■

RESULTS

100 LAPS (195.421 MILES)

1	Stirling MOSS	Lotus 18	2h45m50.100s
2	Richie GINTHER	Ferrari 156	2h45m53.700s
3	Phil HILL	Ferrari 156	2h46m31.400s
4	Wolfgang VON TRIPS	Ferrari 156	98 laps
5	Dan GURNEY	Porsche 718	98 laps
6	Bruce McLAREN	Cooper T55	95 laps

WINNING SPEED 70.704mph

FASTEST LAP MOSS and GINTHER, 1m36.30s (73.055mph)

POLE POSITION MOSS, 1m39.100s (70.991mph)

LAP LEADERS GINTHER 1-13, MOSS 14-100

JIM CLARK | 1963 BELGIAN GP | JUNE 9 LOTUS 25

NON-STOP CLARK AT SPA

He hated the place. It spooked him, particularly when it rained. But that didn't stop him winning there – four times in a row. On this occasion he conquered his demons and the conditions

BY GREGOR GRANT

Phil Hill's ATS (26) and Jo Siffert's Lotus-BRM are regular visitors to the pits during the race. Both men will retire at about half-distance

LEADING FROM START to finish, Jimmy Clark (Lotus-Climax) won the 23rd Grand Prix of Belgium at Spa-Francorchamps last Sunday. This was his second consecutive victory in a race won three times by Juan Fangio, and twice by the late Alberto Ascari. It was also the fourth success for a British-built racing car.

Graham Hill (BRM) held second place for 16 of the 32 laps, only to retire with gearbox failure. Into second place went Dan Gurney (Brabham-Climax), but two laps from the end he was overtaken by Bruce McLaren (Cooper-Climax), the only other driver except the winner to complete the full distance.

Richie Ginther (BRM), Jo Bonnier (Cooper-Climax) and Carel Godin de Beaufort (Porsche) were the only other survivors of the 20 starters.

The closing seven laps were run in diabolical conditions, drivers being blinded by torrential rain and almost losing themselves in the heavy mists which blanketed the Ardennes during the height of the storm.

Neither Ferrari nor ATS had a finisher, but Tony Settember was very unlucky to go off course during the worst of the storm, when his Scirocco-BRM was in eighth. However, he was classified as a finisher. Also unlucky was that promising newcomer Chris Amon, who succumbed to an oil leak when well placed.

McLaren's second place opens up the world championship, for he now leads with 10 points, against the nine collected each by Graham Hill, Clark and Ginther.

PRACTICE

Evening practice on Friday was held in glorious weather, best times being returned by Willy Mairesse (Ferrari), 3mins 56.2secs, Jack Brabham (Brabham-Climax), 3mins 56.6secs, Tony Maggs (Cooper-Climax), 3mins 57.1secs, John Surtees (Ferrari) 3mins 57.9secs, and Bruce McLaren, 3mins 58.3secs.

Ireland (4mins 5.3secs) had difficulty finding gears on the beautifully made BRP-BRM. Ginther (4mins 4.5secs) was trying a new six-speed gearbox on his BRM, but this did not seem to be au fait and it was replaced with the old five-speeder.

ATS arrived late, Phil Hill and Giancarlo Baghetti putting in a few slowish laps. The cars' V8 engines sounded tremendous, but the chassis looked to be more crudely finished than one would expect. Colotti six-speed gears are enclosed in a 'elektron' casing of ATS manufacture. The Dunlop disc brakes had strictly non-Dunlop modifications, and during a visit to their headquarters, mechanics

The front row of (from left) Willy Mairesse, Dan Gurney and Graham Hill is about to get a surprise. Half-hidden by Mairesse is Clark, making a rocket start from the third row

were busy welding and reshaping the seats-cum-fuel tanks. The engine, with its finned cylinder head alloy castings, is a beautiful piece of work. Four d/c Webers were fitted, but it is intended to replace these with Lucas pi equipment in time for Silverstone – and possibly Zandvoort.

The Scirocco-BRM is a workmanlike machine, with a tubular frame reinforced by a metal centre section which also comprises the petrol tanks. A Colotti gearbox is used.

Gurney's Brabham-Climax was not holding the road too well, so the Repco boys spent most of Friday night sorting this out. They must have worked to good purpose, for Dan's time of 3mins 55.0secs on Saturday afternoon was beaten only by Graham Hill (BRM), who did 3mins 54.3secs. Jim Clark's official 1500cc lap record of 3mins 55.6secs was also bettered by Mairesse (Ferrari), 3mins 55.3secs. Other good times were achieved by Maggs, 3mins 56.0secs, McLaren, 3mins 56.2secs, Brabham 3mins 56.6secs, Ireland 3mins 56.9secs, Clark 3mins 57.1secs, Ginther 3mins 57.6secs, and Surtees 3mins 57.9secs.

Trevor Taylor had a tremendous accident at Stavelot, when a wheel rim split and deflated the tyre at around 140mph. The monocoque Lotus demolished the wooden observer's box, and was completely wrecked. Taylor cut his face and suffered bruises, but was soon back at the pits to take out the practice car to qualify it.

De Beaufort flew out to Stuttgart to get another engine for his Porsche. Hill's BRM engine had valve-cap trouble and had to be changed for an older unit. The gearbox also was not in as good a nick as the Owen boys would have liked.

No one was clear as to how Jim Hall (Lotus-BRM), Jo Siffert (Lotus-BRM), de Beaufort and Settember could ensure qualification, but all 20 arrivals were in the published starting grid, so the RACB officials must have been satisfied. Anyway, Hall's 4mins 0.1sec was a good effort, as was Siffert's 4mins 2.3 secs.

RACE

Big, dirty black clouds and the threat of thunderstorms did not deter a huge crowd making an early start to the circuit. Heavy rain scattered the good people, but the majority stayed put at their chosen vantage points.

After the usual parades and things had taken place, the 20 cars were pushed onto the starting grid. Shortly after 3.30pm the flag was raised, and with a throaty roar from the 18 V8s and two V6s, the Belgian Grand Prix was on.

Jim Clark made one of those picture starts: from the third row, he was in first spot long before the end of the pits, and as the field streamed up Eau Rouge, his Lotus-Climax led from Graham Hill's BRM and Tony Maggs's Cooper-Climax. Brabham, sitting on Maggs's tail, streaked through into third place just before Stavelot, and Gurney and Mairesse were also soon crowding the young South African.

Clark pulled away from Hill on the Masta Straight, but down towards the Source hairpin the BRM was right up again on the Lotus.

Past the pits, the race order was Clark, G Hill, Brabham, Gurney, Mairesse, McLaren, Surtees, Maggs, Ginther, Amon, Taylor, Ireland, Siffert, Bonnier, de Beaufort, Bianchi, P Hill, Settember, Hall and Baghetti.

Mairesse bombed past Gurney at Malmédy, and at Stavelot pinched third place from Brabham. As this news came through the PA system the stands cheered. However, at the start of lap two Clark and Hill had pulled out a sizeable lead over the Ferrari, and McLaren had tacked his Cooper onto Brabham's Brabham. Jo Bonnier, in the blue Walker Cooper, was making rapid progress and had whistled past Taylor, Siffert and Ireland to slipstream Maggs.

At La Source there was a peculiar mix-up when de Beaufort signalled Bianchi through, but

Jack Brabham's BT7, John Surtees's Ferrari 156 and Bruce McLaren's Cooper T66 tackle La Source hairpin as they battle for third place early in the race

the Lola somehow became tangled up with the orange Porsche, and both cars came to a halt. The Dutchman quickly reversed, and there appeared to have been a little bit of stock-car stuff, as de Beaufort hurtled past the pits with a slight bump on the nose of his car, and Bianchi trundled into the pits with the front end looking more than somewhat second-hand.

There were unexpected wet patches on the circuit, and times were far below the training figures. Clark's second lap took precisely 4mins 18.5secs.

As the rest of the starters screeched down the hill towards Eau Rouge, Parnell's mechanics worked madly to straighten Bianchi's Lola. Reg was all for retiring the car, which had a bent torque rod as well as bodywork damage. But Bianchi eventually rejoined the race, minus the nose piece of the Lola.

The other Parnell Lola, in the hands of 19-year-old Chris Amon, was being conducted extremely well, but smoke was coming out of its rear end. He had worked himself up into ninth place, close behind Ginther's BRM. Surtees had slipped ahead of Gurney to take sixth place.

Jim Clark was steadily becoming faster and faster, and by four laps had made 5secs on the world champion. Then Mairesse ran completely out of brakes at La Source, and tried to demolish a billboard. He sorted himself out, but dropped back to fifth place, behind Brabham and Surtees, with McLaren a few yards behind. Into the pits came Bianchi to have more damage rectified, and Phil Hill stopped to see what could be done about finding some gears on his ATS.

Jim Clark was having himself a ball, building

'There appeared to have been a little bit of stock-car stuff, as de Beaufort hurtled past the pits with a slight bump on the nose'

up a formidable lead over the BRM. Mairesse came in to have his Ferrari seen to. Siffert also halted, to be followed by Baghetti, Trevor Taylor with oil pressure bothers, and finally Bianchi, again to have things straightened out. With five laps chalked up, the order was:

1, Clark (Lotus-Climax), 21m 41.5s
2, G Hill (BRM), 21m 49.5s
3, Brabham (Brabham-Climax), 22m 25.6s
4, Surtees (Ferrari), 22m 26.3s
5, McLaren (Cooper-Climax), 22m 26.8s
6, Mairesse (Ferrari), 22m 35.2s
7, Gurney (Brabham); 8, Amon (Lola); 9, Ginther (BRM); 10, Ireland (BRP-BRM); 11, Bonnier (Cooper); 12, Maggs (Cooper); 13, Siffert (Lotus-BRM); 14 Hall (Lotus-BRM); 15, de Beaufort (Porsche); 16, Settember (Scirocco-BRM); 17, Baghetti (ATS); 18, Bianchi (Lola); 19, P Hill (ATS)

Taylor's car was pushed into the dead car park, as mechanics worked on three red cars: Mairesse's Ferrari, Baghetti's ATS, and Siffert's Lotus-BRM.

Surtees shot up into third place at Stavelot, but Brabham and McLaren were giving him no peace. Behind, Gurney, Amon and Ginther were in line ahead, whilst Bonnier and Maggs were having a private battle.

Clark steadily forged ahead of Hill's BRM, and Brabham's engine appeared to be firing on just one bank, and he struggled to climb the hill after Eau Rouge, with team-mate Gurney closing fast on the driver-constructor. Maggs took Bonnier, but they were nose to tail as they streaked by the pits.

By lap eight, Clark had widened the gap over Graham Hill to 15secs. Surtees was 10.5secs in front of McLaren, followed by Gurney, Amon, Ginther, Bonnier and Maggs.

Ex-mechanic Graham Hill was a very hands-on racer. His inveterate last-minute tinkering would often drive his mechanics to distraction, but his mechanical knowledge regularly brought him advantages, too

Into the pits went Jack Brabham to investigate serious petrol starvation. Later Phil Hill again stopped to try to find out why the gears wouldn't engage properly. The ATS sounded glorious, but it was obvious that there were a few problems still to be sorted out before the Bologna folk can offer stiffer opposition to their rivals.

At the end of lap eight, Clark was 17secs ahead of Hill, and was about to lap Settember's Scirocco, which was going far better than many of the more expensive pieces of Formula 1 machinery. Tony was not being foolish, and decided not to have a straight dice with the experienced de Beaufort, and to concentrate instead on bringing the Goldhawk Road machine to the finish.

Lap nine, and Jim had stretched his lead over Graham. McLaren put up five fingers as he swept past the Cooper pits, so presumably one of his six speeds were missing. Anyway, he had dropped 9secs to Surtees in one lap, and was being threatened by Gurney, who was motoring magnificently in his new Brabham.

Jim Clark doubled the Scirocco, and began to close up rapidly on de Beaufort. The Dutchman was enjoying himself hugely, and had worked his orange Porsche up to 11th place. Mairesse rejoined the race, only to abandon two laps later with unspecified troubles, as well as a damaged gearbox.

Ten laps completed, and the order was:

1, Clark (Lotus), 42m 35.8s

2, G Hill (BRM), 42m 55.0s

3, Surtees (Ferrari), 43m 21.4s

4, Gurney (Brabham), 43m 44.3s

5, McLaren (Cooper), 43m 57.1s

Chris Amon, putting up a brave show, had to call it a day with a loss of oil from a mysterious leak. Baghetti, who had gone out again with his ATS, stopped for yet another transmission sort-out, did another lap, then vanished from the fray. Ireland was also in gearbox trouble, making two pit-stops, then a final one. Brabham also came in on his 10th lap to try to cure injector pump troubles.

With Hall doubled by Clark on lap 11, there were now only eight cars on the same lap. Maggs had pushed past Bonnier. Graham Hill began to cut down Jim Clark's lead slightly, but 12.4secs on lap 13 was the nearest that he ever got to the Border Scot.

It was on this lap that Surtees stopped to investigate apparent fuel starvation. Jo Siffert's Lotus-BRM had front-suspension bothers and the Swiss halted a couple of times to check the car.

So far, Clark had turned fastest lap with 4mins 4.0secs — very quick when one realises that many parts of the circuit were wet.

The race was now nearing half-distance, and the 15-lap order was:

1, Clark (Lotus), 1h 02m 34.8s

2, G Hill (BRM), 1h 03m 10.5s

3, Gurney (Brabham), 1h 04m 01s

4, Ginther (BRM), 1h 05m 02.2s

5, McLaren (Cooper), 1h 05m 02.9s

6, Maggs (Cooper); 7, Bonnier (Cooper); 8, Hall (Lotus-BRM); 9, de Beaufort (Porsche); 10, Settember (Scirocco-BRM); 11, Surtees (Ferrari); 12, Bianchi (Lola); 13, Siffert (Lotus-BRM); 14, Brabham (Brabham)

Ginther and McLaren were travelling in close company, and Maggs and Bonnier were still dicing for sixth place and a championship point.

As Jim Clark was tearing up Eau Rouge on his 16th lap, Hill came through over 26sec behind, the BRM not sounding too healthy. On the previous lap there had been a noticeable splutter. On lap 17 the world champion had dropped to 38.5secs behind the Lotus, and the BRM was seen no more. Gearbox trouble — very rare for Owen machines — had intervened, and Hill's race was run.

Hill, Phil, suffering from continual transmission troubles, finally abandoned the remaining ATS. Graham's exit left Gurney in second, 1min 31.5secs behind Clark.

It was raining pretty hard in the pits area, but just before it came on, Jim Clark got down to 3mins 58.1secs: this was on his 16th lap.

Surtees had started off again, five laps in arrears, and Baghetti walked in from Blanchimont, where he'd abandoned his ATS with broken gears.

It was reported over the PA that Bianchi and Hall had touched, and that the Texan had gone off the road. He was unhurt, but the Lotus-BRM was badly bent.

Clark was absolutely out on his own, and there was nothing that Gurney and Co could do but hope. On lap 18, McLaren wrested third place from Ginther, whose engine was inclined to a spot of popping and banging.

Maggs gradually pulled away from Bonnier, who was doubled on lap 19 by Clark. Surtees was still circulating in ninth place, but the Ferrari engine sounded very sick.

At 20 laps — a dozen to go — the order was:

WHAT HAPPENED NEXT...

More wins for Clark. Lots of them. Often on the same set of Dunlop tyres! Victories in Holland, France, Britain, Italy, Mexico and South Africa made him a dominant champion. He also scored his only second place – ever! – behind Surtees in Germany.

Urgh! Clark's grimace to *Autosport* photographer George Phillips says it all. The race finished in torrential conditions and ought to have been stopped earlier – even drivers raised in Scotland thought so!

1, Clark (Lotus), 1h 23m 43.8s
2, Gurney (Brabham), 1h 25m 47.2s
3, McLaren (Cooper), 1h 26m 59.6s
4, Ginther (BRM), 1h 27m 09.7s
5, Maggs (Cooper), 1h 27m 14.4s
6, Bonnier (Cooper), 19 laps
7, de Beaufort (Porsche); 8, Settember (Scirocco-BRM); 9, Surtees (Ferrari); 10, Bianchi (Lola); 11, Siffert (Lotus-BRM)

It was now largely processional, and Clark added Ginther to his score on lap 21 – leaving only four cars on the same lap.

The sky had darkened and there were ominous flashes of lightning and rumbling of thunder. As Clark started his 24th lap after doubling Maggs, the heavens opened and it began to rain push-rods. It was an eerie setting to a grand prix, with brilliant forked lightning accompanied by crashes of thunder which drowned the sound of exhausts.

Surtees finally packed it up, the Ferrari's fuel injection system having developed a fractured pipe. Bianchi completed an adventurous day by leaving the road and hurling the Lola against the side of a house. Settember, still in eighth place, stopped to pick up a visor.

Down came the lap times as the unfortunate drivers crouched behind their windscreens and peered through the increasing mist and gloom. Clark came down from 4mins to 6m 40s (126.900km/h) – or 52.5mph slower.

As the cars toured slowly past accompanied by bow-waves, Brabham optimistically dived into the fray, some 15 laps in arrears. Jack certainly chose the most diabolical conditions to see how his car handled in the wet! Sensibly, he soon returned to the pits.

Off the course shot Tony Settember at Masta, whilst Siffert went into a fantastic slide on the descent from Blanchimont, and wrecked the red Lotus-BRM. Both drivers were unhurt.

Bonnier stopped for a visor, and upped anchor just as de Beaufort came into the Source. Gurney, never having driven a Brabham in the wet, became progressively slower as the roads ran like rivers, and thick mist cut visibility down to a few yards.

Maggs went missing, then turned up at the pits with the nose of his Cooper bashed in – a result of an excursion amongst some wood piles. He went to restart, but mechanics spotted oil pouring out of the damaged cooler, and that was that.

McLaren, on seven cylinders, stayed in front of Clark, but eventually the Lotus man doubled the Cooper. Both came up on Gurney and, before the Californian fully realised what had happened, he had lost his second place, and had also been lapped by Clark

Conditions were so appalling that both Colin Chapman and Tony Rudd tried to persuade the organizers to stop the race, but this was refused. Frogmen's equipment could quite well have been issued to the six survivors, who were completely hidden by spray.

Graham Hill, looking as soaking wet as the photographers, had a big cheer as he walked back to his pit from La Source.

With one lap to go, McLaren managed to overtake Clark to get back on the same lap. Ginther, whose fuel injection equipment had played up to slow him when he was duelling with McLaren, was sailing safely in fourth place, followed by Bonnier and the indefatigable de Beaufort.

Then, to the great relief of the stormbound pilots, the race was over, with Team Lotus jumping for joy as Jim Clark received the chequered flag. McLaren had to do another lap, for he passed through a few moments before the winner.

The pits area was thronged with well-wishers – none too safe, as sudden braking on the soaking road could quite easily have caused an incident!

Clark's average speed was the slowest race to be run at Spa-Francorchamps since 1954. ■

RESULTS

32 LAPS (280.363 MILES)

1	Jim CLARK	Lotus 25	2h27m47.60s
2	Bruce McLAREN	Cooper T66	2h32m41.60s
3	Dan GURNEY	Brabham BT7	31 laps
4	Richie GINTHER	BRM P57	31 laps
5	Joachim BONNIER	Cooper T60	30 laps
6	Carel DE BEAUFORT	Porsche 718	30 laps

WINNING SPEED 113.819mph

FASTEST LAP CLARK, 3m58.10s (132.469mph)

POLE POSITION Graham HILL, 3m54.10s (134.732mph)

LAP LEADERS CLARK 1-32

JOHN SURTEES **RINGMEISTER!**

The 14-mile Nürburgring was deemed the greatest test of a GP driver. That being so, this ex-motorbike world champion was a match for even Jim Clark. High praise

BY GREGOR GRANT

IN A DISPLAY of driving virtuosity that wore down the entire opposition, John Surtees in his V8 Ferrari repeated his 1963 success in last Sunday's German Grand Prix at thc Nürburgring. Not only was this the fastest race ever run on the Eifel circuit, but Surtees set up a new lap record with a sizzling 8mins 39secs, 98.3mph – 8secs quicker than his 1963 figures.

One by one his rivals dropped out of the running, first Jim Clark and then Dan Gurney. Graham Hill gamely flogged his anything-but-healthy sounding BRM round for a thoroughly deserved second place to give him 32 points in the world championship to Clark's 30.

Into third place came Lorenzo Bandini in the V6 Ferrari, followed by the independent Swiss driver Jo Siffert (Brabham-BRM). Maurice Trintignant took fifth place in his blue BRM, and Tony Maggs collected a championship point with his Centro-Sud BRM.

Of the 22 starters, only nine were running at the end, but 14 were classified. Japan's Honda went extremely well for a first appearance, but was eliminated after 11 laps when Ronnie Bucknum left the road. His best lap was 9mins 22secs.

To the motor racing man, the Nürburgring offers the greatest of all challenges. This 14.2 miles of specially constructed roadway contains every possible hazard, twisting and turning amidst the wooded slopes of the Eifel Mountains. While some may know the circuit better than others, it is almost impossible to learn it throughout its entire length. Drivers are content to familiarise themselves with the most difficult sections – particularly the many blind corners which are inevitable with this type of road circuit.

The weather is one of the most trying features. Crowds at the start area may be basking in brilliant sunshine, while over at Adenau it can be pouring with rain. The vagaries of mountain climates can, and do, cause surface conditions to change rapidly, and on the Nürburgring one must always be on the lookout for slippery patches under the trees, which remain as a constant threat long after most of the circuit has dried out. Consequently, there is no time for relaxing concentration, and 15 laps of the 'Ring at racing speeds requires a high standard of physical fitness and mental alertness. Truly, *der Nürburgring* does sort out the men from the boys!

It is also a stern test of the machinery, and it is sobering to realise that the modern 1.5-litre unsupercharged Grand Prix car is over 14mph faster than the almost mythical blown cars of the 1930s. John Surtees's winning speed aboard the Ferrari was 96.6mph, and the fastest recorded in the so-called Golden Era was Rudi Caracciola's 82.15mph in 1937 with the 5.6-litre Mercedes-Benz.

ENTRY

So for the 26th *Grosser Preis von Deutschland* camc thc main contenders for the world championship, with the addition of Honda, plus several independents. The organisers had invited all the drivers who had scored points in the current championship series. Of the regulars, the only notable absentees were BRP.

German driver Gerhard Mitter had a Lotus 25, entered by Team Lotus. The Owen Organization had entered four BRMs for Graham Hill, Richie Ginther, Dickie Attwood and Maurice Trintignant, but Attwood's four-wheel-drive machine did not appear. Mike Hailwood had made a remarkable recovery from his East German motorcycle crash and took his place, along with Chris Amon, in the Parnell team.

Honda had already been on the circuit prior to the official training and had learned a great deal. For example, the suspension had to be modified to eliminate bottoming, which was so pronounced that Ronnie Bucknum lost practically the entire exhaust system.

Ferrari's V12 was not produced, and there was a V8 for John Surtees and a V6 for Lorenzo Bandini. Edgar Barth was in Rob Walker's Cooper. Graham Hill's car was the earlier monocoque BRM, the latest one not being ready after its Solitude shunt. Both Centro-Sud BRMs had been re-cellulosed Italian red.

PRACTICE

Wonderful weather accompanied the opening practice on Friday, and it was very hot indeed. John Surtees's official 1963 lap record was the target, namely 8mins 47secs in the V6 Ferrari. He improved on this with the V8 by 1.8secs, but was 0.6secs slower than Graham Hill. Next best was Dan Gurney with 8mins 47.8secs, followed by Lorenzo Bandini, 8mins 49.3secs, and Jim Clark, 9mins 4.1secs. Fastest of the independent drivers was Bob Anderson (9mins 13secs).

Bucknum managed only one timed lap with the Honda, not taking any chances with 10mins 4.1secs – considerably slower than six of the 904 Porsches taking part in the GT race. The Honda sounded very crisp, but I am inclined to think that several of the Japanese horses had escaped from the stable. Still, these are early days, and it was a splendid effort to appear at all.

Saturday's weather was anything but promising, with heavy rain in the early morning, and lowering skies over the Eifels. Yet when the Formula 1 cars came out onto the circuit, the roads were practically bone dry, and the rain obligingly

DUNLOP

Surtees leads Jim Clark's Lotus 33 (top); Clark, the world champion, had started the season in fine form, but as of now his grip on the title is starting to slip (above); Honda's mechanics prepare the RA271 prior to the company's GP debut (right)

held off. It was a day of remarkable speeds, for with their 13in Dunlop equipment, no fewer than six of the factory drivers cracked the lap record: Surtees returned 8mins 38.4secs, Clark, 8mins 38.8secs, Gurney, 8mins 39.3secs, Bandini, 8mins 42.6secs, Hill, 8mins 43.8secs, and Brabham, 8mins 46.6secs. McLaren did 8mins 47.1secs, while Amon was quickest of the independents with 8mins 54secs. Ferrari must certainly have sorted out the V6 'Aero', for Bandini was no less than 4.4secs underneath Surtees's last year's record, also done with a V6.

Ronnie Bucknum managed a 9mins 34.3secs with the Honda, but had engine bothers, leaving the Japs with a problem. Five laps were necessary to ensure qualification, and it was a good thing that the organisers had laid on a special evening session, which would not count for grid positions, but only for qualification. As Mitter had also not done his requisite number of laps, the organisers were obviously determined to bend over backwards to ensure the participation of both drivers. As it so happened, both completed the necessary laps.

It was not a good day for BRM, both Hill and Ginther having some sort of gear selection trouble which led to inadvertent over-revving and burst motors. So the men with the Day-Glo overalls were faced with a couple of engine changes.

The unfortunate Carel Godin de Beaufort lost his Porsche at Bergwerk and hit a tree. The big Dutchman was taken to hospital at Coblenz with serious head and spine injuries, to which he succumbed.

Bob Anderson was in trouble with his normally ultra-reliable Brabham and had to abandon out on the circuit. Phil Hill also had bothers with his Cooper, while American Peter Revson had a most odd-looking Lotus-BRM after losing the nosepiece in an off-course excursion.

RACE

Race-day did not look too promising, with grey skies and a cold wind. However, the locals thought that the rain would hold off, and the thousands of people who had camped all round the 'Ring were joined soon after dawn by folk from every possible part of Europe. By 8am the roads were absolutely choked with traffic, but so many people wanted to see the five-lap bicycle race that traffic was kept on the move and hold-ups were nothing like those of last year.

Incidentally, that bike race was really something. Pedalling the reverse way around the 'Ring for 70 miles is not my idea of pleasure, but I must say it was a spectacle, with the closely bunched heroes followed by their large cavalcade and preceded by motorcycle cops.

As the locals had predicted, the rain held off, but it was real brass-monkey weather, especially in the draughty tribunes. The crowds had thickened as starting hour approached, and the official handout mentioned 310,000 people as being present.

Our photographer Frankie Penn was delighted that he was given an official police pass by press officer Reinert which really worked. In point of fact, *Herr* Schmidt, the Nürburgring boss, must have talked to the rozzer chief, for the men in green were unbelievably co-operative and scrupulously polite. Providing one had the correct pass, there was no bother at all (Monza please copy!). Penn was completely dumbfounded. Since the advent of *Presseleiter* Reinert, he was saluted and shaken by the hand by the police instead of being bawled out and threatened with a term in the pokey.

Dick von Frankenberg and Anthony Marsh gave out last-minute information over the PA in German and English respectively as the cars were wheeled to the grid. Unlike circuits with fairly restricted start areas, there was no dummy section at the Nürburgring, the cars being allocated 4-3-4 order on the grid proper.

At the two-minute signal, engines were started and mechanics scurried off the grid. Twenty-two multi-cylinder engines make plenty of noise, and as Dr von Diergart (President of AvD) raised the West German flag, the shriek of exhausts was deafening. Jim Clark had a last-minute fiddle with his gears, but as the flag swept down, the field went off to a perfect start.

Bandini momentarily occupied the lead, but as the pack snarled down to the South Curve, Clark, Gurney and Surtees were in front. Into the North Curve, Clark led by a few inches from Gurney, with Surtees almost wheel to wheel with the Brabham. This trio went ahead, and towards Adenau there was a second group comprising Graham Hill, Jack Brabham, Lorenzo Bandini and Phil Hill, but at the Karussell Jo Bonnier had taken Phil Hill.

In the tribunes, the crowds waited for the first arrival, keeping their eyes glued to the Dunlop electronic scoreboard. Up they hurtled to the Tiergarten, and then past the start area, with Clark leading Surtees by 0.5sec, and Gurney very close behind. The order at the end of the first tour was Clark, Surtees, Gurney, G Hill – a slight interval – and then Brabham leading a tight bunch that consisted of Bandini, McLaren, Ginther, Bonnier and Amon. As the last of this group poured past the back of the pits, came Siffert, Maggs, Baghetti, Trintignant, Spence, Barth, but there was no sign of Hailwood. Into the pits went Mitter, Revson and Anderson, the first pair to change plugs and the Brabham driver to replenish his radiator. Hailwood had stopped with engine bothers at Tiergarten, and abandoned.

Surtees managed to take Clark for the lead, with Gurney very close behind. The three leaders were all under 8mins 50secs for the standing lap, and as they tore past the pits to start the third tour, the Ferrari had a 1.5secs advantage over the world champion's Lotus. Hill had come much closer to Gurney, and there was a considerable gap before Brabham, McLaren and Bandini came past.

Meanwhile, Anderson had stopped at his pit to add water, and in eighth Ginther stormed past ahead of Amon and Siffert. A short pause, and then we had Maggs, Trintignant, Bucknum, Spence and Barth, with Baghetti pitting with a broken throttle. Mechanics worked on the car, but eventually the BRM was pushed away. Phil Hill was out, too, with engine trouble, and Bonnier had also been forced to abandon. Before two laps had been completed the field had already been depleted by three.

Gurney was really trying, and at Breidscheid

he had taken second place from Clark, who was being sorely pressed by Graham Hill. John Surtees was definitely in the groove, the Ferrari sounding magnificent and the ex-motorcyclist driving with the skill that makes world champions.

Lap three, and the Ferrari whistled by the pits with Gurney in close attendance. A gap of 4.5secs, and then came Clark, with Hill in his slipstream. A pause, and Brabham, Bandini and McLaren screamed through almost nose to tail. As Amon hurried past, Ginther came in to have the plugs replaced to try to cure a misfire. The field had spread out somewhat, with Siffert, Maggs and Trintignant in line ahead, pursued by Bucknum, Spence and Barth, and at the tail-end, Mitter and Revson.

Surtees and Gurney were side by side when they went into the North Curve, and at the Karussell, the American was in front. Similarly Clark and Hill were duelling, passing and repassing between the South Curve and Karussell. Brabham, McLaren and Bandini were at it hammer and tongs, too.

Barth, battling with Bucknum and Spence, abandoned at Bergwerk with an engine failure.

'The crowds gasped as Gurney took Surtees at the North Curve, but as they disappeared over the rise they were side by side'

Anderson restarted, but he was reported to be in suspension trouble and made a third pit stop, long after the leaders had completed their fourth lap.

Gurney had about a second over Surtees as they stormed past the pits, while Hill had snapped into third ahead of Clark. Some 23secs behind came Brabham and Bandini. Into the pits went McLaren, to abandon with a broken valve spring.

The Gurney-Surtees and Hill-Clark duels went on with no holds barred. At the end of lap five, the Ferrari was just inches in front of the Brabham, both over 10secs in front of Hill, who was gradually pulling away from Clark. The crowds gasped as Gurney took Surtees on the inside of the North Curve, but as they disappeared over the rise they were again side by side.

With six laps completed, the leaders were still fighting it out, and roared into the South Curve wheel to wheel. Again Gurney tried to nip in the inside at the North Curve, but just failed to out-accelerate the Ferrari. Revson had been doubled, while Anderson called it a day and motored straight through the tunnel and into the paddock to retire.

John Surtees, driving an inspired race, set up a new lap record on his seventh tour of 8mins 45secs and had pulled out a lead over Gurney of 3secs. Graham Hill came through securely in third place, but where was Clark? Out onto the pit front went Chapman and the anxious mechanics. Then the world champion glided into his pit with a dead engine, to abandon with a suspected broken valve.

This put Brabham into fourth place, followed by Bandini, and then by Siffert and Amon, who were putting up a magnificent show. Maggs was really motoring aboard the Centro-Sud BRM, and Trintignant was putting up a splendid exhibition.

Eight laps gone, and another lap record to Surtees with 8mins 43secs.

The race order was as follows:

1, Surtees (Ferrari), 1h 10m 41.2s
2, Gurney (Brabham), 1h 10m 46.3s
3, G Hill (BRM), 1h 11m 7.1s
4, Brabham (Brabham); 5, Bandini (Ferrari); 6, Siffert (Brabham-BRM); 7, Amon (Lotus-BRM); 8, Maggs (BRM); 9, Trintignant (BRM); 10, Spence (Lotus); 11, Bucknum (Honda); 12, Ginther (BRM); 13, Mitter (Lotus); 14, Revson (Lotus-BRM), 7 laps

As Surtees hurtled down behind the pits, he was pointing to his offside-rear wheel. Then, as the scoreboard flashed his arrival at Karussell, there was an unexpected lapse of time before Gurney's number was illuminated. The American had eased off as the water temperature needle went off the clock. He'd dropped to 15secs behind the Ferrari.

Jack Brabham, seeing a red car in his mirrors, thought that it was Surtees about to double him, so he waved the car on as they sped uphill to the tribunes. To his chagrin, it was Bandini, so a stern chase ensued.

Surtees was 15.5secs ahead of Gurney, then a similar interval and Hill tore past, his engine sounding rough. Brabham was trying everything to retrieve his fourth place from Bandini and finally managed to squeeze ahead after a spot of dodgem motoring at the North Curve.

Then came reports that Gurney was falling back again. Graham Hill passed the slowing Brabham, and was 15secs ahead when they reached the Karussell. Surtees was by then 40secs to the good. Surtees and Hill duly went through to start lap 11, and into the pits went Gurney. His mechanics could not remove the radiator header-tank cap, so gallons of water were sloshed over the engine in an attempt to bring down the temperature.

Team-mate Jack Brabham went through, with Bandini in close attendance, while both Siffert and Amon had passed by the time Gurney restarted. By this time, Surtees had doubled Mitter, and then Bucknum, whose Honda had been overtaken for 12th place by Ginther in his rough-sounding BRM. The Japanese car had been going remarkably well for a first-ever race appearance, and Bucknum was driving extremely well.

Gurney's efforts to keep with Surtees had resulted in a new lap record of 8mins 42.9secs. The new figure did not stand for long: on his 11th lap, John Surtees produced an astonishing 8mins 39secs to lead Graham Hill by 46secs.

By lap 12, the Ferrari was 55secs in front of the BRM. We had to wait 3mins 48secs before Bandini appeared – with no Brabham! Later it was learned that the Australian had broken his crown wheel-and-pinion just before the Karussell.

This was also an unlucky lap for Chris Amon, who, after a splendid drive, had to abandon at his pit because of a broken rear suspension radius rod. Bucknum went off the road. He bent the Honda more than somewhat, but escaped without injury.

Dan Gurney made another pit stop, and eventually set off slowly in last place, behind Mitter.

Trintignant, going like the clappers, caught and passed Maggs for fifth behind Siffert, who had been circulating most impressively. Ginther moved into seventh as he overtook Mike Spence, whose Lotus sounded as rough as did the BRM.

Graham Hill, 64secs behind Surtees on lap 13, was also suffering from a stuttering power-unit and there were anxious faces in the BRM pit.

One lap to go, and Surtees managed to double sixth-place man Maggs. As the Ferrari screamed past the pits it sounded as if it could go on indefinitely. All that was left was to follow his progress on the Dunlop scoreboard. Graham Hill duly appeared about 68secs behind, his engine sounding rougher than ever.

All eyes were on the indicator board, as the progress of Surtees was closely followed. Safely through Karussell, then the Swallowtail. Up the rise through Tiergarten, and he was nearly home. The crowds chattered excitedly as the ever-rising engine note was heard. However, it was Trintignant's BRM. A few yards behind came the winning Ferrari to take the chequered flag.

Trintignant had just managed to avoid being doubled, but this meant he had to do another lap, although, on road position, he had already been classified fifth. Graham Hill, looking very tired, came over the line to take a well-earned second place and six points to put him two points ahead of Clark in the world championship.

Ferrari, already overjoyed by Surtees's second successive victory here, went almost mad with excitement as Bandini finished in third place. Then came Siffert and, a lap behind, Maggs, Ginther, Spence and Mitter in that order. Dan Gurney got a big hand as he finished in 10th place.

So there remained only Trintignant to arrive. The minutes passed, and the blue BRM appeared on the home straight, being pushed by the gallant Frenchman. With his fifth place assured, he was not disqualified, but, of course, was credited with only 14 laps. ■

RESULTS

15 LAPS (212.602 MILES)

1	John SURTEES	Ferrari 158	2h12m04.80s
2	Graham HILL	BRM P261	2h13m20.40s
3	Lorenzo BANDINI	Ferrari 156	2h16m57.60s
4	Jo SIFFERT	Brabham BT11	2h17m27.90s
5	Maurice TRINTIGNANT	BRM P57	14 laps
6	Tony MAGGS	BRM P57	14 laps

WINNING SPEED 96.579mph

FASTEST LAP SURTEES, 8m39.00s (98.313mph)

POLE POSITION SURTEES, 8m38.40s (98.427mph)

LAP LEADERS Jim CLARK 1; SURTEES 2-3, 5-15; GURNEY 4

Bruce McLaren's Cooper T73 is made to look insignificant by the Nürburgring; Surtees takes the plaudits – and bears the weighty wreath – on the podium (below)

WHAT HAPPENED NEXT...

Surtees, Hill and Clark went to the final round in Mexico each with a chance of becoming champion. Clark was a lap away from achieving this when he retired; Hill was involved in a controversial late clash with Bandini; and Surtees became the first – and so far only – to win world titles on two and four wheels.

ELL SHELL
SHE
3
3

Graham Hill's GREATEST

Senna won it six times, but there can only be one Mr Monaco – the Londoner who perfectly blended on-track performance with off-track flamboyance

BY GREGOR GRANT

GRAHAM HILL SCORED a dramatic victory for BRM in the finest race ever seen at Monte Carlo. This was a motor racing classic, the huge crowd popping up and down with excitement as Hill caught and passed the Maranello cars after an early incident at the Chicane when he stopped, thinking his car was about to catch fire. Lap records fell time after time as Bandini in the flat-12, and Surtees in the V8 fought tooth and nail to hold off the Londoner.

Graham, who had led for the opening 24 laps, followed closely by his brilliant team-mate, Jackie Stewart, climbed steadily from fifth spot to take Surtees on lap 54, and then head Bandini on lap 65. Twelve tours later John Surtees snapped past Bandini to attempt to set about Hill. A stern chase ensued, but the flying BRM prevailed to take the chequered flag at an average speed of 74.37mph, as compared with his 1964 average of 72.68mph. Surtees had plenty of drama one lap from the end when his Ferrari spluttered to a standstill with an almost bone-dry petrol tank. Bandini struggled to the finish with a sick-sounding engine to take second place ahead of Stewart. Surtees was finally classified fourth, and next in order came Bruce McLaren (Cooper-Coventry Climax) and Jo Siffert (Brabham-BRM). During his final assault Hill brought the Monaco lap record down to 1min 31.7secs, 76.72mph.

Dickie Attwood, who drove a splendid race with a Lotus-BRM, had a wheel hub carrier break going towards the Gasometer Hairpin. He hit the straw bales but was uninjured. However, it was Paul Hawkins who supplied the most spectacular accident when his Lotus slithered through the Chicane backwards, and finished up in the waters of the harbour with its intrepid pilot swimming to safety still wearing his crash hat and goggles.

Jack Brabham led for nine laps, but his 32-valve engine blew up in the biggest possible way on lap 43. Of the 16 starters, 10 were classified at the finish.

PRACTICE

With the defection of Team Lotus [to the Indianapolis 500] and the cancellation of invitations to others, only 17 entries were received to fill the 16 places on the grid. With six places assured to the 1964 placemen, the battle to qualify lay between Rindt's Cooper-Coventry Climax and the Honda of Ronnie Bucknum, as Ginther, although he was slower than both, had an assured start.

The insistence by the organizers on a minimum of 60 completed laps to qualify for full starting money, and the fact that Mike Spence and Pedro Rodriguez would have had to qualify anyway, doubtless led to the withdrawal of Lotus, which was rather hard lines on Spence and also on the far-travelled Mexican who had driven so well at Silverstone.

Jochen Rindt was extremely unlucky. The car just wouldn't get maximum rpm, and mechanics tried everything possible to put it right. Alas, when the trouble was traced – throttles not opening fully – it was too late and the Austrian's best was 1min 37.5secs, as compared to Bucknum's 1min 37secs. Ginther, plagued by various troubles, including a broken universal joint, could do no better than 1min 39.7secs.

Best time of the three sessions was put up by Graham Hill with 1min 32.5secs, 0.4secs faster than Jackie Stewart who had set the pace in the earlier trials. Jack Brabham was 0.1sec quicker than Stewart, so shared the front row of the grid with Hill. Bandini's 12-cylinder Ferrari was next with 1min 33secs, then Surtees with 1min 33.2secs. Easily quickest of the independents was Dickie Attwood with a superb 1min 33.9secs in the Parnell Lotus-BRM.

The gasworks has gone, and the swimming pool is in place – but won't become a familiar part of the circuit until 1972

Jack Brabham's Brabham BT11 leads the Cooper T77 of Bruce McLaren around the Station Hairpin. The former was holding the lead when his Coventry Climax engine blew up on lap 43

RACE

Race-day dawned dull, with heavy clouds hanging over the mountains. However the natives said that it would not rain. The Principality was packed to the limit, and parking space was problematical anywhere near the circuit.

The crowds were early to settle into their favourite vantage spots, and seemed to be bigger than ever when Prince Rainier and Princess Grace of Monaco arrived with their entourage. It was a pity that the parade of past winners and machines was slightly disorganized, these intriguing cars becoming rather mixed up with

'It was a superb start, with the howl of 13 V8s and three 12s shattering the ears as they scrambled past the Royal Box'

a fleet of Peugeots. Dominating the procession was the big supercharged Mercedes-Benz driven by Hermann Lang. Then we had Louis Chiron in a somewhat scruffy 2.3 Bugatti, Juan Fangio in the W196 Mercedes, Manzon (Gordini), Brivio (Alfa Romeo P2), Taruffi (2.7 Ferrari), Farina (250F Maserati) and Moss (2.5 Lotus-Climax), the last car being the property of Tom Wheatcroft. An Alfa Romeo Type 158 was also present, also driven by Fangio.

Anyway the sight and sound of these machines of a past era was nostalgic, bringing back memories of many hard-fought races on the Monaco circuit.

Then it was time for the depart, with Chiron darting about waving his blue flag in all directions.

It was a superb start, with the howl of 13 V8s and three 12s shattering the ears as they scrambled past the Royal Box and into Ste Devote, led by Hill, Stewart, Bandini and Brabham. Last away was Bucknum (Honda). Up to the Casino they streamed, and then down past the Metropole and the Station (which no longer exists!) to reach the seafront, hurl themselves through the tunnel to emerge at the Chicane, along past the Tabac towards the pits and the notorious Gasometer Hairpin to start it all over again. (The Gasometer has also vanished from the scene!)

Hill, Stewart, Bandini, Surtees, Brabham, McLaren, Attwood, Siffert, Anderson, Hulme, Gardner, Bonnier, Hailwood and Hawkins – that was the order at the end of that electrifying first lap. Bringing up a belated rear were the two Hondas, and Ginther drove his straight into the pits to abandon with a broken universal coupling.

The pace was fast and furious, with the BRMs of Hill and Stewart leading the Ferraris and Brabham's Brabham. A few yards behind, Attwood was tailing McLaren. The sorting-out process was beginning, and already white patches on tyres showed contact with the high kerbs of Monaco. Hill and Stewart seemed to be determined to get well out in front and stay there. At any rate, they were both drawing away from Bandini and Surtees at around 1sec per lap, getting down to 1min 34.1secs on the second tour. John Surtees seemed to be content to let Bandini make the running for Ferrari. Brabham had dropped back slightly, being threatened by McLaren and Attwood, with Anderson leading the duelling Siffert and Hulme. Although obviously not a serious contender (so far at any rate), Bucknum's Honda sounded far healthier than ever before, and certainly appeared to have plenty of steam up the rise to the Casino.

At the end of 10 laps the BRM pair had pulled out 11secs over the Ferraris, and Brabham was starting to edge nearer to the red cars. Into the pits went Mike Hailwood to retire with mechanical problems to leave 14 cars on the circuit. The average had shot up to 117.548km/h, and on the 12th lap the leaders had already doubled the Honda, and four laps later Hawkins had also been lapped.

Driving with almost robot-like precision, Hill and Stewart forged ahead, while Brabham closed on Surtees and Attwood on McLaren. Twenty laps and the race order was:

1, Graham Hill (BRM), 31m 55.5s; 2, Jackie Stewart (BRM), 31m 57.6s; 3, Lorenzo Bandini (Ferrari), 32m 11.6s; 4, John Surtees (Ferrari), 32m 12.2s; 5, Jack Brabham (Brabham-CC), 32m 13.2s

Next time round Bonnier had been doubled. Dickie Attwood had taken McLaren on lap 17 easily to lead the independent brigade. Bob Anderson was challenging Denny Hulme, who had managed to shake off Siffert.

The Ferraris of Lorenzo Bandini and John Surtees (18) chase Hill into Casino Square. Note, the pavement was not out of bounds for pedestrians; Hill brakes hard for Mirabeau (bottom)

Just as the race seemed to be settling into a BRM procession and a Ferrari-Brabham scrap, Graham Hill was seen to come to an abrupt halt at the Chicane. Apparently, after fiercely braking to avoid Anderson's slowing Brabham, he thought that his engine had caught fire, but this was not so, and he restarted in fifth place. This left Jackie Stewart in command, some 16secs in front of Bandini and Co. Lap 27 and Brabham had forced his way past Surtees and was looking for the slightest opportunity to take Bandini.

BRM had a shock on lap 30 when Bandini came through in the lead pursued by the tenacious Brabham, the watchful Surtees and a wide gap before Stewart and Hill appeared. Stewart had done it all wrong at Beau Rivage, and from a BRM lead of 17secs, the pair had now fallen 11secs behind the race leaders. Bob Anderson, overtaken first by Gardner and then by Siffert, stopped at his pits to investigate a mysterious lack of power, and Frank Gardner's effort came to an abrupt end when the engine mounting bolts came adrift and the radiator started to fall off.

Bandini desperately fought to hold off Brabham, and Surtees kept well within striking distance. Jackie Stewart signalled Hill to go ahead just past the pits, and the Londoner set off like a scalded cat to see what could be done about catching the leaders.

As the unfortunate Bucknum came to rest with his gear linkage adrift, a tremendous roar went up from the crowd as Jack Brabham slipped ahead of Bandini at the hairpin to take the lead. One could feel tension all over the circuit as the battle raged in front, and Graham Hill began almost imperceptibly to close up on John Surtees. Attwood and McLaren were still duelling merrily, with Bruce retaking the Parnell car on lap 36. Strung out behind came Hulme, Siffert, Bonnier and Hawkins.

Hill got down to 1min 34.6secs, and on the 40th lap he was only 4secs behind Surtees. In point of fact, less than 1.5secs separated Brabham and the two Ferraris. However, Dame Fortune once again struck at the Australian. Coming down towards the hairpin on the 43rd lap his engine blew up in a monumental way, and that was that. Apparently he had been driving with no rev-counter – not the ideal way to race.

'Stewart signalled Hill to go ahead, and the Londoner took off like a scalded cat to see what could be done about the leaders'

Into the lead swept the red machines of Italy with Graham Hill in hot pursuit. The Londoner's progress was meteoric. Using all his immense skill, he was steadily cutting down the gap between the BRM and the Ferraris as Stewart held fourth place.

Attwood, whose driving had been most impressive throughout, had his race end almost in disaster as a wheel hub carrier broke approaching the hairpin. Off came the wheel, and the Lotus-BRM charged the bales, scattering straw in all directions. Firefighters rushed to the scene as Attwood stepped out completely unhurt.

Bandini had now doubled Siffert, which left only half a dozen cars on the same lap. This came down to five on the 48th tour when Hulme also had to give way. The Ferrari pit kept their charges informed of the threat from Graham Hill. Surtees moved closer to Bandini with a 1min 34.1secs, but a couple of laps later Hill

The Ferraris give valiant chase (left), but Hill ups his pace (above) to secure his third Monaco win (below). That's an inflatable neck brace Hill is wearing

WHAT HAPPENED NEXT...

Jim Clark and Lotus returned victorious from Indy to dominate the rest of the GP season. The Scot, however, would never win in Monte Carlo, whereas Hill would prevail twice more – in 1968 and 1969.

was down to 1min 33.9sec, and then, on the 50th tour to complete half-distance, he produced a 1min 33.3secs. The positions were:

1, Bandini (Ferrari), 1h 20m 10.6s; 2, Surtees (Ferrari), 1h 20m 11.2s; 3, Hill (BRM), 1h 20m 12.1s; 4 Stewart (BRM), 1h 20m 26.5s; 5, McLaren (Cooper-CC); 6, Hulme (Brabham-CC); 7, Siffert (Brabham-BRM); 8, Bonnier (Brabham-CC); 9, Hawkins (Lotus-CC); 10, Anderson (Brabham-CC)

Three laps later and Hill had snatched second place from Surtees at the Station. McLaren had also been doubled by Bandini. The excitement was tremendous as Hill hounded Bandini. The Italian was keeping surprisingly cool, driving really well and naturally anxious to avoid any repetition of the Mexican incident.

All eyes were on the struggle going on in front. Hill, chin jutting out and inscrutable as ever, was driving "10-10", never putting a wheel wrong and getting the utmost from his splendidly prepared BRM, Jackie Stewart had fallen back from the contest but was doing a grand job of work holding fourth place, well capable of coming to grips with the Ferraris should anything happen to Hill.

'Folk like Fangio shook their heads as these cars lapped the torturous circuit at averages not dreamed possible in their day'

On lap 58 Surtees made a desperate effort to regain second place with a new lap record of 1min 33secs. However, next time around, this was equalled by Hill, so the gap remained the same. Bandini was beginning to look a trifle weary with the pressure ever increasing from Hill. To have a couple of world champions breathing up your exhaust pipes can be pretty unnerving.

Jackie Stewart's BRM occasionally twitched under braking, looking as though a wheel might have been damaged when he spun at Beau Rivage and clonked the kerb earlier on. Anyway, he was gallantly plugging on, secure in fourth place.

It was obvious that Bandini would have to give way sooner or later. Winding on the flat-12 to the limit, he set a new lap record on his 63rd circuit with 1min 32.9secs. Two tours later and Hill had equalled this, and next time around Graham was down to 1min 32.7secs, having taken the lead from Bandini at the Station. Programmes were waved and the Londoner was cheered all the way round the circuit. This put Bandini on his mettle and the young Italian gave his car the stick to equal Hill's new record and once again get close to the back wheels of the BRM. Graham replied with 1min 32.5secs, which was immediately equalled by Bandini on lap 67. Not to be outdone, John Surtees did the same on lap *soixante-neuf.*

With this spate of record-breaking, the crowds could hardly contain themselves. All restraint was thrown to the winds and the yelling and cheering was just like a football game. Seventy laps, and only 2.5secs separated the trio; the race average was 118.614 km/h. Hill's time was 1hr 51mins 17.6secs, and it is interesting to recall that in 1964, when in the lead, his time for the same distance was 1hr 52mins 31secs.

Ferrari were becoming more anxious and out went the lap signals for Surtees to do something about the flying BRM. Then, on the 77th lap, Surtees drew alongside Bandini at the pits and forged ahead at Ste Devote. The chase was on in earnest – two great drivers in two superbly prepared cars. For lap after lap Graham held a 2-3secs lead and a tired-looking Bandini gradually dropped out of the contest. The crowd had now quietened down considerably, realising the tense struggle going on between the two champions.

With 20 laps still to do, Hill's slender lead remained the same. On lap 82, Graham once again broke the record, this time with 1min 31.7secs, 76.72mph. Folk like Fangio shook their heads as these cars lapped the tortuous circuit at averages not dreamed possible in their day.

Then came drama at the Chicane. Paul Hawkins seemed to have something lock up, the Lotus spun, shot backwards through the hay bales and, narrowly missing a huge solid bollard, shot backwards into the waters of the harbour to disappear in a cloud of steam and foam. Hawkins quickly surfaced and with powerful strokes speedily swam to safety as speedboats and frogmen arrived to the rescue. Said the Australian laconically: "That's one way of cooling one's ardour!"

Bandini's car was sounding somewhat breathless. Surtees's efforts did not reduce the gap and in fact Hill began to edge ahead. Denny Hulme, after a splendid drive, came into the pits with some wheel trouble with only eight laps still to be covered.

Two laps remaining and Hill had a 7secs advantage – an impossible task for the Ferrari driver unless something happened to Hill's BRM.

Actually it happened to the Ferrari, for with one lap to go the red car stammered to a standstill having run out of petrol. As Graham hurtled on his way to victory for the third successive year, Surtees edged the silent Ferrari round to the finishing line on the starter motor, with Chiron jumping up and down like a yo-yo to ensure that no Ferrari mechanics laid a hand on the machine.

Bandini duly completed his 100 laps, as did Stewart, so to Surtees went fourth place, having covered one more lap than Bruce McLaren and Jo Siffert. Into seventh place came Bonnier, having driven an unspectacular race throughout.

A deliriously happy Graham Hill toured round after being congratulated by Prince Rainier and Princess Grace. There was plenty doing in the old town that night. Following a victory celebration with Louis and Jean Stanley as hosts, the Tip Top and other spots were invaded by BRM for the third time in three years. ■

RESULTS

100 LAPS (195.421 MILES)

1	Graham HILL	BRM P261	2h37m39.60s
2	Lorenzo BANDINI	Ferrari 1512	2h38m43.60s
3	Jackie STEWART	BRM P261	2h39m21.50s
4	John SURTEES	Ferrari 158	99 laps
5	Bruce McLAREN	Cooper T77	99 laps
6	Jo SIFFERT	Brabham BT11	98 laps

WINNING SPEED 74.371mph

FASTEST LAP HILL, 1m31.70s (76.719mph)

POLE POSITION HILL, 1m32.50s (76.056mph)

LAP LEADERS HILL 1-24, 65-100; STEWART 25-29; BANDINI 30-33, 43-64; BRABHAM 34-42

Stewart's second **win in the wet**

The Scot copped a lot of flak for his safety crusade, but even his critics had to respect his skill and bravery. The Nürburgring was at its elemental worst – but Jackie was at his inspirational best

BY PATRICK McNALLY

JACKIE STEWART | 1968 GERMAN GP | AUGUST 4
MATRA MS10

A heavy crash in practice put Jackie Oliver on the back foot. He finished 11th in his oddly handling, just-rebuilt Lotus 49B

JACKIE STEWART COMPLETELY dominated the German Grand Prix at the Nürburgring last Sunday to win at an average speed of 86.87mph, giving Ken Tyrrell's Matra-Ford its second Grand Prix win in the wet this year. Stewart, who was still driving with one hand in a special support, took the lead halfway round the first lap and held it right through to the finish, setting fastest lap in the process.

One of the features of the race, which was run in atrociously wet conditions, was the battle for second place between Graham Hill's Lotus 49B and Chris Amon's Ferrari, which was resolved when Amon suffered differential trouble and spun with only three laps to go. Jochen Rindt took third place in a four-cam Brabham ahead of Jacky Ickx in the second of the works Ferraris. Graham Hill still leads the World Championship with 30 points, although Jackie Stewart has now moved up to second place ahead of Ickx.

ENTRY

The vast expanses of the Nürburgring need no restrictions on size of entry, so it wasn't surprising to find that the AvD had gathered together the biggest entry of the season. In typical Teutonic fashion they had included Kurt Ahrens in a third Repco-Brabham and Hubert Hahne in a 2.1-litre Lola-BMW, requiring Vic Elford, Jackie Oliver, Piers Courage and Silvio Moser to compete for the three remaining places on the grid, despite the fact that all four have already gained championship points – a ridiculous situation. Although Jo Bonnier was entered he decided not to run, as his McLaren-BRM is at the moment still uncompetitive.

Most formidable among the contenders were the Ferraris. SEFAC had brought along three cars as usual, including a brand-new car, 0015, for Jacky Ickx. Chris Amon was to drive the same car he used at Brands Hatch, 0011, but old 0007 had been left at Maranello and Ickx's Rouen-conquering car, 0009, was the spare on this occasion. The two veteran cars had been stripped and rebuilt, but the specification of all three remained identical.

After their initial domination of the British Grand Prix, the Team Lotus cars were basically similar, although Oliver's old-type ex-Tasman, ex-Siffert 49 had been brought up to 49B spec using bits off the car he demolished at Rouen. The only thing still original was the monocoque centre section, which had been cut about to take the different pick-up points, fitted with a cross member to take the rear suspension, and now carried a Hewland FG400 gearbox. Graham Hill's car had needed new rear uprights and driveshafts after the British Grand Prix, and Lotus had made up some shafts using parts from Mercedes and BRD bits in an effort to find transmission joints that could take the increased loads incurred by the use of the wing. Both Lotuses were fitted with steel-braided brake lines to give a harder pedal. Jo Siffert's British GP-winning Rob Walker Lotus 49B had also had its transmission strengthened, and all three cars had been fitted with struts from the bottom of their bellhousing adaptor plates to the cross member to try to distribute the loads more evenly.

The McLarens appeared in their usual form, Denny Hulme's unaltered since Brands save for the omission of the rear aerofoil. Bruce McLaren's car was the original M7A/1 which had been fitted with 13in wheels and the original front suspension geometry. M7A/2 had been brought along as a spare, easily recognizable by its extra lines of rivets down the sides of the monocoque.

Brabhams had joined the three-car set: the usual BT26s and a new but incomplete four-cammer as a spare. They also had the old BT24 twin-cam for Kurt Ahrens to drive under the Caltex Racing banner. Brabham has been busy testing at Goodwood and the fuel system has now been changed as a result, with altered pick-ups and a new catch tank for the overflow; the wings on both cars were also higher.

Completely unchanged, bar wider wheels, were the BRMs for Pedro Rodriguez and Richard Attwood, although Piers Courage's Parnell car had grown an aerofoil above its engine. John Surtees's Honda featured a longer exhaust system and a brand-new engine, RA301 E803. The car was

A tunnel brought the cars from the paddock to the track (left); Jean-Pierre Beltoise would crash his Matra (above); conditions were dire, as – Vic Elford's Cooper looms out of the murk (below)

sitting higher than before to allow for the 'Ring's bad bumps, and a new aerofoil had been added. Contrary to popular belief the old aerofoil on the Honda had been rubber-mounted, and its failure was due to poor materials.

Matra Sports arrived with its usual pair of V12 MS11s for Jean-Pierre Beltoise. The newer of the two was fitted with an aerofoil whose pitch was controlled by a small electric motor coupled to operate when the brakes were applied; there was also an override switch. The older car was still running with the original six-pipe exhaust and a mass of rather untidy plumbing over its gearbox, indicating that they haven't had time at Vélizy to update it.

Ken Tyrrell's Matra International MS10 for Jackie Stewart featured new magnesium front uprights designed to reduce camber change on lock, but was otherwise unchanged. A second car was brought along as usual, and Johnny Servoz-Gavin had been busy learning the circuit all week, though there was no official entry for him. Tyrrell tried to get another entry accepted, without success.

Official lap record-holder Dan Gurney brought along the Eagle, unaltered since Brands, although a brand-new engine had been fitted. The Eagle had the honour of having the widest rear wheels in the race, measuring 16.25in across and shod with Goodyear's widest tyre yet with a 13.2in footprint.

Cooper-BRMs appeared for Lucien Bianchi, who knows the 'Ring well, and Vic Elford, who is equally knowledgeable. The Coopers were unchanged bar the addition of the large aerofoils above the engines. Hubert Hahne was entered in an official BMW 2.1-litre car; this was basically a Lola T100, reworked somewhat and fitted with the old Apfelbeck 16-valve F2 engine bored and stroked and fitted with a Hewland gearbox.

PRACTICE

The ever-changeable weather made a mockery of practice. In theory there were three practice sessions, two on Friday and one on Saturday, but the little weathermen excelled themselves. Friday's morning session was reduced to a fog-shrouded farce, while the afternoon session had to be called off because of lack of visibility.

On Saturday it rained and the mist was still thick round the circuit, and it looked as if there would be no practice at all that day; but towards the end of the afternoon the mist lifted slightly and the organizers decided, after consulting the GPDA, that the cars could go out after all. The AvD then decided to run a further session on Sunday morning; conditions for this were no better, for although the visibility had improved, the track was virtually awash after heavy overnight rain.

In the first session on Friday the track was damp and patches of mist made drivers doubly cautious. Little were they to know that these were the best conditions they were to experience. Jacky Ickx, who knows the 'Ring inside out, soon showed his worth to Ferrari by getting round in 9m 4s, over 10secs faster than team-mate Chris Amon, who was next fastest. Chris had the benefit of a day's testing here the previous month and it was serving him well, for he only did one complete lap!

After the Ferraris came Jochen Rindt in the four-cam Brabham. He only did a few laps before deciding that his engine needed changing; nevertheless his time of 9m 31.9s made him third just ahead of Hill, who also did few laps.

The Honda gave John Surtees a nasty moment when the throttle stuck open thanks to the return springs fouling. 'Big John' brought the Japanese car back to the pits on the ignition switch and had no further opportunity for practice; however his time of 9m 57.8s made him sixth-fastest, much to his surprise. Vic Elford was the one to astound the pundits, getting the Cooper-BRM round 0.8secs quicker than Surtees – yet another to demonstrate the value of an intimate circuit knowledge.

Piers Courage was the fastest BRM by far; his 10m 0.1s was 19secs faster than Pedro Rodriguez and over a minute quicker than Richard Attwood in the works cars. Jo Siffert got round in 10m 3.4s in the Walker Lotus, but Jackie Oliver's car was still being screwed together in the paddock.

Jack Brabham saw no reason to hurry at this stage, as his time of 10m 38.4s indicated; neither

Crowd roaring.
Engines screaming.
Quiet words.
Make it happen.
at&t
WILLIAMS
OFFICIAL PARTNER

did Gurney, who just wanted to make sure that the Eagle was on all 12. Kurt Ahrens, having his first Formula 1 drive for Brabham, very sensibly took it easy and his time was not indicative of his ability. Both Lucien Bianchi in the Cooper-BRM and Jean-Pierre Beltoise in the Matra V12 doddled round, as did Hubert Hahne in the Lola-BMW.

This first practice session did not give a fair indication of what we could expect, for everybody was anticipating better conditions. Jackie Stewart, Denny Hulme and Bruce McLaren did not even bother to do a complete lap – they must have been kicking themselves the following day. The Friday afternoon session was finally abandoned after the cars had sat waiting in front of their pits for the weather to clear.

On Saturday morning the cars didn't even get as far as the pits, and it wasn't until 3pm that word came through that the circuit was open for practice. Once again the drivers were disinclined to have a real go, still hoping that Sunday morning would provide a dry track they could actually see.

Jackie Stewart decided he had better get in a few laps and, on a soaking track, set fastest time in 10m 0.4s in the Matra-Ford, on the same type of grooved Dunlop tyre he used to win at Zandvoort. Next quickest was Ickx in the Ferrari, whose time was almost exactly a minute slower than his previous day's best and 4secs slower than Stewart – the Ferrari was on grooved Firestone YB11s.

Both Jochen Rindt and Dan Gurney looked very spectacular, their cars sliding wildly on the slippery track, but both got down to exactly the same time – 10m 13.9s. Rindt tried out the new car just in case either he or Jack were forced to use it for the race. The Eagle's handling was not pleasing the Californian, who was also troubled by damp ignition which made the engine sound flat.

Jackie Oliver was having an unhappy time with what was virtually a new Lotus 49B, and came in to comment after being black-flagged: "As if the mist and rain aren't enough, some b------ has dropped oil all round the track"; then he found out he was the culprit, as his catch tank was filling up and pumping oil out through its breather. Teammate Graham Hill was more fortunate, and his time of 10m 14.6s made him fifth-fastest.

John Surtees was finding even less traction with the Honda than his competitors and was once again wondering whether his limited-slip was the culprit, for Hill, on identical tyres, had succeeded in out-accelerating the Honda from one corner while John just got wheelspin. When asked what he thought of the conditions by a newsman, John's reply was the understatement of the year: "It's not very nice out there." Chris Amon certainly didn't like the wet, yet his time of 10m 17.4s in the Ferrari was nearly half a second faster than Surtees.

Jack Brabham tried hard in his four-cam, but the conditions were against him and he was half a dozen seconds slower than Surtees, and only just faster than Elford, who was thriving on the difficult track. Jack's engine eventually ran out of oil, and the spare engine from the new BT26 had to be fitted to his car. Elford had a big spin going into the South Curve, but, although he left the track, the car was undamaged. He and Lucien Bianchi tried the large aerofoils Cooper had brought and commented on the improved stability, although Bianchi did not go that quickly as he only did a couple of laps.

There was an appreciable gap in the times after Elford, with Siffert and Pedro Rodriguez next up. Richard Attwood was only 7.5secs slower than Pedro with a 10m 48.2s, but Courage, already assured of a good place on the grid, didn't bother to try hard. BRMs tried various rollbars and damper settings but conditions made it impossible to appreciate any improvement.

The McLaren pair were very unhappy. Denny Hulme was the faster with 10m 52.9s, but Bruce McLaren couldn't set a time, his Ford V8 engine

Stewart ran the Matra with and without wings during practice. Presumably Graham Hill removed the brolly before setting off (top)

sooting plugs all the while. Hahne tried some very narrow Dunlops on the BMW-Lola and recorded a creditable 10m 56.5s, although compatriot Kurt Ahrens had trouble with the twin-cam Brabham and was not competitive. Unhappiest of all, however, was Jean-Pierre Beltolse, who only completed a couple of laps in the Matra, which doesn't seem to be showing its Zandvoort form these days.

The question of qualification never came up for Silvio Moser, for the oil pump seized on his Vogele Brabham and damaged the bearings.

For the additional practice session on Sunday morning the track was awash, deep water lying in places, and mud washed across the circuit made it all the more slippery. The Ferraris, Cooper-BRMs and Jo Siffert decided the session would serve no useful purpose and didn't go out.

Despite the near-impossible conditions, Jackie Stewart hurried the Matra-Ford round, eventually getting down to 9m 54.2s, a pretty impressive performance. The Tyrrell team even found time to try a wing, but Jackie said he couldn't feel any great difference. However, Friday's times meant that Ferrari had the pole position, with Jochen Rindt also on the front row. Graham Hill's time put him on the second row with Vic Elford, and John Surtees and Piers Courage shared the third row with Jackie Stewart.

Denny Hulme and Jean-Pierre Beltoise both improved their times, Denny getting down to 10m 16s for a place on row five, while JPB managed 10m 17.3s on the very last lap of practice, which moved him up from the rear of the grid to the same row. Jackie Oliver, worried that everybody else was going quicker, got down to 10m 18.7s and then, in one last final fling, put the Lotus into the hedge on the third of the fast right-handers going down to the bridge before Adenau Crossing, tearing off two wheels. Although the race was due to start only two-and-a-half hours later, somehow or other the Lotus boys managed to repair the car in time.

Gurney's Eagle still seemed to be handling oddly and the American driver was unable to improve on his Saturday's best, but Bruce McLaren used the extra session to good purpose, improving his time by nearly 30s. Neither Hill nor Rindt could improve on their times, while Surtees contented himself with trying out a variety of wet-weather tyres. Hubert Hahne was again impressive and improved to 10m 42.9s in the Lola-BMW.

RACE

Undeterred by atrocious weather, the crowds flocked to the circuit, their enthusiasm undampened. Because of the morning practice the start was delayed for 45 minutes; despite reports that the weather was lifting, there was no sign of a break, and the starting area was still covered by a white and very wet blanket of mist and rain. There was hardly a spectator to be seen, for they were all hidden under an undulating colourful mass of umbrellas. At 2.30pm the cars lined up on the dummy grid, which was a bit of a shambles. The start procedure had to be seen to be believed; the order to start engines came 10mins before the start, and by the time the cars moved forward onto the proper grid most of them were on the boil.

When the flag finally dropped, the cars roared towards the South Curve, sending up great white plumes. Poleman Jacky Ickx was a trifle heavy on the throttle and provoked too much wheelspin, so it was Graham Hill's Lotus, coming through from the second row, which took the initiative. Chris Amon's Ferrari and Jackie Stewart's Matra were close behind the Lotus as all three tore into the North Curve, while behind them Dan Gurney, Jochen Rindt and Jacky Ickx were dicing furiously. Stewart was determined to get the lead, and as they went into Adenau Crossing he had passed Amon's Ferrari and was right on Hill's tail. By the Schwalbenschwanz the young Scot had taken the lead, and as they roared pass the pits at the end of their first lap the Tyrrell Matra-Ford was already 8secs ahead.

Amon was now locked in combat with Hill, while behind them Rindt was leading Gurney and Ickx. Surtees had been behind the Gurney Eagle, but his engine was off song and, when Ickx had passed him, he came in for a plug change. Piers Courage lay seventh ahead of Jack Brabham and Denny Hulme, who was leading Siffert, Rodriguez, Beltoise, Ahrens, Oliver, Bianchi, McLaren, Hahne and Attwood. Vic Elford went off at Schwalbenschwanz when blinded by spray, the Cooper-BRM spinning into a couple of stout posts and wiping off a front and a rear wheel; Vic was unhurt.

By the second lap Stewart had pulled a further 25secs ahead, the blue Matra solitary but secure at the head of the field. Amon was no closer to Hill, and both were drawing away slightly from the Gurney/Ickx duo. Brabham had passed Courage's BRM, which was being challenged by Hulme's McLaren. Siffert in the Walker Lotus was having a hard time staying ahead of Pedro Rodriguez, who

Practice was blighted by the bad weather. Stewart and Hill wait in the pits for conditions to improve – they never did

was being pushed along by JPB's Matra. Ahrens, Oliver and Hahne were some way further back, leading Bianchi, McLaren and Attwood.

By lap three Stewart was 37secs in front of Hill. Amon was third and Rindt's four-cam Brabham still lay fourth, but Ickx's Ferrari was now in fifth place having passed Gurney at the Flugplatz. The Eagle then punctured a front tyre at the Karussell when the Californian got a wheel on the grass and hit a sharp rock which gashed the sidewall. Dan continued to the pits to change the wheel, and when he restarted he was behind everybody bar Surtees, who was in the pits again trying to find out what was wrong with the Honda's engine.

Denny Hulme got past Piers Courage to claim seventh place, slipping by the BRM as they went into the North Turn, while further back Siffert was in danger of being taken by Pedro's BRM and the French Matra. Ahrens, Oliver and Hahne were in close company, the works Lotus slowed drastically by its accident; although it had been rebuilt in time for the start, its geometry was way out and Oliver was running with toe-in as well as about 10 degrees of negative camber on the left rear wheel.

The two Ford V8-engined cars of Stewart and Hill continued to lead, but the gap between them had grown to 59secs. All eyes were now on Amon, who was having a big go to get by Hill and had closed to 1.7secs. Ickx was pressing Rindt hard, and both were moving up towards the leaders. Jack Brabham now lay sixth, from Hulme and Courage and Rodriguez. Siffert was in the pits with engine trouble. The Walker mechanics changed the plugs to no avail, for, like Surtees's Honda, the car had boiled on the line and was US; Siffert and Surtees did a few more laps before retiring.

With five laps completed the scene looked set for another Stewart victory. The Scotsman's lead was now 67secs and there was no-one to challenge him in the entire field. Graham Hill seemed well able to hold Amon at bay, while Rindt's lead over Ickx suddenly lengthened dramatically when the Belgian, whose visor was completely misted-up, arrived at North Turn quicker than he expected and spun away valuable seconds. However, the second Ferrari was in little danger from Jack Brabham,

'He turned its nose down the hill, engaged starter and gear at the same time and rejoined the race. This cost Mr Hill a minute and a few grey hairs to boot'

for the latter was nearly 2mins in arrears, still leading the group consisting of Hulme and Courage, who were fast being joined by Pedro Rodriguez. Oliver, despite rear-wheel steering, had passed the German pair of Ahrens and Hahne. Lucien Bianchi retired the second Cooper at this stage, as a leaking fuel bag had covered him in petrol and he decided he had had quite enough.

By half-distance there was no doubt that Stewart was master of the situation. The Ford-engined Matra was sounding as strong as ever and was 90secs ahead of Hill and Amon, who were still scrapping furiously for second, and still running virtually nose to tail. Rindt was a solitary fourth, for Ickx had lost further time by coming into the pits to discard his visor; he arrived too quickly to stop and continued without protection for his eyes. Jack Brabham was being made to work hard for sixth place by the scrap behind him, still led by Hulme, from Courage, Rodriguez and Beltoise, all fighting every inch of the way.

With eight laps completed – only six to go – Stewart set the seal on his domination by again setting fastest lap, 9m 36s, and drawing away still further from the Hill/Amon battle. Further down the field Brabham, despite problems with a sticking throttle, had drawn away from Hulme, who was now being pressed really hard by Rodriguez, who had passed Courage. Gurney was coming up fast through the backmarkers and was now in 13th place, about to pass Oliver's Lotus.

Stewart continued his relentless pace, which now saw him hold a 1m 52s advantage. Amon was still very close to Hill, but Rindt was catching both of them, sliding the four-cam Brabham wildly out of the chicane. The hottest battle was still between Hulme, Rodriguez and Courage; Jean-Pierre Beltoise had left the road just before the right-hander below the Karussell, the Matra's fuel system being damaged when the car struck a bank. Apparently JPB had been trying to pass Courage and left his braking too late. Ickx, who was still lying in a secure fifth, had been into the pits again to collect his now-clean visor, for the rain was still coming down hard and the young Ferrari driver was almost blinded.

With three laps to go Stewart's engine sounded as healthy as ever, and although he was now

Jochen Rindt's Brabham harries Elford through the Karussell. The Austrian (opposite, left) would eventually join Stewart and Hill on the podium

WHAT HAPPENED NEXT...

Graham Hill took the title after a three-way finale with Stewart and Denny Hulme. But the following year, still driving a Ken Tyrrell-run Matra, Stewart won six GPs to clinch the first of his three titles.

over 2mins ahead of the Lotus/Ferrari duel, he still didn't ease up. As they went into their 12th lap Amon looked as if he was going to pass the Lotus at any moment, for he was only a length behind and pulling out of the spray as if to overtake. But the cruel luck which has dogged Amon throughout the season struck again. Something was apparently amiss with his limited-slip diff, and going into the second part of the North Turn the Ferrari spun wildly on the slippery surface, finishing up on the grass bank, undamaged but stuck firm in the mud. However, Amon's pursuit of the Lotus had confirmed his ability as a wet-weather driver

Graham Hill, not realizing Amon was no longer behind him (all he could see in his mirrors was spray), continued to press on, and in his efforts spun in the esses after Hohe Acht, stalling in the middle of the road. Glancing nervously over his shoulder, expecting Amon's Ferrari to come hurtling out of the mist at any moment, the Londoner got out of the car – which had refused to start on the button – turned its nose down the hill, engaged the starter and a gear at the same time and rejoined the race. This series of manoeuvres cost Mr Hill a minute – and probably gave him a few grey hairs to boot.

There had been other place changes that lap, for Rodriguez had passed Hulme as they went down to Adenau Crossing, the McLaren driver letting the Mexican through; until then he had been unaware of the speed at which he was being caught, as he couldn't see his own pit signals.

As Stewart started his last lap he had it in the bag, for his lead over Hill's Lotus was a fraction under 4mins. Hill on the other hand had Rindt hard on his heels, and was having to work overtime to hold his place. But the Austrian's efforts came to nought, for the enormous sheet of spray created by Hill's Lotus made it far too dangerous to pass. Pedro Rodriguez had closed right up on Brabham, but he too found the spray too much and decided it was safer to stay where he was.

Shortly before the finish Stewart came up to lap Oliver just before Adenauer Forst; he didn't see the Lotus until he was almost on top of it and suddenly saw the wing emerging from the spray ahead; he had to brake violently and gave himself a nasty moment.

As the final minutes ticked by the tension was unbearable, but the Tyrrell team need not have worried, for Stewart is not one to make foolish mistakes. As the Matra appeared over the brow hats shot into the air in triumph – they had won again. Now all the attention turned to Hill – could he hold off Rindt? Four minutes after Stewart had crossed the line, Hill flashed across it, too, still 6secs ahead of Jochen. Jacky Ickx took a lonely fourth place for Ferrari, but only 10secs separated Brabham, Rodriguez and Hulme, who filled the next three places.

Dunlop was delighted with its second Grand Prix victory of the year; its 226 compound seems an ideal wet-weather tyre. They are fortunate that Stewart demonstrates its potential so convincingly. The last time anyone could remember a race being run here in such dreadful conditions was in 1936, when Bernd Rosemeyer won a fog-bound Eifelrennen in an Auto Union. ■

RESULTS

14 LAPS (198.646 MILES)

1	Jackie STEWART	Matra MS10	2h19m03.20s
2	Graham HILL	Lotus 49B	2h23m06.40s
3	Jochen RINDT	Brabham BT26	2h23m12.60s
4	Jacky ICKX	Ferrari 312	2h24m58.40s
5	Jack BRABHAM	Brabham BT26	2h25m24.30s
6	Pedro RODRIGUEZ	BRM P133	2h25m28.20s

WINNING SPEED 85.714mph

FASTEST LAP STEWART, 9m36.00s (88.681mph)

POLE POSITION ICKX, 9m04.00s (93.898mph)

LAP LEADER STEWART 1-14

RINDT WINS AS BRABHAM CRASHES AT LAST CORNER

The leader was the wise old bird who liked to win at the slowest possible speed. The chaser was the young tearaway whose speed was ferocious but whose winning record in F1 was poor...

BY PATRICK McNALLY

JOCHEN RINDT | 1970 MONACO GP | MAY 10 LOTUS 49C

Rindt, his wick finally up, harries Henri Pescarolo's Matra into Casino Square. They are battling for fourth – a victory for either man looks very unlikely...

IN THE MOST sensational finish at Monte Carlo since the war, Jochen Rindt scored a last-ditch victory for Gold Leaf Team Lotus when Jack Brabham, who had led for nearly two-thirds of the distance, crashed into the barrier on the last corner of the last lap. He restarted to take second place ahead of Henri Pescarolo, who gave Matra their best result this year with a fine third.

From the start Jackie Stewart's Tyrrell March ran away from Chris Amon and Brabham, pulling out a handsome lead until ignition trouble forced him into the pits. Amon tailed Brabham until the rear suspension of his works March failed, and his team-mate Jo Siffert went well after a slow start until his fuel injection started to play up. The Matra of Jean-Pierre Beltoise was also up with the leaders again until retiring, this time with transmission failure, while Denny Hulme finished a dogged fourth in his McLaren after losing bottom gear.

Jacky Ickx had the Ferrari lying fourth at the start but broke a driveshaft, while Graham Hill scored two more championship points with fifth place in a Lotus borrowed from non-qualifier John Miles after crashing his Rob Walker car in practice

In the last desperate lap as he closed on Brabham Rindt set a tremendous new lap record of 1m 23.1s in the old Lotus 49C. Brabham's second place puts him in the lead of the world championship points table from Stewart.

PRACTICE

As usual there were three days of practice: Thursday afternoon, Friday early in the morning, and Saturday afternoon before the Formula 3 final. There was to have been a qualification race after Saturday's practice, but after a strenuous protest from the drivers, the organisers were given a dignified let-out when they were advised by the CSI that it was contrary to Article 138 of the Sporting Code, which states that drivers in grands prix may not drive in two races in less than 24 hours.

That would seem to be the last we will hear of the qualifying race idea. Instead there was an extra 30mins qualifying session for non-seeded drivers, these final times not qualifying for grid positions. The cancellation of the qualifying race itself had been predictable, but it seems a pity that all the constructors, entrants and organisers haven't yet got together to thrash out this whole qualification question. Many people think that the arguments for every driver having to qualify if there are a restricted number of places on the grid are very strong. As it turned out, Surtees and Rodriguez of the seeded drivers were slower than Stommelen and Servoz-Gavin, who did not qualify.

The first practice was held in ideal weather conditions, but times were not that impressive, as the circuit, which had been resurfaced in many places, was too dusty for the tyres to get hot enough to generate maximum adhesion. Nevertheless four drivers got below Piers Courage's official 1969 lap record of 1m 25.8s (although Stewart had done a 1m 25.1s in that race before retiring). Fastest was Stewart, who tried some special qualifying tyres near the end of the session and put in three consecutive quick times: the fastest was 1m 24.1s, although Tyrrell's own watch got a better time.

Amon had at one time been the quickest in the works March, the new Firestone YB17s obviously helping a great deal, but Chris's best was a full half-second slower than Jackie's. Towards the end of practice he left the road at Mirabeau, creasing the monocoque slightly and damaging the suspension. The New Zealander had been baulked

'Stewart looked impressive in the wet, coming through the Tabac inches from the guard rail, sliding hard but under superb control'

by Pedro Rodriguez's BRM, which was having ignition trouble, and had been so busy letting the Mexican know he was in the way that he forgot to brake for the corner until too late – and he was honest enough to admit it!

Third-fastest was Hulme, who was in great form after his recent 169mph laps at the Brickyard; looking neater than either Stewart or Amon he wheeled the M14A around in 1m 25.1s. Denny was finding that his Goodyear G20s were not getting to grips with the new surface like they usually do, due to the dust.

Beltoise in the V12 Matra was again impressive and, under the watchful eye of Matra director Jean-Luc Lagardère, was half a second slower than Hulme. The 15in rear wheels seemed to have no adverse effect on handling – though on this particular occasion the 13s might have been better as the tyres would have heated up quicker. Anyway, Bruno Morin of Matra said that this was the first time so far that the MS120 had needed no sorting at all in the handling department before a race. Team-mate Pescarolo got in very little practice: first he was on the wrong mix of tyres, and then, just when he wanted to get really going, the fuel system played up.

As ever, Brabham was very fast and, despite locking brakes, was fifth-quickest, 0.2sec slower than Beltoise. The BT33's brake balance seemed to have gone haywire; first the fronts would lock on, and then, without touching the balance bar, the same thing would happen at the rear. Very twitchy!

Rindt had been one of the fastest early on, but just when the track was getting quick, the engine in his Lotus 49 blew and he had to stand by and watch others go faster than his 1m 25.9s. The second works Lotus was not particularly fast, as Miles was busy learning the circuit (he had never raced at Monaco, even in F3) and was wisely content to do this without the fireworks which might have resulted in a broken car.

The surprise of practice was Peterson, who managed very well in Antique Automobiles' March in spite of a disconcertingly poor brake pedal.

Friday morning's practice was a washout. The times would be of no real significance, but Stewart certainly looked the most impressive in the wet, coming through the Tabac inches from the guard rail, the blue car sliding hard but under superb control. The world champion's quickest lap was 1m 37.1s, which was over 2.5secs better than his nearest rival, that other great wet-weather driver, Pedro Rodriguez.

Brabham did more laps than most, making sure his brakes were better, and right at the end of practice, when the rain was falling heavily, he did a couple of laps with an umbrella held over the cockpit, to the great amusement of all.

Rindt was content to see that his new engine worked properly, while Amon tried the lightweight car, fitted with all the bits off his crashed car, and pronounced it sorted.

Despite the threat of rain the track remained more or less dry for the final day's practice. An added hazard was a pool of water, formed by waves breaking over the promenade wall, that ebbed and flowed just before the tunnel. Halfway through the session came another change of rules: all times set in any practice session were to be counted for qualification, a sensible decision taken at a stupid time.

The Formula 3 heats had left a good deal of rubber and oil on the road, and to start with times were slow. It wasn't until right at the end of the session that Stewart put in three really good laps, the best of which was 1m 24.0s, which assured him of pole position. Amon was also on the front row by virtue of his Thursday time, though the New Zealander wasn't able to "get it together" in either the lightweight car or his original one, which had now been repaired. Later that evening the March mechanics got busy transferring the engine and suspension bits back on to 701-001.

Neither did Hulme improve on his Thursday time, not that he was having any troubles, he just never went out when the track was suitable. Denny

was content to spectate for much of the time as he was already on the second row alongside Brabham. The Australian was still unsure of his brakes, and though he got down to 1m 25.4s, he never got both a clear and dry track to show his potential.

After two pretty unsuccessful days of training Ickx really got the Ferrari buzzing in this final session, rewarding the large number of Ferrari fans among the spectators with 1m 25.5s—third-fastest time of the day and fifth overall. This put him on the third row alongside Beltoise in the Matra; two non-Cosworth cars so high on the grid was indicative that Northampton's total supremacy is now seriously challenged.

Beltoise had a trouble-free session but still wasn't quite as fast as he had been on the first day. Pescarolo did extremely well to record exactly the same time as his Matra team-mate in this session, 1m 25.7s, which put him on the fourth row with Rindt's Lotus. Henri's effort was all the more commendable because throughout the session his V12 continued to suffer from fuel starvation, and it wasn't until right at the end of the day that a stray pop rivet was discovered to be blocking open a non-return valve.

Rindt's fortunes were not improving in the veteran Lotus 49, and it was only his good time in the first practice which saw him so far up the grid. During the final day's training the Austrian was disappointingly slow, the car handling badly after changes to camber settings. Late on Saturday the Lotus boys were busy resetting the car trying to get it as it had been previously.

One of the closest-kept secrets of practice was that Stewart and Brabham were using only four of the five speeds in their DG300 gearboxes. Brabham had had a special first gear cut at considerable expense by Hewland, while Stewart had managed to gear with readily available cogs. This meant more widely spaced ratios but cut out several gearchanges per lap, with resulting reduction of strain on gearbox, driveshafts and driver. As fifth was not needed, Stewart had a special fifth only 500rpm or so higher than fourth as a spare should fourth fail. On the Brabham the spring-loading on fifth and reverse was increased to avoid inadvertent selection.

RACE

On the morning of the race the circuit was a dismal sight, for it had rained all night and showed no signs of stopping. Then, just after midday, the sun suddenly poked through the clouds to brighten the hearts of everyone, and the track was soon bone dry.

The cars formed up with all the usual pomp and ceremony, a colourful parade of majorettes smacking somewhat of Indy. There were no overnight changes to the grid, except that Graham Hill was right at the back, behind the BRMs, in John Miles's car (duly painted blue) as his own had proved irreparable.

As the cars moved forward from the dummy grid the Tyrrell camp got their first hint of trouble when Stewart's engine refused to fire, and this held up the proceedings for a few minutes. Finally Jackie's V8 burst into life and they moved forward in neat formation, a colourful collection set against the background that only Monaco can offer.

As Paul Frère raised the flag aloft, Brabham was already creeping forward from the second row. Down came the tricolor and off they swept in a cloud of rubber smoke, with Stewart leading Amon and Brabham up the hill, hounded by the rest of the pack. Hill made a terrific start from the back of the grid and had passed the two BRMs.

When they came into sight again the blue Tyrrell March was already several lengths ahead of Amon's similar works car, with Brabham inches behind; then came Ickx in the Ferrari, pursued by Beltoise in the leading Matra, Hulme's McLaren, Rindt's Lotus and Courage in the de Tomaso, all in a tight bunch.

After two laps Stewart's advantage was already 2secs, while the scrap behind him continued to be led by Amon and Brabham, who were still nose

Brabham leaps a kerb in his bid to stay ahead of Chris Amon's March 701 (left); the tunnel was a true tunnel in 1970, lit by arc lights and strings of bulbs (above)

to tail. Beltoise slipped by Ickx at the Gasworks Hairpin to claim fourth place in a heart-stopping manoeuvre, for there were cars filling the whole track as this bunch went through; Hulme, Rindt, Pescarolo, Courage, Siffert and McLaren continued to dive inside and outside each other but maintained their positions.

Stewart's progress continued to draw him away from the rest, and after five laps he was as many seconds ahead. Amon continued to hold Brabham at bay, to the Australian's disgust. Jack was already waving his fist every time they went through the hairpin. JPB was staying with these two, the Matra sounding superb, but there still was nothing to choose between Ickx, Hulme, Pescarolo and Rindt, who formed a long chain as they all accelerated out of Casino Square and down to the Station Hairpin.

There seemed no stopping the Scot who, after ten laps, was 8secs ahead and very much master of the situation; however the battle behind him was growing more intense, as Brabham vainly searched for a way past the red March that blocked his path. The Matra continued to harry both of them, for it was being pushed all the time by Ickx, and even after the Ferrari went out with a broken driveshaft UJ on lap 11, the Frenchman stayed right with the Brabham/March battle. Ickx's departure saw Hulme move into fifth place, a second or so behind, the New Zealander still shadowed by the other Matra, Rindt and Courage, who had succeeded in pulling away from Siffert.

As Stewart continued to increase his advantage, setting a new lap record of 1m 25.0s, Brabham was going nearly mad trying to pass Amon, for he obviously felt he was being held up while Stewart was getting away unhindered. Brabham attempted the inside of the Gasworks on lap 17, but didn't make it and had to brake hard; this nearly let Beltoise by, the two cars accelerating past the pits side by side. McLaren's dice with Siffert came to a sudden halt: Bruce misjudged the Chicane and clouted the right-front suspension, damaging a wheel and the top pick-up point. After a lap or so in the pits, when the wheel was changed. Bruce rejoined, but the car wouldn't handle and he retired.

'A couple of laps later, accompanied by a sigh of disappointment from the stands, the fourth-placed Matra came into the pit'

The order after 20 laps was Stewart, Amon, Brabham, Beltoise, Hulme, 'Pesca', Rindt, Courage, Siffert, Peterson, Oliver, Hill and Rodriguez. The Tyrrell car was 11.4secs ahead of Amon, who was less than 1sec in front of Brabham, who was keeping the pressure on, and had now done a 1m 24.9s lap. The Matra had fallen back a little and was 3.8secs behind, but still less than 30secs covered the first nine drivers. The vast crowd (estimated at 120,000), having braved the early morning rain to pick their vantage points, were being rewarded by some really close motor racing.

A couple of laps later, accompanied by a sigh of disappointment from the stands, the fourth-placed Matra came into the pit and JPB pulled off his helmet: the crown wheel-and-pinion had failed. Seconds before this, Brabham had finally managed to get inside Amon at the Gasworks and was now firmly in second, although 14secs behind Stewart.

On lap 24 Stewart got down to 1m 24.6s as he continued to draw away from Brabham and Amon. There was now a small gap to Hulme, who was now having a hard time fending off Pescarolo and Rindt. Courage was in seventh place, fighting for every inch of the road with an equally determined Siffert, and this was bringing them both closer to Rindt and Co.

The dramatic change came after 27 laps, when Stewart's engine, although he was now settling down to a steady drive with his comfortable lead, suddenly went rough. After a slow lap, which let

Bruce McLaren negotiates Tabac. He will retire his McLaren because of suspension damage (above); the shocked Brabham team, including a youthful Ron Dennis, ponder what might have been (right)

Brabham and Amon by, he came into the pits. The Tyrrell mechanics changed the dreaded black box and the rotor arm in double-quick time, but Jackie still lost a couple of laps. He rejoined at unabated speed and, although at the tail of the field, did many more laps before the engine went right off again and he retired rather than blow the whole thing asunder.

With no Stewart, the race suddenly came very much to life. Brabham and Amon were now battling for first, and the others knew the position, too, as pit boards flashed the message that the dominating Stewart was out and that they were in with a chance. Hulme was now third, albeit still with constant attention from the surviving Matra and Rindt, while just behind them Siffert had succeeded in passing Courage.

The reason why Courage had dropped behind Siffert became apparent on lap 36 when he brought the de Tomaso in with steering that was seizing up. Although the rack was changed in record time, poor Piers was out of the fight. The de Tomaso went back into the race way behind but kept lapping at a healthy rate until finally its brakes started to fail, although Piers kept it going to the end.

It was at this time that Rindt began to go places. He picked off Pescarolo under braking for the Gasworks Hairpin, and set off after Hulme with a vengeance, showing his determination in a new lap record of 1m 24.3s. As half-distance came up on the board 10 cars were still running: Brabham, Amon, Hulme, Rindt, Pescarolo, Siffert, Hill, Oliver, Peterson and Rodriguez. The gap between Brabham and Amon was 2.6secs, Hulme was 11.9secs behind Amon, with Rindt pinned to his tail. Further back Hill had moved ahead of Oliver, whose BRM had gone sick; two laps later 'Ollie' retired with a blown engine.

'With the help of a marshal he extracted the BT33 to claim second – with his poor helper still on the car's nose for the first few yards!'

While Brabham continued to lead Amon by a couple of seconds, Rindt now snatched third place from Hulme and began to catch the Brabham/March duo, if only fractionally. Siffert was also in a hurry and, having gradually closed on Pescarolo, left the Matra behind on lap 44. 'Seppi' pulled up into fourth place four laps later when he passed Hulme, who was being slowed by the loss of first gear, making negotiating the hairpins awkward.

The distance between Brabham and Amon was remaining constant, although Amon lost time when he got caught up behind Rodriguez's BRM, which cost him 2secs at least, for he couldn't get by for an entire lap despite shaking his fist at every available occasion. Rindt had an easier passage through the slower cars and was now only 9secs behind Amon, driving like one inspired.

Then, with only 20 laps to go, Amon found his car handling most oddly. He slowly brought the car round to the pits as Brabham disappeared into the distance. A bolt had fallen out of a bottom-rear wishbone pick-up and the rear wheel was steering the car: Amon's hopes of a GP victory were once again dashed.

But there was still plenty of action, for Jochen Rindt was only 13secs down on Brabham, with Siffert going just as quickly and making a tremendous bid to catch the Austrian. Now it was Seppi's turn to break the lap record with a 1m 24.1s. But he was also out of luck. With only 18 laps to go the second works March started to pop and bang with fuel starvation.

Brabham, fully informed of the speed of Rindt by his pit, still seemed to have the race well sewn up, and he was holding the Lotus at 13secs' distance on lap 65. But Jochen redoubled his efforts, and the gap was 10secs with the same number of laps to go. However, when Jochen started to close at a couple of seconds per lap, experienced

WHAT HAPPENED NEXT...

Armed with the new Lotus 72, Rindt won four GPs in a row – including when leader Brabham ran out of fuel on the last lap in Britain! Tragically, the Austrian was killed at Monza and would ultimately become F1's only posthumous world champion.

spectators thought Brabham was doing his usual trick of winning by the smallest possible margin.

Then, with only four laps to go, Rindt closed dramatically when Brabham got caught behind the ailing works March; Seppi was swerving all over the road trying to get the fuel pumps to pick up better. As they went into their last lap the two cars were separated by a mere 1.5secs. Still it looked a certain Brabham victory, for it is one thing to catch 'Black Jack', and quite another thing to pass him.

With the crowd beside themselves with excitement, egging Rindt on for all they were worth, the two cars raced round a couple of lengths apart, sweeping through Tabac for the last time and coming up to lap Courage and Peterson (who kept well out of the way) just before the Gasworks Hairpin, the final corner of the race.

Brabham, presumably anxious not 'to leave the door open' for Rindt, took the inside line – and for some inexplicable reason left his braking too late, locked up all four wheels and skated straight on into the guard rail. Jochen, who had been poised to try to get round the Brabham on the outside, shot by the crippled car and passed the open-mouthed man with the chequered flag (who was so surprised he forgot to drop it!) in what must be the most dramatic finish at Monaco since the pre-war battle between Varzi and Nuvolari.

Afterwards Brabham said that although his brakes were not up to par by the end of the race, the cause of his accident was missing his braking point after lapping the slower cars. With the help of a marshal he managed to extract the slightly crumpled BT33 and set off to claim second place – with his poor unfortunate helper still on the nose of the car for the first few yards! Meanwhile, almost at once came the news that on that last incredible lap the tigering Rindt had chopped another massive chunk off the lap record in his chase of Brabham, leaving it at a fantastic 1m 23.2s! There was talk that Jack might be disqualified because of the outside assistance received after his accident, but in the excitement this was apparently forgotten.

The last few laps saw the ailing Siffert passed by both Pescarolo and Hulme, and when the Swiss driver finally stopped at the Chicane, Hill, Rodriguez and Peterson also got by. Pedro's progress after his early pit stop had brought him up with Peterson, whom he passed with 10 laps still to go to claim a championship point for BRM. Matra took third place, Pescarolo finishing 30secs behind Brabham after circulating for some time in company with Hill and Rodriguez, who were both on different laps.

A tired Hulme brought his four-speed McLaren home fourth, still on the same lap as the winner, while the indomitable Hill did extremely well to bring his borrowed Lotus home fifth.

As a postscript to this astonishing race, 20 minutes after the flag fell, thunder roared, lightning flashed, the heavens opened and a hailstorm of such ferocity ensued that the track was completely awash in a matter of minutes. If the race had still been going, the final laps would have been reduced to a complete shambles. ■

RESULTS

80 LAPS (156.337 MILES)

1	Jochen RINDT	Lotus 49C	1h54m36.60s
2	Jack BRABHAM	Brabham BT33	1h54m59.70s
3	Henri PESCAROLO	Matra MS120	1h55m28.00s
4	Denny HULME	McLaren M14A	1h56m04.90s
5	Graham HILL	Lotus 49C	79 laps
6	Pedro RODRIGUEZ	BRM P153	78 laps

WINNING SPEED 81.845mph

FASTEST LAP RINDT, 1m23.20s (84.557mph)

POLE POSITION Jackie STEWART, 1m24.00s (83.752mph)

LAP LEADERS STEWART 1-27; BRABHAM 28-79; RINDT 80

Hunt's Lord of the Dunes

A team run by public school playboys. A driver tarnished by a reputation for crashing, for buckling under pressure. Surely they couldn't hope to beat the mighty Ferrari...

BY PETE LYONS

AURORA
AFX
DUCKHAMS

HIS LORDSHIP ALEXANDER, virtue triumphant incarnate, almost floated onto the back of the flower-garlanded victory lorry and, his face shining with effervescent ecstasy, rode backwards along the entire row of pits saluting his rival F1 teams with a peculiarly English digital gesture. In front, facing the right way and waving in a more sober manner, but his face similarly incandescent, James Hunt set off on his 76th lap of the Dutch GP – his first Grand Prix victory. It had been a long, long time coming. But every line of his face proclaimed what a worthwhile wait it had been.

James Hunt and Hesketh Racing had beaten Niki Lauda and Scuderia Ferrari. Had blown them off using brains and cool skill, by not quite a second – on the one circuit in all the world most notoriously a Ferrari circuit.

It was beautiful.

PRACTICE

Anyone who remembered last year, and was paying attention this year, could be forgiven for wondering why anybody but Ferrari bothered coming to Holland. Last year's race had been a complete walkover for the 'fire engines' and pre-race testing this year had suggested that whatever were the magic combinations of ingredients inside the Maranello cars that made them peculiarly well suited for the Zandvoort circuit, they had not been lost. Any lingering stubborn optimist must have lost all hope well before the end of official practice, when the time sheets showed the Ferraris still supreme by an almost ridiculous margin. Niki Lauda was so firmly on pole that he had nobody to race but himself. His luck had turned good so often recently – after the bad spate last year – that there was only one slim ground upon which any partisan of the British Ford Cosworth V8 could entertain any notion of his failing to tot up his fourth consecutive GP: namely, the historical fact that hardly ever has anyone accomplished such a thing.

Ferrari arrived in their accustomed force, their huge red transporter and their trio of magnetically red racing cars stationed boldly in the centre of the paddock. On the 312Ts there was very little changed – as very little needed changing. There were some different wings to try and also some revised exhaust pipes, but essentially Lauda and Clay Regazzoni had the same fearsome weapons with which to win the Dutch battle as Niki had used to win the Monegasque, Belgian, and Swedish battles before.

Right from the first 90-minute-long session of Friday practice the 'Ts' were quickest, 'Regga' doing a 1m 20.57s and Niki a 1m 20.58s; take that, Eengleesh! The best Briton at the end of that period was James Hunt, at 1m 20.97s. Not really in the same league at all. The afternoon cemented the story: Hunt improved by 0.27s, but Lauda improved, too – by 0.23s. The gap between best Ferrari and best Ford was 0.36 of a second. After 75 laps of the race…

Ferrari did not purchase this superiority without some cost. Toward the end of the afternoon session Lauda had a giant moment in the middle of the lap, a big wild lurching slide, and came into the pits for investigation. The mechanics found that in the rear suspension subframe a bolt threaded into a bush in the gearbox casting had pulled loose.

Next day there was another drama, when the same driver's nose piece started to fall apart all by itself; he also, at the end of the day, reported that there was a new and worrying vibration developing inside the engine. But he had further consolidated his pole position: his 1m 20.29s was this time better than the best Ford Cosworth entry (Emerson Fittipaldi's McLaren this time) by 0.62s.

The last flowering of F1's amateur spirit as Hunt accepts the chequer. Hesketh's carefree image, however, belied the talent and determination that lay therein

A gap of 0.62 seconds, applied to the final grid sheet covered all those places from Hunt's third place to Jacques Laffite's 15th. Well, if it wasn't going to be much of a race overall, it was going to be one hell of a 'Formula Ford' dice!

There was a bit of drama with 'delaminating' tyre treads; more there was quite a lot of trouble with mismatching tyre sizes, as at Sweden and earlier this year. The Hesketh crew were particularly bothered by it: "You can find yourself suddenly oversteering to the left and understeering to the right," said James. A lot of painstaking effort was devoted to trying to match up equal pairs. The Hesketh team also devoted some time to practice pit stops/wheel changes – shades of Monaco! – and to race-tuning the spare car, just in case. They didn't bother themselves over much about trying to go quicker, and in fact Hunt's Friday time stood good for third on the grid; he was content to be merely ninth-fastest in the last Friday session.

RACE

For some Dutch reason there was to be no race-morning practice session. It was lucky then that Hunt's metering unit had packed up during the last few minutes of practice. And after much soul-searching the Ferrari team had decided to change Lauda's engine – and Regazzoni's too. There was now no chance to see if the new ones were going to run properly.

But the no-practice plan was modified by the weather. Practice had been dry and pleasant, and although late on Saturday evening a heavy rainstorm had blown over the circuit, creating fears (or hopes) for a wet race, Sunday morning was sunny and warm. Sunday mid-day, though, was another story. A stiff northerly breeze was gradually bringing down cloud to darken the sky, the temperature dropped, and right at noon the first light spots of rain started. They rapidly coalesced into a heavy downpour.

After a Renault 5 race, the F1s were let out to splash tentatively

Lord Alex, 'Hunt the Shunt', 'Bubbles' and Harvey, aka Hesketh Racing (top); Jochen Mass, Tom Pryce and Carlos Reutemann slip and slide (above)

round and round and in and out. The scheduled starting time of 14.15hrs came up and was disregarded; this was more important. For one thing, many drivers had never even run at Zandvoort before, and it was vital that they find out what happened to water drainage in the wet.

But was it going to stay wet? By the end of the practice, a few minutes past the scheduled race time, the rain had let up. The sky was still dull, the visibility was still low, the wind was still blowing – what would it bring?

There were several teams on the point of gambling on dry conditions. As they formed up on the grid after their single exploratory lap, the track surface on the racing line looked pretty well dry, that is the 'faster side' of the main straight looked dry compared to the pits' side. Lauda on pole had a wetter path ahead than Regga. But the wind was drying it all very quickly. What to do?

What decided everyone was a resumption of rain. For a moment as they stood on the grid dithering, there was a sprinkle, and everyone firmly decided on wet tyres. Then they went to the line.

Lauda got off well, Regga lagged ("I lost concentration"), Scheckter started perfectly. The Tyrrell had to jink left by the Ferrari, which put it onto the wet grass at the roadside for a few metres and Jody had to lift off. "Otherwise I expect I could have beaten Niki into the first corner," he said. But as the thundering, splashing horde arrived it was still Lauda in front, the apex of a ragged triangle of nose wings, glistening knobby tyres and tall comets of spray. Scheckter did get in second, Hunt was on the inside and probably third from Regga, and then it was impossible to sort them out.

It was in fact very wet on around the circuit, and faced with dense balls of churning water everyone quickly settled into a single file with breathing space up to the next man, and as the cars slithered away and their tentatively rasping engines died away, their tall multi-coloured airboxes zipping through the wet grass on the sand dunes looked like so many dorsal fins of monstrous sharks.

Well strung out (we've been spoilt by so many good opening laps in the last couple of years!), they completed their first lap: Lauda with his comet, and Scheckter with his, and then Regazzoni who had stayed third from Hunt after all; Mass was next (he had looked especially good in the wet practice) and then Pryce and then Emerson, but Reutemann was whipping out and overtaking him into Tarzan at the start of the second lap.

The rain was over almost immediately it had started, and now commenced a drying process that was not false. More quickly than seemed possible the surface of the road lost its sheen, and the comets of mist dwindled, and within only half a dozen laps it was clearly going to be another race like Monaco where everybody's lap chart gets scrambled up.

As he had at Monaco, Hunt was the first to make up his mind to stop. "It's quite a tricky decision to make," he explained later, "because although the racing line may be dry enough for slicks, you have only two very narrow dry strips in which to run and if you go only a few inches off line you're on wet." But there is an obvious advantage in getting power down through smooth tyres on a dry surface as soon as possible, and at the end of the seventh lap James boldly broke away from his fourth place and veered into the pits. Mass followed him in, and both Hesketh and McLaren pit work was rapid, and they rejoined after only about half a minute stationary in about 19th and 20th places.

After that it was wholesale. In succeeding laps Reutemann came in, then Emerson, then Jarier, then Peterson and Pace and Scheckter and Evans and Pryce and Laffite… Lauda held on to his lead until the end of the 13th lap, before relinquishing it to Regazzoni; the pit work at Ferrari was good, too, and he rejoined the string of mixed-up cars just as Hunt was coming by – but the difference in speed sent the Hesketh ahead through Tarzan.

Bystanders, paying close attention and discussing it with each other, agreed it was, after Regga's stop, James who was leading the race. That vitally prompt decision to change tyres had paid off. The seconds he'd gained running in those two "narrow dry strips", although his stop had been a few seconds longer than necessary (the team had, after their bad Monaco performance, determinedly worked at a methodical rate and invested those few seconds in being sure not to fumble) had made all the difference. He was ahead of the fearsome Ferrari by about 10 seconds. Now the thing to watch was whether he could hold it at that.

What nobody knew, what everyone had to wait and see about, was how well everyone was suited to the rapidly drying conditions. It was no good thinking about practice times, it was another day now, and the performance potential shown earlier would be modified by the chance settings arrived at individually now.

'The thundering, splashing horde arrived… a ragged triangle of nose wings, glistening knobbly tyres and tall comets of spray'

Hesketh had chosen to set the car up for dry conditions; they were in fact all set to gamble on starting on dry tyres when the little 'spoiler' rain came along on the grid. So now, as it went their way, their driver found his car responding properly and he was fast. Ferrari however had chosen more of a compromise, and their overwhelming speed advantage had gone. Lauda was quick still, but not really any quicker than anyone else.

Besides, there was Jarier. The UOP Shadow had come out right on the Ferrari's tail and was running very strongly, and after a couple of laps weighing things up, Jean-Pierre pulled by. So here was mighty Ferrari well and truly succumbing to the revenge of the Fords!

Niki did not give up, he gave chase instead. As hard as he knew how he pressed Jean-Pierre, and the two of them became a familiar sight as lap after lap they appeared at the head of the pits straight still locked in tight one-two formation. They were both doing everything to break it up as a formation, from their separate points of view; on one memorable lap they came braking violently together into Tarzan and Niki locked up a front tyre in a long, screeching puff of smoke – but that was OK, JP was doing exactly the same a hand's breadth out to the front and the outside! It looked like a well-trained dual ballet step.

All the while Hunt was holding his place out in front; in terms of distance on the track it meant that as the pair of second-place cars locked into their dice came hurtling into the braking zone at the end of the pit wall, the white Hesketh was around out of the banked corner and passing along the opposing straight exactly opposite. It was the sort of stasis that could break up at any instant, but also could go on all the way to the end of the race.

It did break up. Lauda, after 43 laps of the race, managed finally to scratch by Jarier at the end of the straight. The next time around a pair of backmarkers, van Lennep coming around to lap Lombardi, separated them and Niki looked like having broken free. The next time around he was free – no Jean-Pierre.

Apparently the Shadow had run wide over a bit of debris on the track, for at the fast downhill Scheivlak corner halfway round his 45th lap his left-rear tyre suddenly lost all its air. In fact the tyre "exploded" with incredible violence, bursting into fragments so completely that only a few rags were left clinging to the rim. Jarier, whom we have left suspended grotesquely in the middle of a giant accident whilst discussing it, had himself no time to worry about the technicalities of what was happening to him. At the end of a lurid trip across the middle of the corner he picked himself out of a car that was damaged only mildly, about the left rear.

So that was that. It was only a two-car race now, Hunt against Lauda, nobody else looking like challenging them. It was only a matter of seeing if the Ferrari could come good and catch the Hesketh. And it didn't look like it for a while. For lap after lap the interval stayed steady enough to hearten the Eengleesh. Perhaps it was shrinking a little, but not as much as Lauda's pole position would have indicated. It seemed to be shrinking not on speed at all, but on speed through traffic.

Behind there was quite a bit of tussling going on for a while, but gradually various unhappy endings thinned it out. Poor old Jacky Ickx, who had greeted the rainy afternoon with perhaps a ghost of a smile, had no chance to reaffirm his 'Rainmaster' image because on his seventh lap his engine blew up. Exit the Le Mans winner; back to the same old...

Mass's early promise had turned to disappointment because the engine just would not run at anything less than full throttle. In the middle of all the corners it would simply stutter and stumble dreadfully, and after coping with it for most of the race Jochen

RESULTS

75 LAPS (196.944 MILES)

1	James HUNT	Hesketh 308	1h30m38.30s
2	Niki LAUDA	Ferrari 312T	1h30m41.90s
3	Clay REGAZZONI	Ferrari 312T	1h31m13.90s
4	Carlos REUTEMANN	Brabham BT44B	74 laps
5	Carlos PACE	Brabham BT44B	74 laps
6	Tom PRYCE	Shadow DN5	74 laps

WINNING SPEED 110.480mph

FASTEST LAP LAUDA, 1m21.540s (115.934mph)

POLE POSITION LAUDA, 1m20.290s (117.739mph)

LAP LEADERS LAUDA 1-12, HUNT 13-75

Hunt has a steely moment on the podium. Ferrari's Lauda and Clay Regazzoni look surprisingly pleased with their lots; Carlos Reutemann was fourth for Brabham (below)

WHAT HAPPENED NEXT...

Two more wins would be enough to give Lauda the first of his three world titles. However, his 'greatest' year was 1976 when he made a remarkable return after a fiery crash at the 'Ring – only to be beaten to the title by Hunt, now at McLaren, by a point.

suddenly went flying off the road when it cut out entirely. After looking at the bent front suspension, his mechanics then looked at the back and found the little metering unit throttle rod had broken.

Scheckter, who had settled into third place ahead of Regazzoni for most of the distance and was driving with contented patience, suddenly arrived in the pits at a creep with a dead engine. Something massive had broken coming onto the straight.

Two laps after that, the end of the race almost in sight, having in fact driven a very good race, Peterson's engine shut itself off going around Tarzan. When they checked over his car later, the Lotus mechanics with grim-set lips realised that it had simply run out of fuel at a distance consistent with someone having neglected to put in the last five-gallon churn of petrol.

Tom Pryce had brake troubles at the end, the pedal "going to the floor"; it spoilt a very promising early run when he'd charged up from the fifth row to fifth place. Carlos Pace was fifth but not too happy about it, for a baulky wheel had ruined his pit stop. Both he and Carlos Reutemann, one place higher, despite their detail differences, were on wet set-ups, and the fact that Martini Brabhams were the second-most successful Ford cars on the day didn't seem to console anyone. Part of Big Carlos's dim expression came from an incident with Pryce, which had bent his front suspension and produced nasty vibrations.

Regazzoni, running "the *muleta* engine, it was the last one we had, and it was 30 horsepower less" found himself free of challenge by the end and in third place on the leader's lap. About the only thing wrong was a nose fin that had apparently been nerfed somewhere, but closer examination showed that it had not hit anything but been struck by a stone. A missile perhaps half an inch in diameter had clearly hit the leading edge like a bullet, passing completely through the chord and out the trailing edge; the foam-filled aerofoil was so weakened that it gradually bent down.

Now for the real race. Hunt was losing ground to Lauda, little by little. He was having some trouble with backmarkers, and knots of them were occasionally costing him the odd second or two. After all, Dutch flag marshalling has long set a notorious standard, and in very many cases the backmarkers' first indication of the race coming through was the Hesketh nose wing chopping by. Lauda, with forewarned people ahead, was getting through with less delay.

James was also trying to be as careful as he could: "I sometimes had to be pretty brave to get by other cars, because I had to line them up and do it before we got to a bad place – if I'd ever have gotten stuck in the corner onto the straight, for instance, Niki would have been by like a shot." But on the other hand there has been all that stick he's been taking about "falling off the road while leading motor races." At Spain and Argentina this year, and at Argentina last year come to that, he'd let it all down by spinning off. To do it now, after all this, with a Ferrari literally now jammed under his wing, would have been understandable – but not forgiveable.

Lauda did close up, and for many long laps at the closing stage of the race was nose to tail and looking for the slightest error. The confidence of many GP victories under his belt, the ease of a comfortable championship points lead sweetening it, he could afford to wait for 'Hunt the Shunt' to goof.

But James didn't goof. He never put a wheel wrong, he never missed a step in his pattern. As the last five laps began he even began to press harder – "I really settled myself in" – and the Hesketh drew out a little from the Ferrari. Quicker round the fast bends at the back, quicker along the straight, losing ground only in the slow corners now, Hunt came out onto the straight for the 75th time still having made no error. The final corner accomplished, he ran down the straight and took the flag not quite a second to the good. The Hesketh pits exploded.

There were smiles elsewhere, too, it was a popular victory. It was a hard-fought, clean, worthwhile victory, too, one that will always stick in the mind – and that James Hunt and Hesketh had stopped the Ferrari winning streak was not the least of it. ■

HOME BASE FOR MARIO

Not since the death of Jim Clark in 1968 had Lotus boss Colin Chapman felt this close to his number one driver. His famous team had turned a corner

BY JEFF HUTCHINSON

MARIO ANDRETTI | 1977 USA GP WEST | APRIL 3 LOTUS 78

Andretti blurs the Lotus 78 around one of Long Beach's numerous twists and turns

AFTER THE SORT of luck which Mario Andretti and John Player Team Lotus have had so far this season, nobody could begrudge him a home victory at Long Beach last Sunday. Except, perhaps, Jody Scheckter. From the second row of the grid, Scheckter outdragged front-row men Niki Lauda and Andretti to take the lead of the 80-lap race. And there he stayed.

There was nothing that Andretti in second place and Lauda in third could do about it as the trio provided a heart-stopping battle through the streets. Until lap 76, that is. First Andretti, and then Lauda slipped by the Wolf as Scheckter struggled to keep it on the road with a slowly deflating front-right tyre which had given Andretti the chance he needed to slip the Lotus 78 ahead for its overdue first victory.

It was a three-car race, in fact, right from the off. Lauda's Ferrari team-mate Carlos Reutemann put himself out of the race be overshooting at the first turn, which contributed to a mass of confusion and bent cars behind him. These included James Hunt's McLaren, which bounced high over the wheels of John Watson's Brabham, both cars pitting as a result of the incident. Hunt finished a lap down in seventh place, although even without his accident and pit stop he would have been no match for the first three cars, which were also the first three on the grid, well ahead of rest.

PRACTICE

They call it 'The Monaco' of the West', but it is at the track itself, winding bumpily around the numerous blocks of high-rise apartments, with the sea in the background, where the similarity ends. Only at Long Beach could you hear religious freaks yelling across the pit straight about the wages of sin. Only at Long Beach could you see vans decorated from top to bottom with beautifully painted scenes like a mobile Salvador Dali painting; or an enormous black Cadillac with a sticker across its front saying, 'To all you virgins, thanks for nothing'.

Hamburgers, V8-powered trikes, gunslinging cops on Harley-Davidsons, 50ft-high flashing signs on every corner, takeaway anything and 24-hour-a-day signs, short shorts, big breasts, tight T-shirts – yes, dear reader, when you step off the jet at LA airport and drive along the 403 Freeway to downtown Long Beach, you have arrived *somewhere.*

In this land of plenty, anything goes. But sometimes it takes a lot of effort, which is a commodity which Englishman Chris Pook and his committee of the Long Beach Grand Prix Association have plenty of. Otherwise the Unites States Grand Prix West would never have happened. From a quiet city of mostly retired senior citizens on Monday evening, when the first of the teams started to roll into town, Pook's men worked night and day to transform Long Beach into a world championship-status racetrack, a job which was finally completed at 12.15 on Friday afternoon. This was almost three hours behind the scheduled first practice, but it was a miracle all the same.

When practice finally got under way on Friday, the long wait for everything to get rolling was soon forgotten. The coffee shops along Ocean Boulevard emptied, the people came up from the beaches, and those lucky enough to live in overlooking apartments crowded windows and balconies as the crackle of Formula 1 engines bounced around the buildings and filled the air with tingling expectation. Slowly, at first, the 22 drivers felt their way around the busy track. Then, as the corners and kerbs became freshly imprinted in the minds of those drivers who were present last year, and the loose dust was cleared by the big tyres, times began to drop. The Long Beach Grand Prix was on.

Most teams had guessed wrongly on their gearing for this track, so there were lots of complaints up and down the pit lane by the end of the first 90-minute session. Quickest in that session was the Wolf, which made Jody a happy man, even though he was one of the drivers with the wrong gearing. He became a lot less happy at the end of the second session, when he slipped back down to seventh-quickest, although at least he had a good reason for his disappointment. His car had broken a gearbox selector just as he went out for a good time on new tyres.

Quickest at the end of day one was Andretti's Lotus, the black 78 looking very smooth, Mario keeping off the kerbs and only in the tight corners hinting at the oversteer which was causing big problems for most of the field. He was also able to go much deeper under braking compared with most of his leading rivals, and things were looking really good for America's racing hero. He ended up with a best of 1m 22.067s, while in the untimed Saturday session he was only a second off that time on full tanks. Things were looking really good. But it was the final 60 minutes that were going to count for pole, the track getting quicker and quicker as more rubber got laid down.

The tension was even greater for this final hour as the normally clear blue Californian sky clouded over, and all the drivers were keen to get out for a quick time before the rain began to fall. In fact, the clouds came and went without shedding their load, and the final hour became almost as exciting as the race itself.

Andretti looked as dominant as he had all weekend, but just a few minutes before the end it was Niki Lauda who grabbed the pole. With new tyres and a couple of clear laps, he screwed himself up for a maximum effort and lapped in 1m 21.65s to claim his first pole position since Brands Hatch last year. It was a fabulous effort, although one could not help the feeling that it was still Andretti who had the best chance of victory. If Lauda got to the first turn first, it was (as Mario put it) "Going to be an interesting race."

Other than an oversteer problem, which was

reduced by the addition of a large air dam on the back of the wings, the Ferraris had been running well, although one worrying factor had been the breakage of the rear anti-roll bar actuating arm on both cars.

Compared with Lauda, Reutemann was much less smooth, his 312T2 taking to the kerbs quite regularly as the Argentine tried to wind himself up for a quick lap. "Perhaps I am trying too hard. That is the problem. You get too sideways on one corner and that spoils the whole lap," he said, rubbing his chin thoughtfully after it was all over and he had ended up only fourth.

Only three cars got into the 1m 21s, the third being the Wolf of Scheckter. This was being driven in a spectacular fashion but was rarely straying over the kerbs despite some ten-tenths motoring. Jody's time was almost identical to Andretti's and his chances of victory seemed as likely as those of the two men sitting ahead of him on the grid.

Jacques Laffite provided a surprise when he took the Ligier to a very unspectacular second-quickest at the end of the first day, his practice trouble-free despite the engine problems he has suffered in the first few races this year. He looked as though he was going to be right there during the final hour as well, but he did not get the right tyres at the right time and found himself back in fifth place when it counted. But things were looking better than usual for the French team, thanks to the good torque of its V12 Matra engine, which pays dividends on a track like this.

RACE

By eight o'clock on Sunday morning, the estimated 65,000 crowd was already milling about the streets leading to the track, while the mechanics were beginning to haul their equipment up to the pit lane in time for the 10am warm-up session before the 1pm start.

The only problem in the warm-up was that of the Rothmans March of Brian Henton, which blew its engine after an oil line came adrift. Fortunately there was enough time for another engine to be fitted for the race, and the full field of 22 cars made it in time for the pace lap.

The start was signalled by the customary lights suspended high above the track from beneath the starter's rostrum. The lights were *too* high in the case of Lauda, who discovered, much to his horror, that when lined up in the final grid positions, ready for the off, he could not comfortably watch his rev-counter and the lights at the same time. The lights turned green when Lauda was still looking at his rev-counter. In the fraction of a second it took before he saw the green light, the rest of the field was already hard on the throttle.

Scheckter made a beautiful start, and led the field through the first turn from the second row. Andretti held an outside line and found Reutemann and Lauda going through on the inside. But Reutemann left his braking impossibly late and slid straight on, his front wheels locked. Lauda and Andretti managed to cut in behind the locked-up Ferrari and get through, but behind them a chain reaction started which almost ended in disaster.

Watson tried to follow Andretti through and was hit by Hunt's McLaren, which bounced high into the air off the Brabham's front wheel. Luckily the McLaren landed back on its wheels, partially blocking the track alongside the stationary Ferrari, while behind Hunt, Clay Regazzoni and Brambilla touched. Poor Vittorio ended up parked against the same wall on which he had ended his race on the first lap a year ago.

In the chaos, the Ligier slipped through unscathed into fifth, while everybody else somehow made it through the confusion. When the rest of the field were by, both Reutemann and Hunt were able to join in behind, but Brambilla's Surtees was still not out of trouble. The course-workers somehow managed to let go of it after they had pulled it clear of the barriers, and it promptly ran off down the steep hill towards Turn 2 and smashed into the barrier on the other side of the track!

By the end of the first lap the first three cars, thanks to the drama behind them, had opened out a sizeable lead. Scheckter led from Andretti, who had managed to sneak by Lauda again before the main straight. Laffite in the Ligier was holding a narrow advantage from Watson for fourth place, while next came the Copersucar of Emerson Fittipaldi, leading Jean-Pierre Jarier, Alan Jones, Patrick Depailler and Gunnar Nilsson.

Hunt stopped at the McLaren pit to check for possible damage, to find Mass also in the pits with

Jean-Pierre Jarier's Penske (34) and Patrick Depailler's Tyrrell (4) avoided the first-corner crash, but the Surtees of Vittorio Brambilla ran into the back of Clay Regazzoni's Ensign (22); Colin Chapman – check that buckle! – and the Lotus crew nervously await Andretti's arrival (below)

the mechanics hurriedly refastening his seat belts, which had somehow come unfastened. Hunt's car was found to have a kink in the front left top link, but he carried on.

Although the first-corner incident had broken up the field far more quickly than usual, it hardly seemed to matter, for the battle between the first three was enough motor racing to keep anyone's pulse racing, not to mention the heartbeats of the three drivers leading the race. Scheckter, though,

'I put a big flat spot on the tyre, and from then on I had a terrible vibration up through the steering throughout the race'

looked comfortably in control of things. Andretti and Lauda were pinned close on his tail, but not looking as though they could do much about altering the situation.

On lap three Niki made his second mistake of the race. He tried to outbrake Andretti for second place at the end of the straight, and locked a front wheel. "I put a big flat spot on the tyre, and from then on I had a terrible vibration up through the steering throughout the race," he explained later. It wasn't enough to slow his pace by that much, however, and he stayed glued to the Lotus's tail

Reutemann had already caught and passed the March of Alex Ribeiro and was rapidly hauling in Brett Lunger, who was preoccupied with trying to find a way past Henton. As Reutemann rushed into the first hairpin, all set to outbrake Lunger, the latter pulled over to try and do the same thing to Henton. "The next thing I knew was this punch in the back, and I was spinning," said Lunger, who didn't even know who he had hit.

"I thought it was someone with brain-fade," he added. His March was out of the race on the spot with a broken upright, while Reutemann drove slowly around to the pits and retirement with a bent front wishbone.

For a while during the opening laps, it looked as though Watson was going to move up to join the leading cars, but after closing the gap for several laps he started to fall back before finally going to the pits with a slowly deflating front-right tyre, probably caused during the first-corner incident. He rejoined the race at the back and started to battle his way back through the field again, but there was another, final, chapter to come in the sad tale of Watson's weekend.

Laffite moved back into fourth place, which was rapidly becoming more and more distant, while fifth, after passing Fittipaldi on lap six, was Depailler. He was, however, not making much impression on Laffite, already some way ahead, and his problem (like Ronnie Peterson, he'd been held up at the start) was the Tyrrell's cockpit-operated brake adjuster: to arrive at the right balance halfway through the race was no easy task, as Ronnie

WHAT HAPPENED NEXT...

Andretti won in Spain, from pole, and spent the rest of the season as its fastest man, taking three more victories and six more poles. However, it was the cagey Lauda who ended up as the world champion.

The *Bullitt*-like descent of Linden Avenue was a key feature of the circuit (left), as was the brooding presence of the liner *RMS Queen Mary* in the harbour (above)

found out. The Swede overscrewed and managed to lock up a front tyre so badly that he had to stop and change it, which dropped him to the back of the field. Later, any chance of his making up more places by the finish were lost when his car stopped out on the track with a leaking fuel line.

Watson's fraught race finally came to an end on lap 33 when he rolled to a stop with a stalled engine, thinking the electrics had died. It turned out that he had accidentally knocked off the cut-out switch. The mechanics went out to him and got the car going again, but a few laps later he was black-flagged for receiving outside assistance. In any case, his race would soon have ended because of gear selection troubles.

But all the missing cars went out almost unnoticed, for the battle for the lead was still the race that everyone was watching. As the trio started to lap slower traffic, the gaps began to vary slightly. Scheckter, having the advantage over those behind as he came up fast upon the backmarkers, was able to open out a couple of seconds over Andretti and Lauda at one stage. But when Andretti got a clear road ahead of him he was able to nibble away at Scheckter's lead and bring it back to nearer a second. Lauda was also managing to keep the Ferrari within touch of the JPS, and as the race went into the final 20 laps the tension began to rise.

The first hint of trouble came around 15 laps from the end, when Jody rushed past his pit pointing to his front-right tyre. Andretti had closed the gap to just under a second, while Lauda had also closed right up, less than two seconds covering the leading group now

Jody got a breathing space when he came up to lap Jarier, and then Nilsson, these two still nose to tail and having a great battle for seventh. Nilsson missed his chance to help out his team leader as he let Jody through without any problem.

But by that time Mario was starting to realise that he would not need any help to win this race. Jody was beginning to look more and more untidy in his efforts to hold off the hard-pressing Lotus, Andretti waiting to move in for the kill: "I could see a bit of smoke coming from the engine, and I was picking up oil on my visor. I thought he was having engine trouble, so I decided it was time to move."

RESULTS

80 LAPS (161.600 MILES)

1	Mario ANDRETTI	Lotus 78	1h51m35.470s
2	Niki LAUDA	Ferrari 312T2	1h51m36.243s
3	Jody SCHECKTER	Wolf WR1	1h51m40.327s
4	Patrick DEPAILLER	Tyrrell P34	1h52m49.957s
5	Emerson FITTIPALDI	Copersucar FD04	1h52m56.378s
6	Jean-Pierre JARIER	Penske PC4	79 laps

WINNING SPEED 86.889mph

FASTEST LAP LAUDA, 1m22.753s (87.876mph)

POLE POSITION LAUDA, 1m21.650s (89.063mph)

LAP LEADERS SCHECKTER 1-76; ANDRETTI 77-80

Mario did not know that Scheckter's front tyre was slowly deflating, but when Jody was forced to brake early, Andretti went through with just four laps of the race left to run. The crowd were on their feet cheering with excitement.

One lap later Lauda also moved ahead of Jody, and then it was all over. The flag came out and Andretti crossed the line seven-tenths ahead of Lauda, who, despite his vibration problems, had managed to set the fastest lap of the race on the 62nd lap in his chase of the Lotus.

Jody came in another four seconds later, the South African receiving as big a share of the applause as the winner when he drove up the pit lane, as disappointed as anybody could be. But for that punctured front tyre, the race would most certainly have been his. Even Andretti said afterwards that although he could stay with the Wolf in the middle stages of the race, it was only when Scheckter started to slow that he could make a serious bid for the lead.

It was a great day for the Lotus team, and it was a great day for the Wolf men as well. They had led the world's best in only their fifth Formula 1 race, and had finished in the points for the third time, a pretty fantastic achievement. Scheckter is still leading the world championship, with Lauda now equalling his score.

As the mechanics filled their packing cases for the last time before heading for Europe for the summer, there was certainly a lot more to look forward to than there was after the three crushing Ferrari wins of last year. And look how that year turned out! ■

GILLES VILLENEUVE | 1981 MONACO GP | MAY 31 FERRARI 126CK

BOOST FOR FERRARI

It was the colour of a London bus – and handled like one. The turbos were coming, no doubt about it, but it would take a miracle for one to win at this famous street circuit

BY NIGEL ROEBUCK

THIS WAS THE most emotional Grand Prix victory in many a long year. For a long time now Gilles Villeneuve has been hailed as the fastest driver in the world, and for the last year and more he has been proof positive that talent alone does not win races in this era.

On Sunday he won at Monte Carlo after nearly two years away from the laurels — a lifetime for a man of his temperament. As he cruised the Ferrari slowly round to the pits, the crowd let its hair down. Monaco, just a few kilometres from Italy's border, becomes a Maranello suburb over race weekend. They came to see Villeneuve and Ferrari win, and they waved their banners, sounded their horns, thundered their applause, when he did so.

And yet this was not a victory in the Villeneuve tradition, for the race had belonged first to Nelson Piquet, then to Alan Jones. The Brazilian led from the start, then crashed while under pressure from the world champion, who then led comfortably until delayed by fuel pressure problems. Villeneuve, who had hefted the cumbersome Ferrari turbo round with enormous bravura from the start, was then ideally placed to take over, and this he did with five laps to go.

Jones duly stammered over the line in second, after a tremendously courageous drive through which he endured considerable pain from his left thigh, scalded at Zolder a fortnight before. And Jacques Laffite, finishing in the points again, took third with the Ligier JS17, the only other man to complete the full 76 laps.

The tensest part of the weekend came from a chilling duel between Piquet and Jones, which ended when Nelson misjudged a lapping move and hit the barriers at Tabac. There is no love lost between these two men, and everyone was a little uneasy, if highly exhilarated, by their *mano a mano* struggle. Despite the fact that Piquet led Jones until his accident, one always felt that Alan had the upper hand.

The detail apart, we shall remember the 1981 Monaco Grand Prix for three reasons. First, Carlos Reutemann, whose fantastic finishing sequence began with his victory here last year, did not make it to the finish, although he keeps his world championship lead. Second, there can be no doubt that, in Nigel Mansell, Britain at last has a driver of fantastic potential. And third, the Ferrari 126 has won its sixth-ever race. A turbo won at Monaco, having qualified second. And its sister car was also in the points. The rival team managers left the principality with furrowed brows. If it could win here, they mused, it could win anywhere. "The writing," said Frank Williams, always a realist rather than a bleater, "is on the wall…"

Skewed tyre marks, sky-hooked Ferrari, skulking driver. Didier Pironi, after yet another vain effort to match team-mate Villeneuve in qualifying, trudges away from yet another bout of barrier biffery

Carlos Reutemann's amazing run of 15 consecutive points-scoring finishes will end when his Williams FW07C retires with gearbox woes

PRACTICE

Now that all the teams have decided to ignore the rules regarding ground clearance, it was time to find something else to squabble over. At Monte Carlo there were hints of – shh! – cheating. And that, as everyone knows, is entirely different from simply not taking any notice of the rules. After all, none dares to call it treason when all are in on the plot. But cheating – pulling a stunt without telling your buddies – is not cricket at all.

Last weekend the paddock positively buzzed with gossip, and Nelson Piquet seemed to figure in most of it. After his staggering practice time on Thursday, there were suggestions from many quarters that the Brazilian's Brabham might have been a little short in the *avoirdupois* department. On Friday morning, indeed, Jacques Laffite was quoted at length in *L'Equipe*: "He [Piquet] has two cars: one ultra-light, which he only uses in practice, and his race car, which is of normal weight. The practice car has carbon-fibre brake discs which save 12 kilos, and I'm told that the car also has a tiny fuel tank, much lighter than the normal one. That car should be weighed as soon as Piquet stops, before the mechanics can touch it. But no, no one will do anything because it's a Brabham, owned by Bernie Ecclestone, and no one can touch him. Everyone is frightened of him." Strong stuff.

While some howled with utter rage, others remained calm, saying that their main concern was legality in the race rather than in practice. They did concede, however, that the near impossibility of overtaking at Monaco did make pole position more than usually desirable, and that Piquet and Brabham were therefore in an enviable position.

The other controversy surrounding Nelson was that concerned with his stupid public threats to Alan Jones. Perhaps this had its beginnings at Montreal last September, when the two men, vying for the world championship, made contact at the first corner, but it really began to flare after the similar incident at Zolder which put Piquet out of the race. Nelson maintains that Alan deliberately drove him off the road in Belgium, later describing him as "absolutely crazy". After walking back to the pits there, he issued warnings to the Williams team of dire retribution in the future, and he had cooled down but little when he arrived in Monaco, openly saying that if he had a problem in the race, and was back in the field, he would put Jones off the road.

"He's a Latin," commented Alan, drily. "When he doesn't like someone he tells everyone but the person concerned. I'm an Australian. When I don't care for someone I tell them to their face. He hasn't said a word to me."

> *'No one will do anything... it's a Brabham, owned by Ecclestone, and no one can touch him. Everyone is frightened of him'*

When Piquet flashed the spare BT49 round in 1m 25.710s on Thursday, it left his rivals gasping. "I suppose it might be possible for me to get under 1m 26s," mused Villeneuve, "but I don't see myself getting close to Nelson's time."

Villeneuve had surprised the racing community by setting the second-fastest time on Thursday, albeit more than 1sec from the Brabham. Turbos, after all, are not supposed to work too well on tight street circuits. For Monte Carlo the 126CKs were equipped with what Mauro Forghieri called "softer engines", intended to generate torque rather than top-end power, and the mods worked remarkably well. Compared with the Williams, Brabhams and Arrows, the Ferraris looked a little heavy and clumsy out on the circuit, but Villeneuve's genius had every pound of boost working for him, committing himself to great on-rushes of power, and harnessing it with superb reflexes on the steering wheel. It was very dramatic indeed.

On Saturday afternoon a display of yet further virtuosity brought Gilles within seven-hundredths of Piquet's pole time, and this left all and sundry shaking their heads. "What will they do," was the general sentiment, "when we get to places like Dijon and Zeltweg?"

If practice went well for Villeneuve, however, it was a total disaster for Didier Pironi. The Frenchman dominated Monaco last year (although he didn't win it), and arrived last week in determined mood. But nothing went right. On Thursday morning, he shunted his race chassis near Rascasse, and in the afternoon crashed the spare heavily at Massenet, the long left-hander into Casino Square. A further T-car was brought down from the factory that evening.

In Saturday's untimed session, Didier blew an engine in the race car (Ferrari's only engine problem all weekend) and had to revert to the spare for the final hour. Unhappy with the handling, he could set only 17th-best time before spinning once more at Massenet, clouting the kerb and returning sorrowfully and slowly to the pits with a rear tyre flat, wing and rear bodywork tattered. With half an hour of official practice left, last year's pole man was not even in the race...

At the end of practice the name on the lips of everyone was that of Nigel Mansell. In the new Lotus 87 the Englishman was fourth-quickest on Thursday, and that shook the establishment to the core. When he improved his position to third in the last session, the only man to join Piquet and

Villeneuve in the 1m 25s bracket, there was open astonishment. Quite where the Lotus 87 was so quick was difficult to establish, for it understeered alarmingly through the slow corners. "It's a bit of a handful everywhere, quite honestly," grinned Mansell. "All I could do was give it my best shot."

Nigel was almost frighteningly quick into the Swimming Pool complex, handling the new car with extraordinary verve and courage, and the 87's traction seemed at least equal of any other car on the circuit. "If it just had the turning-in ability of the 81," murmured Mansell, very cool about his staggering performance.

The Williams cars are always around the front, of course, although Carlos Reutemann and Alan Jones might have hoped for better than fourth and seventh. The Argentine's time was a result of a deft, precise, elegant demonstration, such as he always puts on here. After Thursday he was way down on times, having fallen foul of 'the 6cm test' in the pit lane, which at Monaco took the form of a laser beam. "It's all a big joke," said Carlos afterwards. "I think if I win on Sunday I will drive the car into the guard rails after the finish…"

How many times has Alan Jones been called "the gritty Australian"? At Monte Carlo he more than lived up to it. With extensive dressings on his scalded thigh, he played down his pain, but privately admitted that "it wasn't very comfortable". Never did it show in his performance, and he would assuredly have started higher than seventh, had his new race chassis not suffered on Saturday from the misfire which would return for the race.

RACE

After the Zolder debacle, everyone was looking for a good, healthy day of motor racing at Monaco, something to restore a little of the sport's prestige and pride. The weather did its best to help. There was in the air none of that rather forbidding, humid, greyness so typical of the Côte d'Azur. Blue skies and sun were in evidence early on Sunday morning, just as in the preceding days. It was hot, and that put everyone in the right frame of mind.

The race not scheduled to start until 3.30pm, there was plenty of time for people to take the sun and enjoy their lunch. Then suddenly, for reasons which sound like something from Peter Ustinov's *Grand Prix of Gibraltar*, the event was in jeopardy. At the Loews Hotel, the skyscraper village on the outside of the Station Hairpin, there was a major kitchen fire which required a lot of putting out. Huge quantities of water splashed out from the basement, right into the tunnel over which part of the hotel is built – and through which the racing cars travel. This was to play a significant part in the events of the afternoon. Not only was it some time before the fire was snuffed out. Surveying the water cascading the tunnel, GPDA President Jody Scheckter had his doubts that the race should be run. Bernie Ecclestone, TV contracts in mind, was keen that it proceed with all possible despatch.

Finally it was agreed that yellow flags would be displayed in the tunnel area throughout the race. A possible overtaking spot had been lost.

After a couple of warm-up laps to check out the somewhat bizarre conditions, the cars formed up on the grid exactly an hour late, at half-past four. The green light flashed…

During the early laps it seemed that Villeneuve might be able to stay with the Brabham, but slowly the gap began to open. After seven laps the Ferrari was two seconds behind, and starting to come under pressure from the remarkable Mansell. Had Gilles' qualifying lap been a one-shot wonder.

"I knew before the race started that we would have a problem with the water in the tunnel," said Gilles afterwards. "In practice the Ferrari was very quick through that section because it could use its horsepower. But we have less grip than the Williams and Brabham, and needed to use all the road. Because of the water, we could not use the 'line' through the tunnel, and had to use the other side of the road. So this section – a very good one for us in practice – now gave us no advantage."

Piquet's advantage stretched still further when his immediate pursuers were badly delayed by Marc Surer's Ensign, being lapped after its pit stop. After 14 laps Nelson was 8secs to the good – and Reutemann was in the pits, having clobbered the back of Mansell's sliding Lotus. The Williams mechanics replaced the car's nose, and Carlos returned to the race, now 17th.

A lap later Mansell, too, came in. His Lotus's rear suspension was quickly checked over, and he went back out, only to return for good after one more lap, retiring with a broken top rocker. A sensational milestone in the Englishman's career was passed, but now his weekend was through.

Nelson Piquet's polesitting Brabham, here rounding La Rascasse, led the race for 53 laps. The Brazilian would succum to pressure from the chasing Williams of Alan Jones and crash at Tabac

Villeneuve leads Nigel Mansell, Reutemann, Riccardo Patrese, Elio de Angelis, Alan Jones, Jacques Laffite and Alain Prost (below); 75 laps later, Villeneuve takes the chequer (right)

Thus, in a couple of laps, Jones had vaulted from fifth to third, and now the world champion lost no time in setting about Villeneuve's Ferrari. For five laps he hovered right behind the French-Canadian before flicking out to the right on the squirt from Casino Square down to Mirabeau. Gilles, unable to match the braking power of the Williams, could have chopped across going into the corner, but did not, seeing little future in trying to block a quicker car for 50-odd laps. Perhaps there also crossed his mind the thought that Alan and Nelson might account for each other.

Once into second place, Jones chipped into Piquet's lead a little, but Nelson seemed well in control, with a cushion of around 7secs. In 10 laps the two of them pulled clear away from Villeneuve, who had also let Patrese by on lap 25. Alas for the Italian, his third place lasted only three laps, the Arrows expiring near Casino Square with a blown engine. Shortly afterward a similar fate befell Elio de Angelis's Lotus, which dropped a lot of oil before pulling off. René Arnoux's Renault found some of it at Station Hairpin, and slid into the barrier.

Immediately after this, there was a major development at the front. As Piquet and Jones began to thread their way through the backmarkers, the Williams was suddenly much closer to the leading Brabham. Alan was working the traffic superbly, and Piquet's 7sec lead was now a tenuous three — and coming down. Jones's driving at this time was something to behold. With Piquet well and truly in his sights, the world champion looked ruthless, merciless, and who can doubt that the Brazilian's earlier theatrical oratory played its part? Indeed, it was difficult not to feel sorry for Piquet. Alan was out to teach him a lesson.

The chase was absorbing. Almost unnoticed went the retirement of Reutemann, his first in over

WHAT HAPPENED NEXT...

After a very open season, three drivers went to the final round – held in a Las Vegas car park! – with a chance of the title. Reutemann and John Watson faded badly, and Piquet's fifth place was enough to clinch the first of his three world championships.

a year, with gearbox problems.

By lap 40 Piquet and Jones were absolutely nose to tail, and one sensed that Alan had the upper hand. All the pressure fell on Nelson, who had to worry about his mirrors, about coming up on traffic, about being boxed in. And under those circumstances he began to look a little flustered, a little ragged. And who could blame him? He was not to be envied. Through Casino Square, their progress was chilling.

The Ferraris, meanwhile, continued splendidly, with Villeneuve pressing on as hard as ever. Pironi frankly admitted afterwards that for him the race had been largely a matter of waiting for others to retire. For the first 25 laps he had struggled with Bruno Giacomelli's wayward Alfa Romeo, almost being collected by the Italian more than once, but now he was up to seventh, hassling Tambay's well-driven Theodore.

Had Piquet something in hand, after all? It had hardly looked that way a little earlier, but now the Brabham was getting away again.

"I was just having a breather, sitting back for a while," said Jones later, and one knew better than to doubt his words. The Australian was working out his strategy, thinking hard about where he would pass – and when. After the race he said that his intention had been to close up on Piquet very quickly indeed, to unsettle him.

In the event, Alan's plans were never needed. On the 53rd lap, with a lead of 3secs, Nelson came up to lap Cheever and Tambay. At Tabac he tried to go inside the Theodore, treading on uncharted, dusty territory. In an instant the Brabham's front wheels were locked, and Nelson skated helplessly into the barrier. Bitterly disappointed with himself, he trudged back to the paddock, where he later had words with Tambay.

After 55 laps only seven cars were out there. Jones led Villeneuve by slightly more than half a minute, with Laffite third, Pironi fourth, Cheever fifth, Tambay sixth and Surer, still going as hard as ever, seventh.

The pattern at the front continued unchanged until lap 67 when Jones pointed the Williams towards pit lane. For some time now – even before Piquet's accident – Alan's engine had emitted a slightly hesitant note. He was in trouble with fuel vaporisation, and figured he had just enough leeway over Villeneuve to dash in for a top-up. When he rejoined, the Ferrari was but 6secs behind, and now he had a battle on his hands.

A whiff of victory is enough for a Villeneuve or a Jones, a sure guarantee that efforts will be redoubled. For five laps Gilles gave all he had, the gap coming down from 6.3s to 4.6 to 3.9 to 2.0. The crowd, predominantly Ferrari freaks, were almost hysterical by now, willing on their man. Both drivers were having problems, Villeneuve with failing brakes, Jones with more vaporisation.

As they rushed in front of the pits on lap 72, the Ferrari cleanly accelerated by the hobbled Williams to the spectators' clearly audible joy. Now Gilles had only to stroke home, Alan to hope and pray for second place; on one lap, it seemed that the Williams might not make it to the top of the hill, so painful was its stammer.

But they made it, both of them. When Gilles took the flag, his reception was one of rapture, of Monza proportions. Jones, some 40secs behind now, was nevertheless close to a minute ahead of Laffite's understeering Ligier, and the rest trooped in behind.

As Villeneuve went off to his press conference amidst a posse of *gendarmes*, a disappointed Jones reflected on his day. Hindsight said that if he had stayed out of the pits he would almost certainly have won. He had driven a quite magnificent race, shrugging off constant pain from his leg, displaying all his greatest qualities to the full. His pursuit of Piquet had been unforgettable. He could have done no more.

Villeneuve looked exhausted as he answered questions in the Ferrari motorhome. "It was one of the most tiring races of my life," he said. "The go-kart ride we all have now is very hard on the driver because he gets pitched around a lot. My helmet kept smashing into the roll-over bar, and I ache all over. But I feel good. And I feel good things are ahead for Ferrari…"

Indeed, this was a good day. ■

RESULTS

76 LAPS (156.407 MILES)

1	Gilles VILLENEUVE	Ferrari 126CK	1h54m23.380s
2	Alan JONES	Williams FW07	1h55m03.290s
3	Jacques LAFFITE	Ligier JS17	1h55m52.620s
4	Didier PIRONI	Ferrari 126CK	75 laps
5	Eddie CHEEVER	Tyrrell 010	74 laps
6	Marc SURER	Ensign N180B	74 laps

WINNING SPEED 82.039mph

FASTEST LAP JONES, 1m27.470s (84.700mph)

POLE POSITION Nelson PIQUET, 1m25.710s (86.440mph)

LAP LEADERS PIQUET 1-53; JONES 54-72; VILLENEUVE 73-76

PROST WINS TWICE

It should in truth have been a comfortable victory. But matters conspired against him – during practice and in the race. Having to sleep on the floor didn't help much either

BY NIGEL ROEBUCK

Shell
CORNER
MOTORSPORT
IMPROVES
THE BREED
FORD
FORD
FORD
FORD
FORD
FORD
FORD
FORD

The Renaults were a dominant forc
René Arnoux leads Prost (above) – b
Alain was ahead when he suffered
puncture and slid to eighth (above righ

ENTRY & PRACTICE

ANY POSSIBILITY OF the new season getting off to a painless start was soon thrown into doubt when, on Wednesday, a free day between testing and practice, the drivers, led by Niki Lauda, Didier Pironi, Jacques Laffite and Gilles Villeneuve, spent hours discussing their objections to the FISA Super Licence application forms.

Some 26 of their number had already signed the forms, having been told they would be necessary to race in South Africa, and without really considering the implications of the various clauses to which they put their names. In particular, two paragraphs were unacceptable to the drivers, who saw the licence as yet another move to restrict their collective and individual freedom.

Having read the offending texts, most team managers and journalists were sympathetic to their case. But that sympathy soon faded when, by 10am on Thursday morning, there were no drivers to be seen anywhere along the pit lane, with the exception of Jochen Mass. He had been staying with friends of his South African wife and had been unaware of what had been planned.

Any former drivers' action has normally collapsed after a short while under pressure from team managers threatening individual action against their drivers. There were the same threats this time, but they fell only on the ears of the press, for, in a brilliant move by the ringleaders of the drivers' action, all the arriving drivers on Thursday were hustled into a waiting coach and whisked out of reach to a pre-arranged hotel in the centre of Johannesburg, 20 miles away.

Many of the drivers, some in overalls, had no idea of what was planned until they were already on the road. Thirty minutes later they were all locked in the conference room of the Sunnyside Park Hotel, which, for the next 24 hours, was to steal the spotlight from the silent and shocked Kyalami track.

Spectators, officials, team managers and mechanics wandered to and fro with an equal feeling of helplessness as the circus lost its act.

Insulated from the pressures of their teams, invaded by news-hungry press, the drivers' solidarity grew stronger by the hour, adding a demand for two drivers with voting powers to be represented on the FISA F1 commission – instead of the one powerless observer which they have at present. Didier Pironi was sent back to Kyalami to present their demands. These were rejected and accompanied by more serious threats of retribution if they did not return to work.

By this time it became apparent that the matter was not going to be settled by the time Thursday's practice had come and gone, and the nervous organisers, seeing a very strong chance that their race might well not take place, began issuing statements saying that, if necessary, the race would be postponed for a week and new drivers be flown out to replace the current ones, who were being threatened with a ban for life.

Not surprisingly, the teams had no intention of filling their cars with inexperienced drivers, and had agreed to pay the organisers $2.5m in damages, which they claimed they would in turn collect from the drivers.

The drivers, however, stood their ground, resisting attempts by team bosses Jackie Oliver and John Macdonald to get into their room on Thursday night to speak with their drivers who they felt might be held under duress.

In fact, they were almost enjoying their camaraderie. Elio de Angelis and Gilles Villeneuve amused the assembly with their piano playing, and Bruno Giacomelli employed his talents as a cartoonist. By 11pm the drivers slipped out of their conference room undetected, and moved into a specially prepared dormitory with mattresses strewn around the floor, sleeping two and three to a bed.

Photographers got a brief chance to get pictures of them in their 'dorm', and another peel of laughter came through the door when

'That sympathy soon faded when, by 10am on Thursday morning, there were no drivers to be seen along the pit lane'

Patrick Tambay remarked that if the combination of Gilles Villeneuve and Alain Prost on the same bed should produce any offspring, he would be the quickest driver the world had ever seen.

By 6am the discussions began again, Niki Lauda holding yet another press conference to inform the world that the situation was unchanged, but that all they needed was a guarantee from Jean-Marie Balestre that he would open negotiations on their demands – then they would turn up for work, although by this time Teo Fabi had broken ranks and left for the track.

Pironi returned to the circuit, and shortly after 10am phoned Lauda to confirm that Balestre had agreed to negotiate with them, and so they got back on their coach and went back to work.

Not surprisingly, there was a cool reception awaiting them from their respective teams, many of whom had heard nothing from their drivers since before the action began. Mo Nunn decided to withdraw his car, while Patrick Tambay, who had been brought in to replace the injured Marc Surer in the second Arrows, decided that he had had enough of all the F1 politics, which he thought he had left behind, and left his seat to Brian Henton for the first of the two planned practice sessions, leaving 30 cars for 26 places.

Bernie Ecclestone looked like carrying out his threat to sack Nelson Piquet when he refused to let him take part in the first of the two sessions, the three Brabhams lined up in the pit lane all wearing number two. "I am worried about his safety. He has hardly slept all night and might not be fit to drive," was Ecclestone's official reason for keeping him out of the car, and it was not until the final – and only – hour of timed practice (after Piquet had been forced to undergo a medical) that he joined the rest of his fellow drivers in the pit lane.

Despite the tense atmosphere, there was a general feeling of relief as the first sound of racing engines reverberated around the rolling green veldt, politics forgotten for a time.

The only incident during the morning's 90-minute session, which was cut short by rain, occurred when Alain Prost punctured a rear tyre and spun into one of the safety walls. The Renault's rear suspension suffered minor damage and was replaced before the final timed session, but his mishap was to have further repercussions on his practice effort.

At the start of the final session, Prost found the revs of his turbo engine slipping lower and lower on the straight, and the team suspected that during his previous incident some dirt had been sucked through the turbo. By the time Prost got set up in the team's spare car he had used up his best set of tyres and any further efforts at claiming pole were spoiled by rain which washed out the last 20 minutes. The man who had set the pace in private practice found himself back on the third row of the grid.

RACE

Although the bright blue South African sky was still dotted with big, white cotton wool clouds, a heavy overnight storm had cleared the air, and when the sun poked through it was oppressively hot. The morning warm-up saw the teams frantically trying to find the best compound tyres with full tanks for the hot track, while the normally aspirated cars were hoping to steal a slight advantage by running softer rubber than the turbos, which were putting much higher loads on their rear tyres with their big power advantage.

Mansell's warm-up was cut short when his Lotus's engine stopped dead, while Eddie Cheever's Talbot-Ligier was still plagued by a misfire which appeared as soon as the engine warmed up. Jean-Pierre Jarier was in a lot of pain with his damaged ribs, and had been heavily bandaged for the race.

Despite all the doubts about the race even taking place until just 24 hours earlier, there was a good crowd of some 85,000 packed around the undulating Kyalami track by the time the cars were ready for the off.

Any fears that poleman René Arnoux might have felt about dicing neck and neck into the first turn with Piquet's Brabham were soon dispelled as the light turned to green. Arnoux made a great start, while Piquet was slow off the line. He even held up his own team-mate, Patrese, as the rest of the field rushed by him down to Crowthorne Corner. Arnoux led the field with Prost already up to second place as they reached the braking area. The Renaults were comfortably through in the lead, with the two Ferraris in their wake, followed by Rosberg (who had made a perfect start), Patrese and the rest of the field.

It didn't take very long for the Renaults to pull out an impressive lead over the rest. The two Ferraris, led by Villeneuve, came next a few seconds behind, with Rosberg struggling to hold off Patrese. Laffite led the next group, with Alboreto, Reutemann, Watson, Salazar, Cheever, Piquet, Lauda and Warwick all bunched up behind and providing some exciting outbraking moves at the end of the straight.

By the end of the third lap, Piquet had moved up to 12th place,

"Okay, which one of us invited Niki back?" Team managers discuss the strike (below); Lauda made an immediate impact upon his F1 return – he drove well, too (right)

and next time around he took 10th from Alboreto. But his drive did not last long. He left his braking too late into Crowthorne, and the Brabham snapped out of line before he could correct it. Instead of taking the corner, he slid straight on and came to rest against the tyre barrier and catch-fencing on the outside of the turn.

"If I crash there just give the marshals a gun and put me out of my misery," Piquet had remarked during practice, but his fears of hurtling into the wall at close on 200mph were unfounded, for the Brabham came to rest almost undamaged and Piquet was left with a long walk back to the pits.

One down, five to go.

That was the thought no doubt going through the minds of people like Rosberg and Reutemann, Rosberg having given way to pressure from Patrese on lap five.

Piquet might have been the first turbo out of the race, but we had already lost two other cars on the first lap. Mansell's Lotus suddenly stopped dead again because of a suspected electrical problem, which also caused trouble for Jarier behind.

"We were all going into Clubhouse Corner when the Lotus slowed and I had to brake. The next thing I knew my car was bouncing up in the air and I landed back on the track with only three wheels, which made it a bit difficult to get around the corner," said Jarier, who ended up in the fencing. At least he didn't have to worry about his ribs any longer.

And then there were four.

A trail of blue smoke around the far side of the track heralded the end of Villeneuve's brief race with a blown engine. So, by lap 10 the two Renaults, now circulating a couple of lengths apart, were almost 10secs ahead of Pironi, who still had several seconds' lead over Patrese in fourth place.

Things had started to go wrong for Rosberg after five laps. "As I went into a corner and changed down, the gear knob came off in my hand and I missed a gear, over-revving the engine. I also dropped the knob, which then rolled around the cockpit floor, getting in the way of my feet and the pedals for the rest of the race," said Keke, who, to add to his woes, was also having to throw his Williams into the corners in order to overcome bad understeer on full tanks.

Reutemann, who had moved up to seventh by this time, took advantage of the situation to move ahead of Rosberg, who was now being pressured hard by Watson. The Williams' engine was also starting to misfire at the top end as a result of its over-revving.

However, fortunately for Rosberg, Watson too was in trouble, his McLaren overheating its front brakes so that his challenge faded again. He trailed a few lengths behind the Williams, so close, yet out of reach, for much of the race.

Lap 11 saw Cheever park his Talbot-Ligier in the pits, his Matra V12 still vaporising its fuel, while a lap later Warwick came to the pits for fresh tyres on his Toleman. The field was rapidly spreading out. By lap 15, the leading cars were already lapping the backmarkers.

'The knob came off in my hand and I missed a gear. I dropped the knob, which rolled around the floor for the rest of the race'

Arnoux, finding his way momentarily blocked by a slower car, was forced to brake. That was all the chance Prost needed, as he arrived at the corner much quicker. He slipped ahead of his teammate to take the lead with no trouble.

And then there were three.

On lap 18, Patrese's race, and BMW's hopes, came to an early end when he rolled into the pits with no oil pressure and a dead engine. Things were beginning to look up for the Cosworth brigade, and we were still not yet a quarter of the way through the race.

After a slow start, Niki Lauda began getting back into his old rhythm, moving up to take Laffite and Alboreto to claim seventh place behind Watson, who was still dogging Rosberg's Williams, which was slowly losing contact with Reutemann ahead.

At the end of lap 24, all the leaders moved up another place when Pironi shot into the pits for fresh Goodyear rubber. His pit crew took a long time before he was back in the race again behind Alboreto, who was about to be lapped by the leader. It took Pironi a few laps to get by the hard-driving Italian, who was doing a great job for the Tyrrell team, while up at the front the order remained static until just after the halfway point.

Prost was driving well within himself, worrying only about the possibility of mechanical problems. His worries were suddenly answered in heart-stopping fashion when his car stepped out of shape as he lined it up for the ultra-fast left-hand Jukskei Sweep on the back of the circuit.

"Another couple of metres into the corner and I would have been off the track and into the fences," explained Prost, whose lightning reactions averted a disaster, although he was still in deep trouble with a flat rear tyre and three-quarters of a lap still to go.

"The next hardest thing was to drive back to the pits at a sensible speed so that it wouldn't damage the car too much," he added, although when he did finally limp in the car had lost most of the remains of the tyre and was riding on the rim.

He sat there in the pits, staring straight ahead, silently tapping the wheel for what to him seemed hours, while four fresh tyres were fitted and the rear suspension was checked for damage. All seemed to be well but for some minor body damage, and he rushed back into the race in eighth place, just over a lap behind Arnoux, who was now holding a good, yet hardly comfortable, lead.

"Overtaking slower traffic I had to keep moving off the line and my tyres were picking up a lot of rubber, making the steering shake badly," reported Arnoux, who at this stage of the race still held a lead of over 40secs from Reutemann. But it was slowly diminishing.

After a somewhat boring middle portion of the race, with the Renaults romping away up at the front, and a well-strung out field behind, the race suddenly took on an exciting new phase as Arnoux's lead began to look shaky. Prost was roaring back through the field, setting a new lap record soon after his stop and pulling in the leading cars by 3secs per lap, unlapping himself in the process.

To add to the interest, Pironi was also moving back up the field. He took Lauda and Rosberg to regain third place and started closing the deficit to Reutemann, as well as watching his own pit signals for the arrival of Prost.

By lap 50, Arnoux's lead over Reutemann had shrunk to 34secs, with Pironi a further 10secs back, and Rosberg and Watson within another 6secs, these two being slowly caught by Lauda, a further

RESULTS

77 LAPS (196.358 MILES)

1	Alain PROST	Renault RE30B	1h32m08.401s
2	Carlos REUTEMANN	Williams FW07C	1h32m23.347s
3	René ARNOUX	Renault RE30B	1h32m36.301s
4	Niki LAUDA	McLaren MP4	1h32m40.514s
5	Keke ROSBERG	Williams FW07C	1h32m54.540s
6	John WATSON	McLaren MP4	1h32m59.394s

WINNING SPEED 127.865mph

FASTEST LAP PROST, 1m08.278s (134.456mph)

POLE POSITION ARNOUX, 1m06.351s (138.361mph)

LAP LEADERS ARNOUX 1-13, 41-67; PROST 14-40, 68-77

Gilles Villeneuve was as spectacular as ever, but his Ferrari retired early (above); after his puncture, Prost unlapped himself to score a remarkable win (right)

10secs away. Things were starting to get interesting.

Prost swept past Lauda on the next lap, and then on laps 54 and 55 he made short work of Watson and Rosberg to claim fourth place. It took him another six laps to wind in Reutemann, and another lap to take Pironi, putting him back in second place with 15 laps to go.

By this time Arnoux had big problems with his tyres, and with nine laps to go Prost retook a lead that was to be his until the finish.

For Pironi, the chances of finishing in the points disappeared when his engine went sick and he was left with no choice but to head for the pits, where more fuel was added. But the misfire continued. He did another slow lap and stopped in the pits again, his chances of finishing well now gone forever.

And then there were two.

Arnoux was fighting to hold his lead over Reutemann, who was slowly drawing in the Renault. (Surprisingly, both the Williams and the Renault pit were surprisingly unaware of the situation.) With four laps to go, Reutemann went ahead to claim second place as Arnoux dropped back to a distant third, almost falling victim to Lauda, who, despite a bad tyre vibration himself, had put on a last effort to pass Watson and then Rosberg, who, in the final laps of the race, was running with hardly any rubber left on his rear-left tyre.

Alboreto came home in seventh place after the best drive of his F1 career, while further back de Angelis brought his Lotus home eighth. He had struggled for the whole race with mediocre handling, although it was good enough to keep him ahead of the two ATS men, Salazar and Winkelhock , both a further lap down and driving a good first race for their team.

Behind these two, Bruno Giacomelli took 11th place with his Alfa Romeo after an early battle with his own team-mate, de Cesaris, who dropped back with a blocked fuel injector, which it took a pit stop to clear. Giacomelli had lost a wheel weight early in the race, and, like most of the Michelin runners, suffered a bad case of numb hands and blisters while trying to hold onto the steering wheel.

This was also the case for Mass in 12th place, the first of the Pirelli runners in his March. "It was so bad that it bent the steering arm," said Mass, who had also been taking a beating inside his tight cockpit. The tough German could hardly walk for the first few minutes after he got out of the car.

'For a professional sport like this, I cannot believe the sort of things that go on. It just leaves me speechless'

Derek Warwick's race in the only other turbo remaining came to a dramatic end when he slid off the road and was knocked out by a catch-fencing post, although he later recovered with no ill effects.

Jacques Laffite's race also faded away, like Cheever's, with fuel vaporisation problems, the Talbot-Ligier stopping after 23 laps.

Eighteen of the 26 starters finished the race, a good average for such a fast circuit in tough conditions.

Then came the bombshell from the organisers, who suspended the drivers because of their previous action. Nigel Mansell summed up everyone's feelings when he said: "For a professional sport like this, I cannot believe the sort of things that go on. It just leaves me speechless." Me too. ■

WHAT HAPPENED NEXT...

The craziest season: 11 different drivers from seven teams stood on top of the podium – and Keke Rosberg was a surprise world champion. But it was all overshadowed by the death of Gilles Villeneuve.

KEKE'S SLICK DECISION

Turbo power hikes were marginalising the once-dominant Cosworth DFV. Maybe, just maybe, given the right conditions and the right driver, it could win. But it was a very long shot

BY NIGEL ROEBUCK

GOODYE

THE TRACK SURFACE is wet, but the rain has almost ceased. Much pondering in the pits: what to do? Wets or not? Green light. A car shoots forward, gains places. After a lap it takes the lead, disappears into the far yonder. Onlookers are aghast. It's a Williams. Not turbocharged. It must be the only car on wets, something like that...

Well, no. Keke Rosberg's car was one of the few to be wearing slicks at the start. Yet such was his aggression and control that, on a very damp track, he left the turbos behind. And they *were* on wets.

The world champion put on a brilliant display at Monaco last Sunday, stamping his total authority on the race from the very first. Despite a severe misfire for much of the way, despite feeling less than wonderful, he saw a chance of nine points – increasingly rare for a non-turbo these days – and snatched it. On the week, however, he was, sadly, only three points up, for the FIA Court of Appeal cancelled his six from Rio. Perhaps that served to strengthen his resolve.

PRACTICE

As most of you sat down to your cornflakes and tea last Thursday morning, there were those in Monte Carlo deciding that they had already had about enough of May 12. By nine o'clock, local time, the entire Theodore contingent, for example, was packing up to go home. Roberto Guerrero's car, hastily fettled to replace the one damaged at Imola, was in trouble from the start, and the Colombian, always excellent on street circuits, was marooned in Casino Square with a broken cv joint. And later in the session Johnny Cecotto, facing the unenviable task of learning Monte Carlo – and setting a good time – all within 60 minutes, creamed his Theodore into the barriers after losing control in the tunnel.

By the end of Thursday there were more long faces. McLaren – Niki Lauda and John Watson – were 22nd and 23rd, ahead only of Salazar's March and the Osellas of Fabi and Ghinzani. In the recent past we have grown accustomed to seeing the red-and-white cars towards the back of a grid – and who could forget what happened at Long Beach? To pull a stunt like that, however, you must first get up onto the wire, and at Monte Carlo there are only 20 starters.

The basic problem has been to wring a truly fast qualifying lap from the McLaren-Michelin equation. As we have seen, keeping up a speedy and consistent pace for two hours – of arriving at a good race set-up – has usually been achieved. Both John and Niki complained of a dire lack of grip on Thursday afternoon, and both were five seconds off the pole. For some time team members have spoken of having to use 'turbo tyres', at the same time accepting that Michelin's current products will be ideal when the TAG V6 comes along.

Through Saturday morning the blue Mediterranean sky was progressively obscured by cloud and, as 1pm approached, large drops of rain sent mechanics scurrying for canopies to cover the cars. In the McLaren pit the cautiously optimistic morning smiles were gone. Unthinkable as it had seemed, Lauda and Watson were not going to qualify for the Monaco Grand Prix. The eternally pragmatic Mr Lauda packed up his gear, summing up the scene crisply and concisely as he did so: "Thursday – shit. Friday – nice weather, no practice. Saturday – rain. Thank you, gentlemen. Good afternoon."

Saturday, therefore, meant nothing – merely that Thursday's times were now the grid. We were denied that frantic scrabble which is final qualifying at Monte Carlo.

Keke Rosberg set the best time in the rain, marginally quicker than René Arnoux's Ferrari and Eddie Cheever's Renault.

It is quite some time since we have seen Formula 1 cars run in the rain and very little wet-weather testing has been done of late. But all the Goodyear teams were delighted with the firm's new radial wets, Patrick Head commenting that in a rainy Williams test session they had proved a couple of seconds faster than the 'cross-plies'.

MARTINI
Agip
motor oils
MAGNETI MARELLI
FLY saudia
ALBILAD
TAG
DENIM
DENIM
NESTE

Since their victory at Imola, Ferrari had tested Goodyear's latest radial slicks, and there were rumours that some might be tried during practice at Monaco. In the event, none was brought, but Arnoux and Tambay were quite happy with what they had.

René, you may remember, was on the pole at Monaco last year, his Renault half a second clear of team-mate Prost, and on Thursday he looked set to put his Ferrari into the same spot, sneaking in one of those awesome one-lap wonders which he seems able to produce so frequently. At the time – 15 minutes into the session – it was well over a second quicker than anyone else's best, but soon it became clear that his old adversary was also in the game, the hillside illuminated scoreboard announcing that Prost's RE40 was now fastest.

Out came Arnoux once more, carving at his time and reducing it to 1m 25.182s. But Prost was not to be denied, shooting round in a magnificent 1m 24.840s. It was not spectacular – Alain never is – but precise and quite uncannily smooth.

Afterwards both men spoke confidently of improving in the final session, but of course they never got the chance. In the rain both Renault and Ferrari handled to their drivers' satisfaction and both said, yes, they would prefer a dry race, but it didn't really matter.

As is increasingly the Renault norm these days, Eddie Cheever qualified third, and had no complaints about his car: "If I'm not quicker, it's because of me. To he honest, I still haven't mastered the technique of getting a turbocharged car through a hairpin properly. I have had this habit of braking too late, which means I don't come into the slow corners cleanly enough. At that point I'm not getting the amount of throttle right – either I give it too much or not enough, it seems. On the speed trap I'm quicker than Alain at the Chicane and other fast corners – but losing out at the hairpins."

Immediately behind Cheever, completing the Renault-Ferrari two-by-two was Patrick Tambay, for whom qualifying was refreshingly undramatic, although he had strong words about the antics of Riccardo Patrese: "Here, you know, everyone has to co-operate – otherwise no one would ever do a fast lap. If you're running slowly, you keep off the line – except him. He's got no respect for anyone."

'Would Rosberg be a real threat in the race? I asked Cheever. "Where's he going to pass me?" came the laconic reply'

That apart, Patrick was quite content: "What I've been working for is a comfortable car for the whole race, getting it balanced so that the tyre wear will be even. There are no pit stops here, so tyre wear will be critical again." Tambay's metering unit went onto 'full rich', bringing the Ferrari to a stop at the end of the wet session, but that, apart from a spectacular blow-up by Arnoux on Saturday morning, summed up the Italian team's troubles.

If there was to be a challenge to Renault and Ferrari, it looked certain to come from Rosberg and the Williams, for the world champion all but equalled Tambay's best during the one dry session, despite feeling well below par with a virus infection. "I started feeling very tired and weak soon after Long Beach," he remarked during practice, "and since then I've been sleeping 12 hours a night. At first, I thought it was just overwork."

For all that, he was immensely impressive in practice, working with all the usual panache and aggression. On Thursday a speed trap had him 18km/h quicker through the Chicane than any other driver! But starting fifth gave him the usual Monaco problems.

Would Rosberg be a real threat in the race? I asked Cheever. "Where's he going to pass me?" came the laconic reply.

All you could say was that if anyone was going to do any overtaking, it would probably be Keke.

RACE

To race morning, then, and a miserable one it was, overcast and very wet until late morning. But eventually the day cheered itself a little, and by 12.30, the start of the warm-up, the track had dried out enough for Tambay to take the Ferrari round in 1m 28.090s. The Frenchman was half a second quicker than Patrese, and then came Arnoux, Prost, Cheever, Rosberg and Piquet. At the bottom of the list was Warwick, whose Toleman coasted to a halt with turbo failure. Other mechanics hard at work included those of Alfa Romeo, changing the engine on de Cesaris's car after an oil leak.

The Monaco Grand Prix always has a late start time, 3.30, and as the minutes passed, everyone kept glancing at the sky. There was no sign of blue, and persistent spots of rain. As race time neared, team managers were in a dilemma: the track was wet, yet the expected downpour hadn't happened. On the grid the psyching began.

If you had a Cosworth, slicks seemed to be a worthwhile gamble, but most of the turbo teams decided on wets, Ferrari (despite Tambay's wish to run slicks) and Brabham changing to them at the last minute. As the cars departed on their final warm-up lap, Warwick's Toleman was the only turbo on slicks.

Williams had no doubts on the subject: both Rosberg and Laffite were on dries (Jacques's a harder compound than Keke's), and would obviously be in good shape if the rain eased. But would they be able to stay with the wet-shod turbos in the early laps?

Rosberg answered that question at the green light, rocketing away in a festival of wheelspin – "It's all that power we have, you know!" By the time the cars reached the Ste Devote chicane, he was up from fifth to second, splitting the Renaults.

I thought back to Cheever's remark of the day before: "Where's he going to pass me?" Answer: during the first five seconds. As Eddie got the power down on the approach to Ste Devote, his car veered away to the left, leaving Keke a clear run through, and only Prost was between the Williams and the lead.

From his position on the outside of the front row, Arnoux made a very poor getaway and was beaten to the first corner by Prost, Rosberg, Cheever, Tambay and de Cesaris, but he quickly set about the task in hand, and by the end of the opening lap was up to fourth.

Lap one: Prost, Rosberg – gap – Cheever, Arnoux, Tambay, de Cesaris, Laffite, Jarier, Piquet, Baldi. Already out were Mansell and Alboreto, who had tangled at the Swimming Pool complex, both cars being tucked safely away behind the wall.

On the wall also was the writing for all who had opted for wets. We were into lap two, and the rain had stopped. More to the point, Rosberg had outbraked Prost into the Ste Devote chicane, and was driving into the middle distance. On a wet road, and on slicks. This was a world champion showing his worth. At the end of lap two he was a couple of seconds clear of Prost, who was himself eight seconds ahead of Cheever, behind whom a queue was forming. Arnoux made a desperate effort to take third place from the American at Ste Devote, squeezing through a gap which did not look as wide as the Ferrari. But that put him all wrong for the exit; he came out wide, and Eddie got the drop on him again as they accelerated up the hill.

On lap four René did get through finally, but was into the pits a lap later for slicks. On his first lap with the new tyres, however, he slid into the barrier before Portier, damaging the left-hand suspension at front and rear, and bursting the rear tyre. Reviving memories of Gilles at Zandvoort four years ago, Arnoux continued in the stricken three-wheeler, and at a remarkable pace. Between the Chicane and Tabac, the wheel began to break up, and it was fortunate that no following driver was hit by a piece of jagged metal. Eventually he did make it to the pits, eventually pushed by marshals, and even returned to the race briefly before parking the remains of the Ferrari. Six laps gone, and one of the pre-race favourites was already out.

Very quickly those on wets got the message. After only four laps Piquet was in for slicks, soon followed by Patrese (lap five), Prost (six), Cheever (eight), Tambay (10), Baldi and Senna (11). And the

Nigel Mansell crosses the Mediterranean aboard his Lotus 92. He was to retire on the opening lap because of a collision with Michele Alboreto's Tyrrell 011

His hands badly blistered, Rosberg gets his better half to hold the trophy (below); Derek Warwick stars in the Toleman TG183B, having started on slicks (right)

result of all this, at the 12-lap mark, was that Kosberg and Laffite were sitting pretty at the front, Keke ahead by an astonishing 25 seconds.

Behind them, though, a new race was taking shape. Surer and Warwick had both started on slicks and, from 12th and 13th places on the opening lap, were now up to third and fourth, just ahead of Prost and Piquet, now charging along after their tyre stops. A magnificent struggle was beginning.

Tambay's Ferrari should have been part of it, but he had lost time

'The engine went completely dead. I thought my race was over. But I let the clutch out – there was the engine again!'

with a spin shortly before changing tyres, and was back in 11th place, behind Patrese, both of them already lapped by Rosberg.

The Surer-Warwick-Prost-Piquet quartet was to hold the spectators' attention for a long time. In truth, there was little else to hold the attention, for the race was already decided.

On the form of practice, we might have expected that Prost, on a virtually dry circuit, would move to the head of this queue, but such was not the case. In a move of incredible confidence and nerve, Piquet slingshot past the Renault on the inside line through the tunnel! And Cheever, now also on slicks, began to catch his team-mate.

"At the start," said Jean Sage afterwards. "Alain's car was on dry settings, but we had put wets on his car. When he came in to change to slicks, the track was not completely dry by any means, so we made some quick adjustments. Unfortunately, we did not guess right and he finished up with a car which was good in neither wet nor dry."

Prost fought on with the RE40, but the real scrap was between Warwick and Piquet, the two of them catching Surer as they battled. Derek and Nelson know all about each other after many a Formula 3 scrap five years ago, and the Brazilian has always said that he rated Warwick as his main competition at that time. In his two years of Grand Prix racing Derek has had precious little actual racing, for his car has rarely lasted long enough to permit it. Now, with the Toleman going splendidly, he was reminding us of Brands last summer, proving how much of a racer he is given half a chance. Several times Piquet took a real lunge at the British car, notably into Mirabeau and once at Portier, and on each occasion Warwick was unimpressed, holding his line and leaving Nelson to sort himself out. It was wonderful stuff to I behold – but how long would it last?

As the 30-lap mark approached, Prost had been left behind as the Toleman and Brabham moved in on Surer's third-place Arrows, and Cheever had his Renault right up behind his team leader's car, passing for sixth place on lap 28.

Alas, Eddie was there only three or four minutes. Coming out of the Chicane he suddenly raised his arm, and Prost was by again. Eddie parked his car. The engine, he said, had simply cut, and he guessed the problem was electrical.

At around this time there were also slight worries for Rosberg, whose lead over Laffite had been trimmed considerably. Was Keke simply rolling it off – or was that a misfire as he accelerated around the pool?

In fact, it was rather more than that – his engine was occasionally cutting out completely. "The first time it happened," he related later, "the engine went completely dead, and I thought that was it, my race was over. But I let the clutch out – and there was the engine again! It kept happening like that, and once I had quite a moment when it suddenly cut in again and spun the back wheels."

As Laffite began to close the gap to Rosberg, we wondered if the two of them might eventually be in a fight for the lead. "We wouldn't have let that happen," said Patrick Head. "They had a huge lead over the rest, and we would have told them to hold station."

Rosberg's problem slowed him sufficiently to allow Patrese and Tambay to unlap themselves. The Brabham and Ferrari were really flying along, Riccardo and Patrick setting new fastest laps all the time. In Tambay's case, this was remarkable. The Ferrari had shed

WHAT HAPPENED NEXT...

Both Prost and Arnoux scored three wins, but a late-season run, including victories at Monza and Brands Hatch, saw Piquet clinch a world title at the final round for the second time in three seasons.

part of its rear wing in the tunnel, and this did nothing to improve its handling. The two of them were running seventh and eighth, with Tambay closing, but Prost looked beyond their reach.

Forty laps: Rosberg — 29secs — Laffite — 41secs — Surer. Not exactly a close battle at the front, but the conflict between Warwick and Piquet had brought them to within a couple of seconds of Surer, and Prost was only four seconds further back. This was a protracted struggle indeed, and the Toleman looked completely at its ease in the middle of it.

"In fact," commented Warwick, "the car was much better than it had looked in practice. I only did two laps with full tanks during practice, but the balance was really good during the race, and the tyres were perfect all through — Pirelli have done a great job recently. I didn't have any real worries about Piquet and Prost, although they were better than me under braking and out of slow corners."

On and on they went, until lap 49. By now Surer, Warwick and Piquet were running almost together, and they came up on Sullivan's Tyrrell, preparing to lap it. At Rascasse, Surer made a small mistake, allowing Warwick closer than ever before. Past the pits they went, and down towards the Ste Devote chicane. Derek to Marc's left. There the two cars touched, the Arrows sliding sideways and hitting the barrier on left and right. As Surer climbed disconsolately out, Warwick restarted, but came in after a single slow lap. Piquet, in the meantime, had threaded the needle-nosed Brabham through the debris, taking up third place.

"It was foolish of me," Derek mused. "I wasn't trying to overtake him — I was nothing like near enough, and getting by on the outside there is out of the question, really. All I was trying to do was pressure him, try and force him into making a mistake. But I suppose he must have thought I was trying to pass because he really came across on me — and we touched.

"I'm annoyed with myself. I shouldn't have put myself in that position. All through I'd been telling myself that patience would pay off, and I'd been going easy on the car. More than anything I feel sad for the team, not getting them any points. All bloody stupid, really."

Piquet's third place became second only five laps later, when Laffite came slowly into the pits, having stripped all the teeth from third gear. Another splendid drive was unrewarded, and Frank's hopes of 15 points were gone.

At 60 laps Rosberg, despite his troubles, had almost a minute's lead over Piquet, with Prost four seconds adrift of the Brabham, and Tambay now up to fourth with the Ferrari, having overtaken Patrese. Immediately afterwards Riccardo brought the car into the pits, reporting a fuel pick-up problem. The mechanics changed his tyres, but no fuel was added. Pressurised refuelling was, of course, not permitted, but fuel could have been added in an attempt to alleviate the problem — as Williams did with Alan Jones's car two years ago. A couple of laps later Patrese's car coughed to a standstill.

In the closing laps Keke was clearly a tired man. Obviously he has been weakened by the virus infection, and his hands were appallingly blistered by kickback through the steering wheel. As the race neared its end he cut his pace considerably, Piquet gaining well over half a minute in the last 15 laps. At the flag the Williams was 18 seconds to the good, and Rosberg had taken a truly memorable victory, won by daring and courage in the first few laps. ■

RESULTS

76 LAPS (156.407 MILES)

1	Keke ROSBERG	Williams FW08C	1h56m38.121s
2	Nelson PIQUET	Brabham BT52	1h56m56.596s
3	Alain PROST	Renault RE40	1h57m09.487s
4	Patrick TAMBAY	Ferrari 126C2B	1h57m42.418s
5	Danny SULLIVAN	Tyrrell 011	74 laps
6	Mauro BALDI	Alfa Romeo 183T	74 laps

WINNING SPEED 80.459mph

FASTEST LAP PIQUET, 1m27.283s (84.882mph)

POLE POSITION PROST, 1m24.840s (87.326mph)

LAP LEADERS PROST 1; ROSBERG 2-76

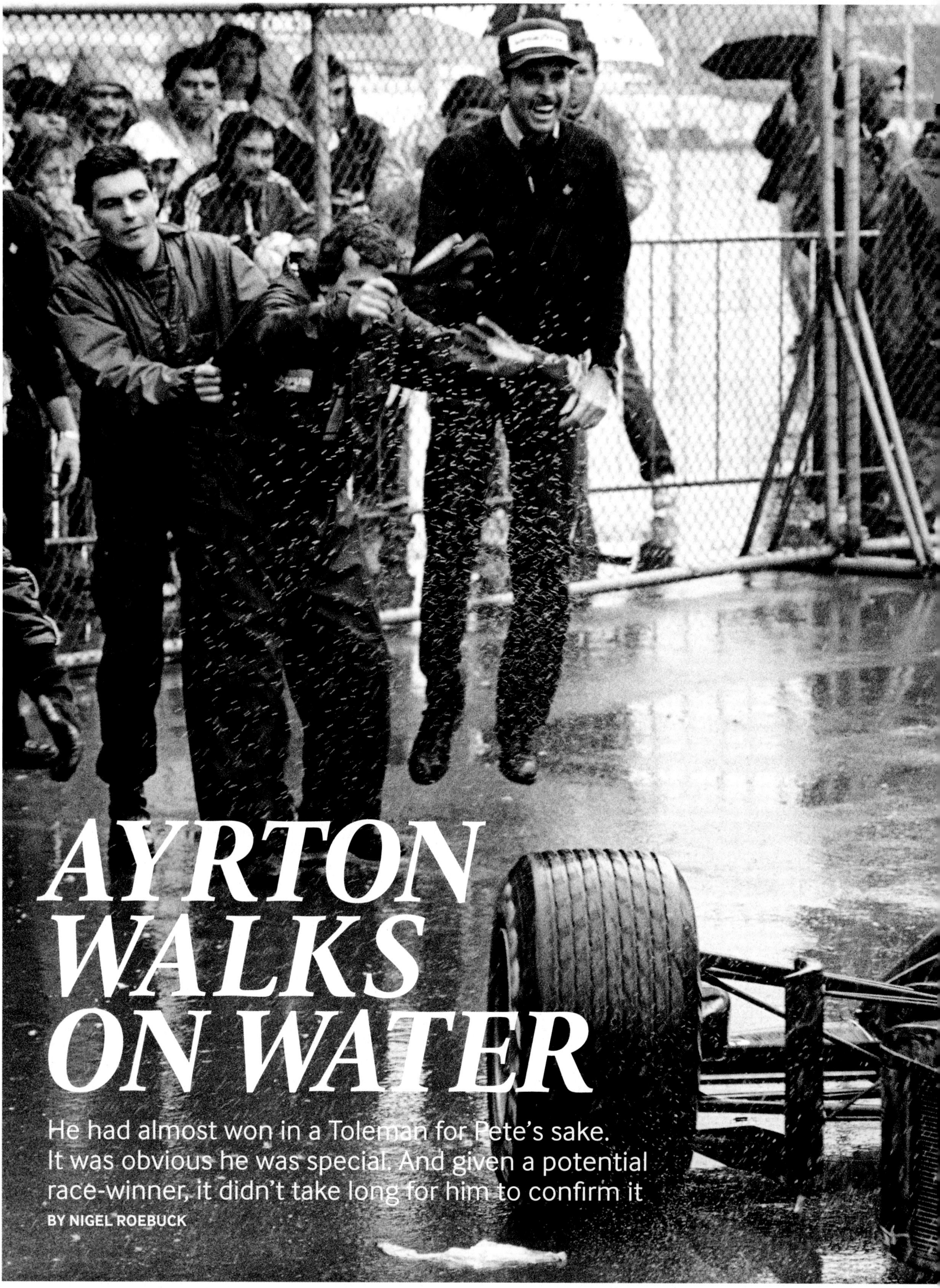

AYRTON WALKS ON WATER

He had almost won in a Toleman for Pete's sake. It was obvious he was special. And given a potential race-winner, it didn't take long for him to confirm it

BY NIGEL ROEBUCK

John Play
r Special
Turbo
RENAULT
GOODYEAR

27
12

Pressure? What pressure? Senna coolly converts his maiden pole to lead into the first corner. He will never be headed

TO CAST YOURSELF onto a wet race track, along which Grand Prix cars are proceeding, is not truly the action of a thinking man. But if you were a Lotus mechanic at half-past four last Sunday afternoon, you were not a thinking man. Your cars had won only once since the days of Mario and Ronnie, and that was out of the blue. Since then they had often taken pole, often led, but this race – this *meeting* – had been dominated by a Lotus, first to last.

Ayrton Senna's victory will be remembered as a classic. From the start he was in a race on his own, and made no mistake worthy of the name in conditions so appalling as to catch out a man of Prost's quality. The Brazilian gave the impression that he could have gone on like that indefinitely. And probably he could. He was mesmeric.

He faced no challenge, as such. Team-mate Elio de Angelis ran second for much of the way, falling back to fourth with a deflating tyre after going briefly off the road. Immediately before, the increasingly confident Michele Alboreto had taken the Ferrari past into the runner-up spot. Patrick Tambay's better-than-expected Renault finished third.

After starting from the pit lane, the legacy of a mistake during the warm-up lap, Nigel Mansell scored the first Williams points of the year with a courageous drive to fifth place, and Stefan Bellof delighted Ken Tyrrell with an irrepressible sixth.

There were but three other classified finishers, Warwick's Renault and Johansson's Ferrari, both delayed by pit stops, and Ghinzani's Osella. There were no points for McLaren, none for Brabham.

In Sunday's conditions the phrase 'tyre war' was redundant. You were on Goodyears, or you were not racing. If you were on Pirellis – even if you were Nelson Piquet in a Brabham-BMW – you were pitifully off the pace, wasting your time. In the circumstances Ghinzani, ninth, deserves some kind of award for valour. Not since the wet race at Zandvoort in 1971, when it was Goodyear's turn to be humbled by Firestone, have we seen a Grand Prix so completely split into two classes.

Or maybe there were three – Pirelli, Goodyear and Senna.

QUALIFYING

The talk, inevitably, was of Ferrari. On Friday morning all conversation seemed caught up with the firing of Arnoux, the hiring of Johansson. A lot of people went to shake Stefan's hand to wish him well, for he is a popular fellow at last presented with a car worthy of him.

"It should give heart to all the young guys with their sights on Formula 1," commented Keke Rosberg, another man who had to wait too long, "because here is someone who has got a top drive on merit. Nothing to do with money – nothing to do with anything but talent. So it still can be done."

At the same time there was general agreement that Arnoux's dismissal could have been handled somewhat better. There were suddenly expressions of sympathy for "poor old René", some of them from mouths never previously heard to utter a word in Arnoux's favour. Opportunities to slag off the ruthless *Commendatore* are rarely passed up.

There were others, too, friends of René in some cases, who expressed a certain relief. The Frenchman has been through a confused time, off form for the last six months, perhaps stale from too much testing, who knows? Unable to match Alboreto, he might have put too much call on sheer bravery. At least he had not hurt himself.

A week in politics, they say, is a long time. How, too, about this business? While Arnoux decided

'The Brazilian gave the impression that he could have gone on like that indefinitely. He probably could. He was mesmeric'

to go to ground, take a couple of months off to consider his future, Johansson took yet another incredulous look at the Prancing Horse patch on his overalls. "I have to keep doing it," he grinned. "It still hasn't really sunk in." A week earlier he had been a Toleman driver with no opportunity to race.

What a time, we all said, to be joining Ferrari, with their car a front-runner again. Alboreto is firm in the belief that he could – should – have won in Rio, and before practice began many considered Michele to be favourite for Estoril.

Wrong. We left Zolder last year believing that the C4 was a genuine challenge to McLaren, and we were wrong that time, too. "The new car was fantastic in Brazil," Alboreto mused, "but here... it feels like a different car. The traction is poor out of the corners, and it's difficult to balance it properly – understeer in, oversteer out. It feels nervous. We are short of downforce."

As in Rio a Lotus was quickest on the opening day, but this time the advantage was maintained through the second. Ayrton Senna, stunning in the Toleman here last October, was the clear pacesetter in both timed sessions. Team-mate de Angelis was fastest on Friday morning, but thereafter Senna was in control, the 97T visibly more stable than anything else through the fourth-gear right-hander at the end of the pit straight. Through the speed trap Ayrton's 192.434mph was beaten only by the Brabham of Piquet – but Nelson's best lap was 2.5secs away. The Lotus, in short, was strong in all areas, its driver more than capable of going with it.

Elio de Angelis holds a slide on his way to fourth (above). In his spray is Alain Prost, who would later, unsighted, spin on a puddle and put his McLaren in the wall; the Lotus crew keeps tabs on Senna (below)

Senna's first pole position, then, in only his second race with Lotus. On Friday the elements helped a bit, occasional splashes of rain, then a brief but fierce downpour ensuring that the Brazilian's time was beyond reach, but on Saturday afternoon Ayrton's first flying lap settled the issue. Later in the session he did one more, and that also would have been good for the front row.

Times were generally slower than expected, the Lotus only seven-tenths inside Piquet's pole time of 1984. True, those ugly rear winglets have been banned, but against that the whole of the previously bumpy pit straight has been resurfaced. Senna was not much inside the time he set during post-race Toleman testing last autumn.

By general consensus, the track was slippery throughout qualifying. "It's very dirty off the line," Piquet remarked, "and it does not seem to have gained much grip this time – not like last year. Then again," he added, "maybe it's something to do with my tyres…" Nelson's Pirelli qualifiers did not please him.

To some extent, though, the track obviously did improve. By Saturday morning Senna found he could run quicker on race tyres than he had managed on qualifiers 24 hours earlier. And one man very much happier on the second day was the ever-present Prost, who put his McLaren on the front row, four-tenths slower than the poleman.

Friday, by Alain's standards, had been a dead loss. After a misfiring morning his engine cut after a couple of slow laps in the timed session. Out he went in the spare McLaren, only fifth, and then came the rain. His second set went unused. But Saturday was much better. In the morning, back in his own car once more, he found the misfire all but vanquished, and in the afternoon smoothly

trimmed away two seconds and more. "I feel happy about the race now," Alain smiled. "I was not running with a lot of boost – not much more than we use in the race, actually – so I was not too good in the straight. But now I have the handling exactly as I like it, and for sure we have a good race set-up." Through the trap Prost was 8mph from Senna, around the lap only four-tenths away. Yes, Sunday did look promising.

Ferrari, as we have said, had their troubles. Amid the euphoria of Johansson's arrival, there was no getting away from the fact that the 156s were, to put it mildly, lively whenever the road turned. During Fiorano testing Alboreto had tried Lotus-type sidepod-mounted winglets, but they weren't seen at Estoril. "I couldn't feel any difference in the grip," Michele reported, "and we lost a bit of straight-line speed." As it was, the Ferraris were very disappointing through the trap, beaten by TAG, Honda and Renault – and 11mph away from Piquet's BMW!

Johansson was nonetheless highly impressed with the Italian V6. "There's a lot of power, believe me. The torque is amazing, as is the response." Most of all, like all drivers new to Ferrari, Stefan raved about the gearbox: "It's superb. I've never come across anything like it."

His two days of baptism were not easy. For most of Friday morning he sat in the garage while the mechanics changed springs and bars. This was his first experience of a 156, and he began qualifying with little practice in it. To make matters worse, a rotor arm failure halted Johansson out on the circuit during his first flying lap. Back to the pits, out in the spare – which was set up for Alboreto, and which he hadn't sat in before.

The following morning he had a spin when the transmission broke, leaving him without drive in the middle of a corner. That meant the T-car again for the final session, and he did well to line up 11th, a second slower than his team-mate. "I need more time in the car," he beamed. "At the moment it feels very nervous, but I'm sure we'll make progress in the Imola test next week."

Derek Warwick put the Renault RE60 into sixth place on the grid, a marked improvement on the car's form in Rio, but still he was less than thrilled. "It's getting a bit like 1982 all over again," he agreed when we spoke about downforce. "Basically, it counts for much more than anything else – and that's what we're short of. The car just doesn't seem to have much grip. I'm quite surprised to be as high as sixth, because on my quickest lap I didn't feel as though I was driving very well – not making

Nigel Mansell had crashed in his first race with Williams. In this, his second, he spins off moments before the off and is forced to start from the pitlane. But he drives superbly to finish fifth in the FW10-Honda

mistakes, exactly, but not flowing. And the car is nervous and twitchy, jumping all over the place."

It was Derek's turn to run the older EF4 engine this weekend, Patrick Tambay having the questionable pleasure of the EF15. Both drivers reckon the new V6 is fundamentally better, but also currently less reliable. Patrick used the spare car for final qualifying, leaving the EF15 in his race chassis for Sunday. He qualified 12th.

RACE

April in Portugal. There was a tune of that name in my childhood 1950s, a light, airy melody, I seem to recall, suggestive of summer's approach. It would not have been appropriate for the Estoril paddock on Sunday morning.

Through practice we had learned to live with murky skies and odd drops of rain, but soon after noon on race-day, grey was going black. The Red Arrows could give us only their secondary programme, and everyone dug out their wet-weather clothes, mildewing since Monaco, another temple of Mediterranean sunshine.

In the grandstand the spectator pondered. Had he spent his week's wages sensibly? And if so, why had nobody joined him?

In the paddock drivers and engineers glanced and grimaced repeatedly at the sky. Crazy when you thought about it, wasn't it? All this testing round the calendar – yet nobody ever tested in the wet. How would Goodyear and Pirelli compare? After two days of dry practice, settings for the race would probably be guesswork.

The Renault mechanics had work of a more immediate kind on their hands. After the warm-up they set upon the spare RE60, transplanting its rear end to Tambay's car (rear suspension failure) and its rear underbody to Warwick's, Derek having spun into a high kerb.

The warm-up, run before the rain arrived, had – surprise! – seen Prost fastest, followed by de Angelis. Third and fourth, though, were the Ferraris of Johansson and Alboreto. As both had said, the cars were indeed excellent on full tanks. Noteworthy, too, after the disappointment of Saturday, was the ninth position of Palmer's Zakspeed.

"Who's using what?" said a Goodyear man in response to my question. "We don't know yet – there's a lot of psyching going on, as usual…" But all that was swept away by the rain. It became a clear-cut matter of companies rather than compounds. Everyone was going to be on wets.

> *'Everyone dug out their wet-weather clothes, mildewing since Monaco, another temple of Mediterranean sunshine*

Would the start be delayed? someone said. No way. Time and TV slots wait for no man. But the drivers were given a few minutes for acclimatisation, during which there were sundry incidents. Mansell had an off, and arrived back at the start-finish area in need of a new nose, now too late to take his place on the grid. He, like Martini, would start from the pit lane, as would Cheever, whose car was pushed off the grid, Eddie sprinting to the Alfa pit to board the 184T-car.

The spectator looked down at the black Lotus before him. This was Senna's first pole position, and in these conditions a good start – and a clear road – was more than usually important. Only the leader would be seeing much in the early laps.

Ayrton did the job, smoothly away without too much wheelspin, but into the first corner there was black-and-gold, rather than the expected red-and-white, in his mirrors. De Angelis had beaten Prost away, and that was going to be important.

On the grid Rosberg, third, had stalled, allowing Elio, fourth, some room with which to work. Although Alboreto, directly behind the stranded Williams, lost little time rounding it, de Angelis momentarily had a clear path down the middle and made the most of it.

In the spray Palmer clipped Rosberg's car, which punctured his right-front tyre. When he came in, the mechanics also discovered a damaged wishbone. Sadly, the Zakspeed's Grand Prix debut was short indeed.

Mansell, Cheever and Martini duly departed from the pit lane to begin their race, and Nigel really got his head down, beginning a splendid drive which would see him eventually in the points. Keke, too, finally got on his way, only to spin on his first lap.

A disastrous start for Williams, but a perfect one for Lotus. At the end of lap one Senna and de Angelis came through one-two, followed by Prost, Alboreto, Warwick, Lauda, de Cesaris, Tambay, Piquet and Johansson.

Ayrton was treading warily, at the same time doing it faster than anyone else. Making the most of his clear view, he was already lapping at a speed beyond his team-mate. After two laps there was a three-second gap between the Lotuses, and Prost's McLaren was a similar distance behind Elio.

Michele Alboreto drove superbly in his Ferrari 156 to finish second and take the lead of the world championship (below); he joins Senna and Patrick Tambay on the podium for another soaking (right)

If one Brazilian looked on course already for victory, the other was facing the most dispiriting afternoon of his racing life. For the first three laps Piquet somehow resisted Johansson's Ferrari, but a queue was forming up behind the Brabham. De Cesaris's Ligier was also falling away. The Pirelli wets, it was clear, were embarrassingly bad. And as conditions worsened, so also did they.

"I would bet," mused one Brabham man afterwards, "that the telex between Chessington and Italy will be glowing red-hot on Monday morning."

Far and away the most imperturbable man on the circuit appeared to be the leader, who revived memories of Pedro Rodriguez as he made his smooth way round. Once or twice the Lotus jinked under braking for the first corner, but never once did it look like escaping from Senna's control. Just occasionally comes a race when one driver makes the rest look ordinary, and this was one such.

After 10 laps Ayrton had nearly 12 seconds over his team-mate, who was under repeated pressure from Prost, the McLaren in turn being caught by Alboreto's Ferrari. Without Senna, I shiveringly thought, we'd have quite a race here.

Fifteen laps on the Pirellis were quite enough for Laffite, who brought in the Ligier, reporting that it was a) dangerous and b) pointless to continue. By now the rain was coming down hard, and the speed differential between Goodyear and Pirelli runners was almost beyond belief. At what looked like walking pace, de Cesaris was having to fight his JS25, and in the end Gérard Larrousse wisely called him in for the day.

Piquet, for his part, never did retire. But the Brabham was frequently in the pits. "It was like a test session, really," said Gordon Murray later. "No point in getting upset – it was far too bad for that! He came in to chat, change his overalls, things like that." Eventually Nelson said he'd like them to know he was driving as hard as he could, but reckoned he was a serious danger to other drivers. At that they called it a day. His best lap in the race was a tenth quicker than Ghinzani's Osella – and seven and a half seconds from Senna's best .

In the confusion of spins and spray it was all too easy to overlook Mansell's progress. Remarkably – considering his delayed start – Nigel had the Williams-Honda up in ninth place after 10 laps. He had gained one place at the expense of Johansson, whose Ferrari debut was proving fraught.

After being punted off by Patrese, Stefan came back superbly to 10th, at that point lapping as quickly as team-mate Alboreto, but on lap 12 he was a victim once more. "Winkelhock spun right in front of me and I couldn't miss him. The nose was damaged, but I thought I'd stay out for a bit. Eventually I had to have it replaced, and then it was just a matter of keeping going to the end," He rejoined in 16th place.

RESULTS

67 LAPS (181.099 MILES)

1	Ayrton SENNA	Lotus 97T	2h00m28.006s
2	Michele ALBORETO	Ferrari 156	2h01m30.984s
3	Patrick TAMBAY	Renault RE60	66 laps
4	Elio DE ANGELIS	Lotus 97T	66 laps
5	Nigel MANSELL	Williams FW10	65 laps
6	Stefan BELLOF	Tyrrell 012	65 laps

WINNING SPEED 90.198mph

FASTEST LAP SENNA, 1m44.121s (93.455mph)

POLE POSITION SENNA, 1m21.007s (120.121mph)

LAP LEADERS SENNA 1-67

Then Rosberg crashed. Coming through the long right-hander onto the pit straight, the car snapped out of control, hit the guard rail and bounced back in the middle of the road, where it came to rest. With the rain really beating down now, there were some anxious moments as drivers swerved around the beached Williams. Keke was quickly out and away, but had bashed his hand on something in the cockpit, the wound requiring several stitches.

"He said the engine was all or nothing," reported one of the mechanics afterwards. "The road was really waterlogged at that point, and the power chimed in at the wrong moment."

At the front there was no change. As the 30-lap mark approached Senna led by more than half a minute, and Prost continued to crowd de Angelis for second place, with Alboreto's beautifully driven Ferrari ever present in their mirrors. "For sure," Alain ruefully said after the race, "I make a big mistake at the start, letting Elio beat me away..."

As the two of them pounded down the pit straight to begin lap 31, the McLaren suddenly began to weave, veering first left, then right, then breaking into a spin. Prost could do nothing to keep it from the wall. Out he stepped, race run.

"It was raining very 'ard just then, with deep puddles, and in the spray it's impossible to see where they are. Once you start aquaplaning at that speed, you are finished." With Lauda apparently out of contention, McLaren were going to lose

WHAT HAPPENED NEXT...

Senna set six more pole positions, but scored only one more victory. Prost, with five wins to his name, fended off a mid-season challenge from Alboreto to become the world champion for the first time.

a race for the first time since Dallas last July.

Conditions had gone from bad to appalling – worse by far, according to Senna, than those at Monaco. At this point, indeed, Ayrton was waving vigorously as he passed the pits, indicating that the race should be stopped. All round the circuit were abandoned cars. Martini's Minardi, after countless spins, was finally out, as was Berger's Arrows. The young Austrian had driven a fine and forceful race, getting ahead of team-mate Boutsen for a while. Baldi's Spirit gave the guard rail a very sizeable thump, and Brundle's Tyrrell, running 10th despite gearbox problems, also spun into retirement.

There were, however, no mistakes from the leader, despite the fact that he was lapping faster than anyone else. An hour into the race he was 40 seconds clear, and interest centred on the battle for second, for Alboreto very definitely had his sights on de Angelis. On lap 43 the Ferrari emerged from the spray and flicked inside the Lotus as they approached the first turn.

Elio made no real attempt to close the door, and it looked as if he had been caught unawares. Immediately he made a rather futile attempt to get back at Michele, but only two corners later left his braking too late and slid wide. On the gravel and slippery grass he did a fine job in keeping control of the Lotus, but while off course punctured a front tyre, which deflated slowly thereafter but did not keep him from reaching the finish.

One of the best drives of the race came from Cheever, always excellent in the wet. From his pit-lane start Eddie had taken the old Alfa 184 up to eighth in the course of only nine laps. A plug change after half an hour had dropped him down the field, but he then clawed back to eighth and looked set to improve further on that. Alack, the car eventually stopped with a dead engine. Electrics, somewhere, they said.

Lap 59 saw a new third-place man, Tambay, who had driven an excellent race from the first. De Angelis, struggling with his soft front tyre, could offer no resistance – indeed he was lapped by team-mate Senna before the end.

'Come in number 12, your two hours are up!' After 67 of the originally scheduled 69 laps, the chequered flag went out to Ayrton – and his moment of triumph could easily have been soured by tragedy. In the manner pioneered by Colin Chapman, some of the Lotus mechanics jumped over the barrier and onto the track to greet their man. Seeing them, Senna slowed and moved to the right immediately after crossing the finish line. Thundering up beside him was Mansell, suddenly with nowhere to go. Nigel lifted off and swerved left, behind the Lotus, then surviving a wild slide on the grass. It was good that Prost's abandoned McLaren was further on down the road.

> ***'I had no spins, but I don't know how. I think I saw the Devil about a million times today… I could have been third or thirteenth'***

Before reaching the first turn Ayrton had flung off his belts, and was waving both arms wildly – the Latin at last. This was his 17th Grand Prix, only his second for Lotus, and he had won it. More than that, he had been in a different class right from the green light. Fastest in both sessions, fastest lap of the race, leader all the way. Full house. Victories like that deserve more than nine points.

"The big danger," he said later, exuberance now gone, "was that the conditions changed all the time. Sometimes the rain was extremely heavy, sometimes not. I couldn't see anything behind me. It was difficult even to keep the car in a straight line sometimes, and for sure the race should have been stopped. Once I nearly spun in front of the pits, like Prost, and I was lucky to stay on the road."

And the car? "Fantastic. I had an engine and gearbox change after the warm-up, and there were no problems at all."

Others were very happy, too. Alboreto's superb drive to second gives him the lead of the world championship, and Tambay was amazed to be third – "I had no spins or anything, but I don't know how. I think I saw the Devil about a million times today... I could have been third or thirteenth."

De Angelis could have hoped for better than fourth, but also drove a fine race. Had not Senna been in the other Lotus, indeed, we might have thought it a very fine race. It will be interesting to see how Elio responds at Imola and beyond.

A finish in the points will have done wonders for Mansell's morale. After his gaff immediately before the start, he drove an excellent and gutsy race to fifth place, finishing ahead of the impressive Bellof, who scored what must be the last point for a Cosworth-powered car! Surely…

The spectator looked on, and considered his afternoon. Had it been worth all the money? On balance, yes, he decided. He was soaked and chilled through, but a Portuguese-speaking driver had won. And one day he would be able to say that he had been there, that day when Ayrton Senna won his first Grand Prix. ■

NIKI LAUDA | 1985 DUTCH GP | AUGUST 25 McLAREN MP4/2B

THE RAT'S REVENGE

All hopes of the world title had gone. Retirement was beckoning. Yet here he was, risking it all in a bid to fend off his team-mate for one last victory

BY NIGEL ROEBUCK

CHAMPION
CHAMPION
MAGNETI MARELLI
West
GITANES
MAREDO
GOODYEAR
benetton
23
27
30
26
22

The Ferrari 156/85s of Stefan Johansson and Michele Alboreto (27) qualified in the middle of the pack. They are chased by Piercarlo Ghinzani's Toleman TG185 (20) and the Alfa 184T (23) of Eddie Cheever, the turbo of which lasted just one lap

NIKI LAUDA SAID during his press conference in Austria that he had lost some of his motivation since winning the championship last year. And that was why he was quitting. His form since rather suggests that he has found it again. Some say that reaching a decision about retirement has freed him to concentrate fully on racing again; he wants his last few drives to be memorable. Others suggest that certain events in Austria have stung him into it.

Whatever the explanation, Lauda's victorious drive here lacked for nothing. Niki was absolutely at the limit in the closing laps. You have to do that when an equal car is behind you, when Alain Prost is driving it, when passing you means another win, another nine points towards the title.

QUALIFYING

There was a weary air pervading the Zandvoort paddock. Nobody enjoys losing two weekends on the trot, and many of the mechanics looked worn out.

Zandvoort is a seaside town, rather tatty at the edges – and the same is true of the circuit. The press facilities I will flatteringly describe as primitive, and the whole place could use a coat or two of paint. Those without a feel for grand prix racing dislike it intensely, for it is not a 'modern facility'.

I love it, and always have; don't mind the stiff North Sea breeze or the dirty sand hills – nor even the fact that people eat herring sandwiches here. The place has atmosphere, and the track provides better racing than any other in Formula 1. Show me a more exhilarating viewing spot than the end of the pit straight, where they brake down from around 200mph for Tarzan.

The debacle of Spa seems yonderly now. The weather that weekend was splendid, you may recall. Since then we have been to Montreal, Detroit, Ricard, Silverstone, the Nürburgring and Zeltweg – and only in France did we have two days of qualifying untouched by rain. In Holland, as in Austria, it was the Saturday we lost: pale grey skies and a steady drizzle through the day. That meant that Nelson Piquet kept his first pole of the season.

Keke Rosberg – galoshes over his driving boots – was to be found under the motorhome awning, mug of coffee in one hand, fag in the other. It was that kind of day.

"So when did you sign the McLaren contract?" I asked. You never have to wait long for a reply from Keke: "Before it was announced."

Then Patrick Head came in: "Keke, I'd like you to do one more run this morning session."

Rosberg drained his cup, stubbed out his cigarette and vanished into the rain.

"Pity about the weather today," he said before dashing. "I made one or two mistakes on my quick lap yesterday. Should've been quicker. Also my top gear was a bit too short. But I doubt if we'd have beaten Nelson. That Brabham on the straight… unbelievable. Out of the last right-hander I should think I was 10-15km/h quicker, but by the end of the straight he was much quicker than me."

During testing Piquet had lapped in 1m12.73s,

Alain Prost chases McLaren team-mate Lauda into Tarzan (above); Nigel Mansell's Williams FW10 finished the race strongly, but was hampered by two tyre stops (right)

more than a second faster than anyone else. He was a fraction off that on his first timed run, but the next produced a startling 1m11.074s, and that no one approached. Still, the car looked wayward, and Nelson confirmed that it felt that way: "The basic problem doesn't change – the car is not so good turning in. But the track is much quicker than when we were here for testing."

The cars are also much quicker than a year ago. Prost had his McLaren on the pole in 1984, lapping in 1m13.567s. This time he circulated in 1m11.801s, and found that good only for third.

"I'm not too concerned," Alain said. "We have our usual problem – not enough qualifying boost, therefore not enough horsepower. Actually I'm quite surprised the time is that quick. On race boost we'll be fine, I think." Alain was the only front-runner to venture out on Saturday afternoon: third in the dry, second in the wet, he looked as strong as ever.

Zeltweg, of course, was a low point for Lotus. Although Senna finished second, he had qualified only 14th, and for once never figured as a possible winner. His Zandvoort weekend got away to a bad start – and an expensive one. During the Friday morning session his car took fire in the early part of the lap. He needed the urgent services of a fire marshal, and therefore decided to drive off down the slip road at the exit of the Hugenholtz hairpin, taking a short cut back to the paddock, where the flames were dealt with.

He may have saved the car, but it was at some cost to his pocket. The stewards considered his action dangerous, and lost no time in fining him $5000, also issuing a severe reprimand. That apart, he was fairly serene on Saturday afternoon.

"We were terrible in Austria during practice, yes, terrible over the bumps," he said. "Here the car is much better – but not as good as it has been at some other tracks. If it's a wet race we could be more competitive than in the dry. The only worry with that is tyre wear…"

Yes, something new. Fears of excessive wet-tyre wear. In the rain Zandvoort is more grippy than most circuits, but its abrasiveness is very hard on tyres. Senna talked of "three stops at least, maybe," and Goodyear's chief anxiety was that there might not be enough wets to go round.

Fifth, half a second behind the Brazilian, was Teo Fabi, maintaining Toleman's recent sparkling practice form. Through the slow corners – Tarzan, Hugenholtz – its turning-in abilities and front-end grip were something to behold, reminiscent of the ground-effect era. After the first session Teo was a little disappointed with his time: "Top gear was too low – I was on the rev-limiter long before the end of the straight. Tomorrow we change." But it rained, and fifth he stayed.

Next to him was – surprise! – a Renault. Patrick Tambay is coping well with the *Régie*'s tribulations, and was quite pleased with his RE60B in Holland: "Not bad at all, really. In Austria I thought we were making some progress at last, and here it seems to be the same. We are still short of grip in the slow corners, but through the quick ones it feels okay. This is a track I like very much."

The fourth row was shared by Nigel Mansell's Williams-Honda (a second slower than Rosberg's sister car) and Thierry Boutsen's Arrows, which made good use of its BMW horsepower down the pit straight. The quiet Belgian seems to be reasserting his position as team leader, and was almost a second up on Gerhard Berger. This was, however, the Austrian's first race at Zandvoort.

Lauda was beaten only by team-mate Prost on Friday morning, but slipped down to 10th in the afternoon. "On my first run," Niki said, "Fabi was running slowly and got in my way. The second was clear, but I was very down on power." Afterwards the McLaren mechanics found that one cylinder was low on compression. Lauda ran only six laps in the wet on Saturday morning, and did not come out in the afternoon.

RACE

There was no real sign of rain in the morning. There was quite a lot of cloud around, but it was patchy in a blue sky. There was also enough breeze to keep the clouds on the move, so thoughts of multiple stops for new wets receded.

Zandvoort's abrasiveness, however, means that tyre wear is always a major factor, and in choosing their compounds several teams budgeted for at least one stop.

The McLarens, you will be amazed to learn, headed the times in the warm-up, a minor surprise being that Lauda was marginally quicker than Prost. Alain tried both his cars, and opted to race his T-car, with the original rear suspension. "Not much in it," he said, "but the spare felt better."

More of a surprise – nay, after qualifying,

a shock – was the presence, in third and fourth, of the Ferraris of Stefan Johansson and Michele Alboreto. "It's just gamesmanship," people said, "and the post-session 'phone call to Maranello will put the Old Man in a good mood. No way they were running on full tanks… "

Stefan said that wasn't the case: "We were on full tanks, but that's no big deal – the cars are always better on full tanks. I wish I could say we'd made a breakthrough, believe me, but we haven't."

A little further down the pit lane there were others with worries more serious. Expressions in the Renault pit were longer even than usual. There was one suggestion indeed that the yellow cars might be withdrawn. A fresh RE60B had been sent to Zandvoort to replace the car destroyed on Friday. So a spare was available, and when the engine in his race car refused to run properly, Tambay took it out. Up to this point Renault had no running whatever on full tanks, and when Patrick put the brakes on for Tarzan at the start of his first quick lap, the left-front suspension broke. He finished up in the tyre wall, quite unhurt but shaken. He was afterwards in an understandable fury. Back in the paddock they discovered that a weld had cleanly snapped in the bottom wishbone.

For the sake of local churchgoers, Zandvoort's race-day schedule is always late, with the warm-up at midday and the race at three. And as the cars formed up on the grid, it was almost with disbelief that we saw Tambay's Renault at the end of pit lane. He had needed more attention to the engine and missed getting onto the grid.

On the final parade lap others, too, had their worries. "I thought for sure I wouldn't finish," Senna said. "All round that lap the engine was on five cylinders. It cleared a bit as we came up to the grid."

At the green light Piquet's Brabham jerked momentarily forward, then stopped, engine stalled. A little further back, on the other side of the track, Boutsen's Arrows was also stationary. All those back of the first three rows, therefore, found themselves accelerating flat out through an unexpected chicane. It seems that no two cars made contact, which was quite remarkable. "My fault," Nelson owned up. "It went up to the limiter, then died. I was lucky not to be hit." While Piquet got a push, Boutsen got himself away, and Tambay was long gone from the pit lane, about to begin a drive of remarkable aggression.

Piquet's Brabham jerked forward, then stopped. 'My fault. It went up to the limiter, then died. I was very lucky not to be hit'

The only man completely unimpeded by the grid dramas was Rosberg, starting second. He made his usual scintillating start, and had a clear lead into Tarzan, followed by Senna and Fabi. Prost, right behind Piquet on the grid, had reacted swiftly to the Brabham's lack of forward motion, but lost out a little as he jinked around it. Still, he was fourth at the first turn. It could have been worse.

We are becoming accustomed to a Rosberg charge in the early laps of a race, and at Zandvoort he really went for it. After one lap Senna's Lotus was well over a second adrift, and Keke finished lap two with almost three seconds' advantage. By now Prost had dispensed with Fabi, and was third.

By lap four a quintet had broken clear of the rest: Rosberg, Senna, Prost, Fabi, Lauda, followed Mansell, Warwick, de Angelis, Surer and both the Ferraris, which were so far showing no sign of repeating their warm-up form.

Keke's lead was out to 3.7 seconds after seven laps, but thereafter Senna and Prost, warring over second, gradually began to reel him in. Lauda had got by Fabi. And the rest were frankly nowhere.

The pace at the front was proving just a little breathless for Fabi's Toleman, and the Italian dropped back from the tail of the first group to the head of the second: Mansell, Warwick, de Angelis. All were being slowly caught by Alboreto, but closing fast on the Ferrari was the amazing Tambay.

From his pit lane start Patrick was up to 10th by lap 14, and showed no signs of leaving it there. Past the pits for the 17th time he was alongside Alboreto and going past. Into Tarzan Michele foolishly tried to sit it out with him, missed his braking point and locked up. The Ferrari weaved first this way, then the other, coming within an ace of clouting the Renault's left-rear wheel. Fortunately for his championship aspirations, Alboreto did not slide into the run-off area, but he came close.

A lap later Fabi was into the pits, the front of his car damaged. The team thought he needed only a new nose cone, but Teo disabused them. He had been off the road and in the air, he said. A loose

Johansson's race ends early in a cloud of smoke, a piston probably (left); Ayrton Senna's Lotus 97T (12) was also hindered by a less-than-perfect V6 turbo (below)

WHAT HAPPENED NEXT...

Prost won the Italian GP, but thereafter the car to have was a Williams-Honda: Mansell was second at Spa, then ended his long wait by winning at Brands Hatch – and then Kyalami; Rosberg won in Adelaide.

rear wheel had caused it. And that, sadly, was that.

Lap 19 was Rosberg's last. Through Bos Uit, the right-hander onto the straight, he trailed smoke. Instantly Prost, Lauda and Senna were by, and Keke was out with his fourth consecutive engine failure.

Now things began to happen quickly. Already de Angelis had been in for new tyres. Like most of the Goodyear runners he had started on Cs all round. So this pointed to a busy afternoon in the pits. The McLarens, though, had gone to the grid with a B on the left-rear, and Warwick's Renault had Bs left, Cs right. Perhaps they'd fare better?

The answer was not long coming. At the end of lap 20 Lauda came in. So that obviously meant tyre changes for everyone. Niki's was a good stop, requiring only 10 seconds. He rejoined in eighth.

Our order, then, was this: Prost, Senna, and then, quite incredibly, the Renaults of Warwick and Tambay! Glory for the *Régie* at last? Alas, *non*. After running fourth for a couple of laps, Patrick failed to materialise at the end of the 23rd. The transmission broken and he had parked up. During the course of his charge he had lapped two seconds faster than the leaders. On lap 16 he went round in 1m17.335s, the fourth-fastest of the race. Only in the late stages did Prost, Lauda and Mansell better it.

Team-mate Warwick lasted little longer. His afternoon may have been less dramatic than Tambay's, but it was also mighty impressive: "It was a pity that I had Nigel in front of me, because the horsepower of that Honda was just unbelievable. Everywhere else I was quicker than him, but down the straight he disappeared."

Soon it was apparent that Derek was in gearbox trouble. Several times out of Tarzan he slowed, freewheeling along in search of third, and on lap 27 he retired: "The bloody oil bung fell out – and then, of course, the oil. I lost third, then fourth, then all of them." Still, for once he had been able to remind everyone of his real worth.

Talking Renaults, however, leads us ahead of our tale. The significant runners pitted like this: Lauda (lap 20), Mansell (24), Senna (26), Alboreto (32) and Prost (33).

"I think maybe I stopped five or six laps too soon," Niki said afterwards. "I would have been in better shape for the closing stages if I had left it a while longer."

For all that, he would not willingly have exchanged stops with his team-mate, for Alain's was disastrously slow. Three of the four were changed in around eight seconds, but at the right-rear there was a cross-thread problem, and by the time Prost got the go signal he had been stationary for nearly 20 seconds. The number two McLaren had gone in with nearly half a minute's lead; it came out in third place, 17 seconds behind Lauda. And to his great credit Alain never sought to use it as an excuse after the race.

After 35 laps, the significant tyre changes all done, the position was this: Lauda, four seconds, Senna, 12.2, Prost. Then came Surer, who had not stopped, de Angelis, Alboreto, Berger and Mansell.

Now the real race began. As in Austria, it was a matter of Prost chasing Lauda, catching and passing him before the laps ran out. At Zeltweg, of course, it never came to that, for Niki retired. It was a race he had truly wanted. "Losing it really sharpened the old Rat's teeth," someone said on Sunday. "That and the press conference, of course."

Still, Prost was closing. While Alboreto displaced de Angelis from fourth, Alain was moving in on Senna for second, recording new fastest laps all the while. By lap 46 he was right up with the Lotus, which had been held up for a whole lap behind Martin Brundle's Tyrrell, and next time round he was through. "I could do nothing about it," Ayrton said. "My engine was terrible today – for the whole race."

Now the McLarens were first and second, 10 seconds apart, and with 23 laps of the race to go. There were no team orders, that much had been agreed. Niki was going to win this if he could, and Alain knew he would have to take it from him.

These two apart, unquestionably the fastest man on the circuit was Mansell, who had by now made two tyre stops, on laps 24 and 39. "My fault," Frank Williams admitted after the race. "He started on Cs, and it was my idea to put him onto Bs at the stop. They were hopeless, and he had to come in again for more Cs." After the second stop Nigel rejoined in ninth place.

'Of course we're still friends. I'm happy to be second to Niki. Maybe we were a little bit crazy in the last few laps, but it was fun'

Fifty laps: Lauda, eight seconds ahead of Prost, then Senna, Alboreto, de Angelis, Mansell, Brundle, Berger. Behind the Arrows now was Surer. After an excellent showing in the first half of the race, Marc's Brabham-BMW now had a broken exhaust, sounding dreadful and becoming more normally aspirated by the lap. He was, though, still ahead of his team-mate.

Having started the best part of a lap adrift, Piquet then had to endure an inordinately long pit stop, in which a set of hard Pirellis was fitted, then removed and replaced by softer ones! At around this point of the race Nelson was lapping very quickly, but still back in 11th place.

By lap 54 it seemed that Prost must do it. In four laps he had reduced Lauda's lead from eight seconds to 3.8. But Niki wasn't done. Thereafter it was a matter of half a second here, a couple of tenths there. With a supreme effort on lap 57 Alain closed the gap to 2.5, setting another record lap – 1m16.538s – in the process. But on lap 60 Niki actually pulled out a quarter-second, recording his best time in the process. This was a race, indeed.

Next time round the McLarens were set to lap de Angelis, and this allowed Prost to close right up. Elio was not obstructive by choice, but Niki had to ease off behind him a fraction as they went into Hugenholtz, whereas Alain had a clear run through. We were now into the last seven or eight laps: surely, from the way he had caught Lauda, Prost had to do it now.

The last 20 miles were quite something. "I was absolutely flat out, on the limit," Niki confirmed later. I asked Steve Nichols, his race engineer, if he had mentioned how much boost he had been running. Steve just grinned, rolling his eyes…

If Lauda had an advantage, it was perhaps on initial acceleration out of slow corners. And maybe a little down the straight, too. More than once Prost was right on his tail approaching Bos Uit, yet was unable to challenge into Tarzan, despite gaining under braking.

It is good that Piquet is not a timid man, for through all this he was running about a hundred yards in front of the McLarens, comfortable enough with his own pace to feel no need to move over for them. What a pity he had stalled.

Piquet's Brabham, however, was one thing, Rothengatter's Osella quite another. Huub was very gentlemanly when the McLarens lapped him at Scheivlak, moving well out of the way, but Alain thought to take Niki unawares immediately afterwards, darting to his left and onto the grass! For a second Prost's car twitched as the left-hand wheels came back on the road, and it looked as though he might slide into Lauda, but all was well.

On the last lap they were as good as tied together, Alain darting left and right, trying to unsettle Niki, looking for a way through. The gap never materialised. Through Bos Uit, coming up to the line, the Frenchman wasn't close enough to think about a slingshot move. At the flag the gap was 0.232 of a second.

"I knew," Niki said, "that the last few laps were going to be hell, that sooner or later I was going to see him in my mirrors. I said I wanted him to get the championship this year, and I do. And I promised that at the end of the season I'll do everything I can to help him." A pause. "But it's not the end of the season yet!"

"Of course we're still friends," said Alain, slightly surprised by an Italian journalist's query. "I was trying very hard to win, but I'm happy to be second to Niki. It was a good race. Maybe we were a little bit crazy in the last few laps, but it was fun."

Zandvoort, as usual, had given us the best race of the year. ■

RESULTS

70 LAPS (184.945 MILES)

1	Niki LAUDA	McLaren MP4/2B	1h32m29.263s
2	Alain PROST	McLaren MP4/2B	1h32m29.495s
3	Ayrton SENNA	Lotus 97T	1h33m17.754s
4	Michele ALBORETO	Ferrari 156/85	1h33m18.100s
5	Elio DE ANGELIS	Lotus 97T	69 laps
6	Nigel MANSELL	Williams FW10	69 laps

WINNING SPEED 119.980mph

FASTEST LAP PROST, 1m16.538s (124.271mph)

POLE POSITION PIQUET, 1m11.074s (133.825mph)

LAP LEADERS Keke ROSBERG 1-19; PROST 20-33; LAUDA 34-70

NIGEL MANSELL | 1989 HUNGARIAN GP | AUGUST 13 FERRARI 640

Nigel's Eastern Bloc-buster

Unusually, the McLarens were struggling, but Mansell looked to have missed his chance due to a poor qualifying. His Ferrari felt good in race set-up – but there were 11 cars ahead of it...

BY NIGEL ROEBUCK

HUNGARIAN TELEVISION
Shell
Philips Car Ster
ONT
CAMPARI
Marlboro
GOOD
USF&G
LEYTON HOUSE
USF&G

Martin Brundle's Brabham spins after contact with Jean Alesi's Tyrrell. Mansell (27) avoids the midfield melee thanks to a strong getaway

FOR THE FIRST time in two years, McLaren-Honda was outpaced. And by a league this was the best race of the season, maybe of several. Nigel Mansell always thought he and the Ferrari would be on the pace in Hungary. On qualifying tyres, though, the car was a disaster – so much so that he spent the last session concentrating on a race set-up. It was a sound gamble, time well spent. Qualifying only 12th, he took the lead from Ayrton Senna with 20 laps to go. Senna was cheerful in defeat. The man in tears was Riccardo Patrese who took pole and led for 52 laps before a radiator burst. According to Nigel this was the best race of his life. He won by passing people – beating them.

QUALIFYING

Friday morning's free practice was, at best, an unusual session. Initially Stefan Johansson led the way and into the last few minutes the unusual theme continued. With 15 minutes to go Alain Prost bumped a Minardi to take fourth! Moments later Piercarlo Ghinzani took fifth. In those dying moments the old order reasserted itself with Prost, Nigel Mansell, Riccardo Patrese, Ayrton Senna and Gerhard Berger all doing quick times.

Alex Caffi sneaked in to take fourth, and the top 10 also featured Luis Sala, Pierluigi Martini and Ghinzani. These lesser-known heroes all had one thing in common – Pirelli rubber – but it was certainly an unexpected list.

The afternoon session, with the official clocks running, was in a similar vein. Caffi led the way. "I saw his time come up on the TV screen," said Gerhard Berger, "and I thought, 'Shit, what's happening now? Alex is good, huh? The best of the young Italians."

But youthful exuberance was put firmly its place just short of the half-hour mark when Mr Experience, Riccardo Patrese (185 GPs and counting) did a blinder of a lap. It was so fast that many had doubts that such a time was possible. The men at Olivetti Longines checked, but it was right. A mere 1.3 seconds faster than Caffi.

"It shouldn't be a shock," smiled Riccardo. "I am fast! The car was perfect, there was a nice balance and I pushed hard. It felt quick." It looked it. This was one of those laps about which drivers dream. Every corner was just so.

The rest piled in with their times, but no one was close to Patrese. A red Italian car was alongside on the front row – but (whisper it and marvel) it wasn't a Ferrari. Caffi had held on to second. Italian youth and Italian experience had outdone everyone, even the mighty McLaren-Honda. Down in the Ferrari pit, if the ground had opened, the team would have been happier. At Scuderia Italia, Caffi beamed like a sports car on the Mulsanne at night. Presumably, he would like it to rain in the second session on Saturday? "Rain?" he said. "No, I don't want rain, I want half a metre of snow. That would be good."

Prost salvaged third for McLaren and Berger upheld Ferrari's honour in fourth, but neither team was having a bundle of laughs. Honda power was not quite as useful as it has been for much of the summer. The Hungaroring is a handling track and no amount of horsepower could mask the fact that the McLaren was not handling well. The imbalance affected both Prost and Senna and neither was exactly ecstatic about being blown off; but blown off they were. Yes, traffic played a part, but that was the same for everyone.

Some reflected their frustration in alarming ways. Mansell felt aggrieved that Jean Alesi had carved him up at one point in free practice. "He finished a quick lap," explained Jean, "and then he stayed in the middle of the road. He is a champion, a top driver. He has a car for winning races. Why he do that?" Jean admitted that he had lost his temper and braked in front of Nigel. "It was very close," he said. No one dared breathe the expression "brake-test", and Nigel didn't want to discuss it, but it was the most overt display of the emotions that were running throughout the field.

The pressure even got to regular iceman Senna, who jumped from his car at the weighing point in the closing seconds of the afternoon session. He sprinted to his garage, jumped into the spare and had managed only a few hundred metres when the flag came out. It had achieved nothing, but a US$5000 fine…

There was still the Saturday official session to get through, of course, and most drivers (all of them being optimists) reckoned that things would be better. The Red Sea of cars would open up and allow them that lap of which they knew they were capable. But the reality was different. Saturday saw no snow, but in the morning Caffi was still up there, second only to Sandro Nannini's Benetton. Behind them the big-hitters continued to look frustrated.

In the afternoon, the track seemed quicker and there were improvements from most runners. There was also more baulking and bad temper.

Ayrton admitted to a couple of mistakes on his fast run but bounced Caffi to the second row. Patrese looked set for another lap in the 1m19s when he encountered Stefano Modena at the end of his lap. Caffi improved, but blew an engine at the end of his fastest lap. Thierry Boutsen carved a slice off his Friday time to sneak up to fourth. But Prost did not improve. "Qualifying was impossible," he said. "I was a full second quicker on race tyres than on qualifiers. I just could not make the front end work."

'I had the race set-up pretty good on Bs and Cs. I felt happy the night before the race: the big problem was starting so far back'

Mansell had a similar problem: "I'm reason–ably happy," he said. "We have gone forward from yesterday, but I could not get the qualifiers to work." He would start 12th on the grid. Team-mate Berger was sixth.

RACE

Mansell and Palmer seemed an unlikely pair to find at the top of the morning warm-up times. Jonathan, only 19th on the grid after two troubled qualifying days, had the Tyrrell set up like Alesi's, and found the handling transformed.

Nigel may have been disconsolate about qualifying 12th, but he had thought his predicament through with the kind of calm logic we associate with Prost. It takes discipline and self-confidence effectively to throw away the last session, to give it over to work on a race set-up, but Mansell figured he had little to lose. He didn't touch qualifying tyres on Saturday afternoon.

"It was frustrating, sliding further and further down the list," he said, "but I couldn't get the car to work on qualifiers, anyway. Over the two days, I'm sure I did more running on race tyres than anyone else, and I had the set-up pretty good on Bs and Cs. I felt pretty happy the night before the race: the big problem was starting so far back."

Berger, fourth in the warm-up, was less content. The handling was reasonably good, but there was a gearbox problem and Gerhard – who has yet to score a point in 1989, and has retired endlessly with gearbox-related troubles – requested it be changed for the race. It was not. And later in the day that would make him very angry.

The McLaren drivers were also in differing frames of mind. Handling was better, but Prost's engine wasn't picking up properly, and the same problem afflicted Boutsen's Williams-Renault. The engine was changed for the race, but then an

Mansell, having looked after his soft rubber, reels in Ayrton Senna. All he needs now is a brilliant piece of opportunism…

electrical glitch meant taking the spare, after all, and it was set up for Patrese. Thierry, a man unusually finicky about set-up, wasn't thrilled. Riccardo, trouble-free in the morning, was relaxed.

In the paddock people said that qualifying was one thing, the race quite another. Just wait, they said; Senna will get Patrese by the first turn; end of story. Well, perhaps. But at least there were wild cards in the pack for once. And another was in the elements. After two days of sun, race morning was hazy and overcast, and spots of rain intermittently fell right up to start time.

Patrese got it right. Into the first corner Senna, as predicted, jinked to the inside, trying to claim the line. But Riccardo confidently chopped across, and Ayrton decided discretion was the better part. Caffi followed them, then Berger, Prost and Boutsen. In the course of the first lap Brundle spun after making smart contact with Alesi's Tyrrell, which pitted for attention to a damaged undertray.

Patrese's first lap was one of which Senna might have been proud. At the end of it, Ayrton trailed the Williams by more than a second, and already a discernible gap was opening between these two and the rest, who were led – and held up – by Caffi, Dallara and Pirelli.

Already Mansell was up from 12th to eighth: "I knew I had to get a good start, make up a lot of places early, and I got around four cars at the first corner. 'Right,' I thought, 'I've survived that; don't blow it.' I got stuck a bit behind Boutsen and Nannini, but I didn't want to push. It was important to keep the tyres in good shape."

Nigel, in the end, had opted for Cs, whereas Patrese, Senna and Prost had gone for Bs. There wasn't a great difference in wear, it was a matter of what worked on which: Ferrari had a little too much oversteer on Bs; McLaren too much push on Cs. Hence their decisions were made for them.

Pirelli's race rubber wasn't wonderful. "There's no grip whatever you run," Brundle said before the race. "So we may as well run the tyre with no grip that's going to last the distance."

Caffi's Dallara was similarly shod, which explained why he needed a fairly brutal technique to keep Berger and Prost behind him. By lap four, Gerhard had made it by, but Alain was twice blocked into the first turn, and it was a surprise that the Honda couldn't more decisively deal with the Cosworth earlier in the pit straight.

'Basically, I had a quiet Sunday afternoon drive for 20 laps or so, until I got a bit annoyed and started to push hard'

"From the start," Prost said, "I had engine problems. The pick-up problem I had in the warm-up was still there, and also the engine was cutting out intermittently. I was slow getting off the corner onto the straight, which made overtaking difficult."

On lap seven, though, the McLaren was past and into fourth, albeit now a long way back of Patrese, Senna and Berger. And Caffi bent himself to the task of holding up Boutsen, Nannini and Mansell, which he managed with some efficiency.

The Senna believers were now beginning to have doubts. Ayrton had seriously threatened Patrese's lead for a couple of laps, but now the Williams had pulled clear again, never less than a second ahead, sometimes more than two. Waiting has never been Senna's game; if he could have passed, he would have done. On the straights he gained a little, but on grip, he said, Riccardo's car had a definite edge. He knew he was in a race this time; Berger was even moving in on his second place. And Prost, with a clear track before him, was catching everyone. The afternoon promised well.

Lap 12 saw Nannini into the pits for tyres. He had no desperate need of new ones, but had grown frustrated with sitting in the queue behind Caffi. Now, he reasoned, might be a smart time to stop. But it dropped him to 19th, gave him a lot to do.

By lap 15 we had a four-car train at the head of the field, for Prost had hitched himself to Patrese, Senna and Berger. And at this point we also had spots of rain: not sufficient to make anyone think of a change to wets, but perhaps a portent of worse to come. For now, though, it made little difference to the pace at the front.

By now Mansell had tired of sitting behind Caffi and Boutsen, and in short order dealt with each: "'Basically, I had a quiet Sunday afternoon drive for 20 laps or so, until I got a bit annoyed and started to push hard. The fuel load had lightened, and my tyres were perfect." It was lap 22, and the Ferrari was nearly 15 seconds adrift of Prost, last man in the leading quartet. A quintet it would

Mansell, in his first season with Ferrari, was revered by the *tifosi*. The honeymoon ended in 1990

soon be. That much was obvious from the speed at which Nigel closed – around a second a lap…

Boutsen, still stuck behind Caffi, followed Nannini's example, and stopped for tyres on lap 22: "I was having to adapt to the handling of the spare, which I didn't like very much. But on new tyres it was much better. I made the right choice."

We might have expected a spate of tyre swaps now, but they did not come. Most of the front-runners were still in good shape, although Berger wasn't sure, and came in on lap 30. The Ferrari mechanics did their work swiftly, sending him out in sixth place. But Gerhard's original set had been quite intact. And this piece of information they radioed to Mansell…

The picture changed fundamentally on lap 41, began to take its ultimate shape. Patrese was still ahead of Senna, but now Mansell was up to third, and Prost… Prost was falling sharply back. "It was hopeless just then," he said. "Cutting out all the time. And the Ferrari was handling much better than we were. I just hoped the engine would make it to the finish. After a few laps the problem disappeared for a bit, then came back, then went…"

Gradually Prost slipped back into Berger's clutches, but Alain had an ally in the shape of Warwick, whose Arrows, while lapped by the leaders after its pit stop, was now working well – well enough to keep Gerhard's Ferrari from passing. Afterwards the Austrian was extremely angry. Not only was he being delayed in his pursuit of Prost, he said, but also being reeled in for fifth place by Warwick's team-mate, Cheever, who, as ever, was coming truly alive on race day. Warwick, unimpressed, felt Berger should have been able to find a way by if he were that much quicker. He, after all, was running every bit as fast as the leaders, had a point to make.

Patrese's dream began to evaporate on lap 51: the water temperature was starting to go up; the power to go down. Down the long pit straight Senna aimed to the right of the Williams, and at last the familiar red-and-white was in front. So that was that. Here came Senna's fifth of the season.

Next time around Mansell, too, was past Patrese, and at the start of lap 54 Riccardo pulled off abruptly. The spectators' applause he probably never heard as he walked back to the pits, tears of rage in his eyes. "I felt quite happy and confident in the lead," he said, "until the temperature began to go up. But eventually I radioed the pits that the engine seemed about to blow, and what should I do? But before they answered, I told them 'I think I stop.'" Something solid had punched a hole through the water radiator. It was as simple as that. As in Montreal, the unfortunate man had perhaps lost a race through no fault of his own.

Senna and Mansell were half a second apart. The two most uncompromising racers in Formula One. This, someone said, might end in tears, leaving nine points for the troubled Prost. At all events, Nigel wouldn't quietly follow Ayrton over the line.

Now we saw that the work of the previous afternoon had been well done. The Hungaroring essentially has just one passing spot, into the first turn, at the end of the pit straight. But all day Mansell had been going by other cars in places off limits to everyone else. The Ferrari was that sharp, that deft. It didn't have the straight-line speed of the McLaren, but it came off the corners better.

RESULTS

77 LAPS (189.851 MILES)

1	Nigel MANSELL	Ferrari 640	1h49m38.650s
2	Ayrton SENNA	McLaren MP4/5	1h50m04.617s
3	Thierry BOUTSEN	Williams FW12C	1h50m17.004s
4	Alain PROST	McLaren MP4/5	1h50m22.827s
5	Eddie CHEEVER	Arrows A11	1h50m23.756s
6	Nelson PIQUET	Lotus 101	1h50m50.689s

WINNING SPEED 103.891mph

FASTEST LAP MANSELL, 1m22.637s (107.411mph)

POLE POSITION PATRESE, 1m19.726s (111.333mph)

LAP LEADERS Riccardo PATRESE 1-52; SENNA 53-57; MANSELL 58-77

"When I passed Prost," Nigel said, "he was very fair about it, and gave me room. I think he was in trouble, anyway. But Senna was different. I knew I'd have to grab any opportunity that came up."

One came up on lap 58. Out of the new right-hander (bypassing the old chicane), the two had Johansson's Onyx in front of them. Stefan had made several stops for attention to his gear linkage, and wasn't going terribly quickly. But he kept over to the left, out of the way. Ayrton, untypically, hesitated a fraction before flicking right to go by. And it cost him dear, for by now Nigel was right there, going for the gap.

They nearly touched, but didn't. And Mansell's momentum was enough to keep him in front along the straight and into the next corner. Putting the Ferrari's superior handling and grip to work, he pulled out enough of a lead to be safe from attack on the pit straight. Senna had led for only six laps. McLarens sometimes fail; rarely are they passed.

Joy in the Ferrari pit was tempered by the realisation that Berger was missing. Gearbox again, as Gerhard had feared after the warm-up, when the pressure in the hydraulic system had been low. His love affair with Maranello is clearly at an end.

Senna made no attempt to get on terms with Mansell in the dying laps; indeed could not. "I had a bad tyre vibration towards the end," he said, and there were suggestions, too, that the Honda V10 had proved unexpectedly thirsty on this occasion.

Boutsen's third was consolation for Williams, but hardly the consequence of a distinguished drive – not in the context of Patrese's performance. Behind Prost in fourth place there were Cheever, deservedly in the points, and Piquet, who ran alone for most of the afternoon.

It hadn't looked like Mansell's day – not even when he'd set fastest time in the warm-up. People don't win GPs from the sixth row, after all. But his drive was perfectly paced, supremely aggressive only when it needed to be. "I think maybe it was the best of my life," he said. "On a par with Silverstone '87, anyway."

Then he dedicated the win to Enzo Ferrari, almost a year after the Old Man's death. Monza will be something else. ■

WHAT HAPPENED NEXT...

McLaren reasserted its domination and Alain Prost secured his third world title. His campaign ended in acrimony however. Not only did he sign for Ferrari for 1990, he refused to take the restart in Adelaide because of the torrential conditions.

Mansell accepts the chequer (above) and shows the emotion involved in his great performance (below). Jonathan Palmer's weekend wasn't quite so productive (left)

NELSON PIQUET | 1990 AUSTRALIAN GP | NOVEMBER 4 BENETTON B190

Dancing in the streets

Wins are like buses, sometimes: you wait ages for one, then two turn up in quick succession. To be honest, he'd been a passenger in the first. This time, though, he was its driver

RACE BY NIGEL ROEBUCK; QUALIFYING BY JOE SAWARD

Ayrton Senna took the lead – from pole position – at the start (right), and was heading for an easy victory when he made a rare mistake at three-quarter distance

NELSON PIQUET IS getting used to this victory press conference business; first Japan, and now Australia. Eighteen points in 14 days. The last few laps were highly diverting, as Nigel Mansell chased him for the lead. Prior to that, it had been processional, with Ayrton Senna holding comfortable sway until lap 62, when he missed a gear, and went off the road.

QUALIFYING

It was probably better to look on Adelaide 1990 as sunny and Cher: the weather was gorgeous, and the American singing star was in town to strut her bits across the stage at the Grand Prix concert. She cruised around town in stretched limos and her bouncers kept everyone amused by threatening to break the legs of photographers. It was nice to see a real prima donna in action. She could teach the F1 boys a few tricks. Alain Prost and (a rather more relaxed) Ayrton Senna seemed to spend most of the early days of the meeting pulling faces, stamping their feet and calling each other "bitch", metaphorically speaking. The papers loved it, but it was rather boring if you happen to be a cynical F1 journalist.

Still, when they put their helmets on and went out onto the track, the quibbling stopped. That was Friday morning, and suddenly the Suzuka silliness faded away. There was too much else to watch.

Ayrton went fastest in the McLaren. It took 40 minutes for him to get close to last year's pole time – and that on a dusty track which saw many cars spinning off. Nigel Mansell did it twice.

In between rotations Nigel beat Senna's time – and the 1989 pole – after 77 minutes. Ayrton came out and promptly went a second quicker: 1m15.713s. That was impressive.

Nigel had another spin and, being the great F1 showman, burned clouds of rubber as he returned to the track – while Ayrton did a second lap in the 1m15s just to make the point.

Senna would remain mighty throughout qualifying. No one ever looked like beating him for pole position. It seemed only a matter of time. It came after 15 minutes of the session, and it was good – a 1m15.719s lap. Everyone else was pottering about in the 1m17s, and it wasn't until the final minutes that Jean Alesi and Alain Prost sidled into the 1m16s. At which point Ayrton went out and took pole down to 1m15.671s.

Simple as that.

"It was the best day I have had all season," Senna said later. "I was so relaxed."

The order behind Senna was: Alain "gripless" Prost, Jean "brakes" Alesi, Riccardo "no grip" Patrese, Nigel "traffic" Mansell, Gerhard "a lot of traffic" Berger, Roberto "oil on the track" Moreno, Thierry "an awful lot of traffic" Boutsen and Nelson "more oil than Roberto" Piquet.

Saturday morning was glorious and even more slippery than the day before, and once again we had cars spinning off here and there.

Gerhard Berger made his bid for glory, but

Senna went out and went a second quicker – only slightly slower than his pole of the previous day.

After 26 minutes Ayrton emerged from the pits to have another blast. He locked brakes, rode kerbs and still recorded a low 1m17s lap. A few moments later Mansell bounced up to second-quickest, but he was still half a second behind Ayrton's Friday best. Next it was Berger, blasting through, giving his all to record the second-quickest time.

It gradually became clear that Ayrton would not need to defend his pole. With four minutes to go, however, there at the end of the pit lane was the familiar sight of number 27 with the alert yellow helmet sticking out of the cockpit.

"I didn't have to go out," agreed Ayrton, "but it was a question of desire – and trying the last set of qualifying tyres for the 1990 championship."

That final lap wasn't one of Ayrton's best. He locked his brakes again and it was a couple of tenths slower than his pole. But still…

To make it a perfect McLaren day, Berger was alongside on the grid: "I lost half a second because my front tyres were insufficiently warmed up."

Mansell and Prost lined up together on the second row, both complaining about a lack of grip.

Alesi was fifth, Patrese's Williams-Renault was sixth, then it was the two Benettons. It had been a dramatic afternoon for Nelson Piquet. A huge wobble on his second qualifying run looked as though he was about to demolish half of South Australia. The run was aborted.

RACE

No question of rain in Adelaide this year, thankfully. The organizers spoke with enthusiasm of the size of the crowd, a fair proportion no doubt seduced in part by the prospect of a free Cher concert after the race. It is estimated, indeed, that as many as 80,000 were on hand to see the lady sing and gyrate, and they can't be blamed for that.

Some, however, left when the 1990 GP season died away, the last engine shut down. Some of them came to Adelaide in the expectation perhaps of further bloodletting – metaphorical, of course – between Senna and Prost. It looked, on paper, like a Senna race, for here Ferrari had not even the hope of better tyre wear, and therefore later pit stops. In Adelaide, it was expected that everyone on Goodyears could go the distance on a single set of soft Ds.

Prost's race day began disastrously, the Ferrari stopping out on the circuit after but one lap, engine blown. But he ran back to the pits, hopping into the T-car, and within a very few laps had set the best time of the session. His mood, though, remained low, as in the previous days. This time it was Alain's turn to walk out of a drivers' meeting, just as Senna had done in Japan. He then missed the traditional 'end of term' photo session in front of the pits.

Why had he walked out? It was in response to a question addressed to the stewards by Ron Dennis, but Prost himself declined to talk about it. Later Piquet voluntarily suggested an explanation of Alain's behaviour: "I think he did it because FISA, for a long time, has promised to take action against drivers who behave badly on the circuit. Look at what Senna did to Alain in Japan – and FISA took no action."

Prost was later reprimanded by the stewards, and the supreme irony is that the latter is to be referred to the newly formed Special Commission for Safety in Formula 1! The risks inherent in one little bloke's walking out of a meeting would seem minimal to most sane minds, but there you are…

It was clear through the morning, though, that Alain was in no real mood to go motor racing this day. He would do the race, and do it well, but the fire in his belly – for this season, anyway – was largely quenched that afternoon at Suzuka.

For all that, he made a great start, perhaps even a slightly premature one, but still found himself unable to find a way between Mansell and Berger, who got away atrociously, then fell back on the good offices of Mr Honda to correct the situation.

All of this was irrelevant to Senna, however, who had left the grid in perfect order, and comfortably led into the first left-right chicane. At the end of the first lap he led easily from Berger, Mansell, Prost, Piquet, Patrese, Alesi, Boutsen and Moreno.

Lap two brought Berger's second mistake of the day, and this time it cost him a place: "I was trying to adjust something on the dashboard, went over a bump, and my hand caught the ignition

Piquet takes the lead from Nigel Mansell's Ferrari (above); McLaren's Gerhard Berger, in pain with his feet, locks up on his way to fourth (left)

switch, and knocked it off..."

Gratefully, Mansell dived by, hard after Senna. What's more, he began to reel him in. The gap was pared, rather than sliced, but by lap 10 the Ferrari was right up with the McLaren. It went no further, however. "The problem was, as soon as I got close to Senna, I got oil and water all over my visor," Mansell said, "and the temperature gauges went up five degrees. On lap 12 he made a mistake at the exit of a corner, and I almost took the lead; but at that pace my tyre consumption was worrying, so I dropped back a bit."

For the spectators, that was a shame, for there was precious little racing going on anywhere in the pack. Patrese was closing a little on Prost, and Boutsen was pushing Alesi, but otherwise each lap was much like another.

Senna and Mansell began to hit traffic as early as lap 15, the likes of Tarquini and Grouillard leaving no easy path for them. Senna, as usual in these circumstances, pulled out a little, but by lap 20 Mansell was up with him once more.

If the Goodyear teams had deemed tyre stops unlikely, the picture was less clear for the Pirelli teams, whose hardest charger, Alesi, came in on lap 22, losing a couple of places in the process. Tyrrell team-mate Nakajima changed soon afterwards.

There was no sign of similar activity from any of the front-runners, however, and over the next 10 laps or so Senna began inexorably easing away from the rest. Mansell was still unthreatened in second, and behind him there was similar stalemate between Piquet, Berger and Prost.

Nelson had served notice of intent almost from the first, having calmly outbraked Prost on lap two, then repeated the move on Berger on lap nine.

"I knew that the car was good on full tanks," Nelson said, "and also that we had a really good brake set-up – which is vital here. Okay, we haven't got the power of Honda or Ferrari perhaps, but we start the race with less fuel than them, which means we hurt the tyres and brakes less in the early laps than they do.

'To maintain the pace of Senna and Mansell would have rooted my rear tyres, I think, so I sat back for a while, took it quite easy'

"All the same," he added, "to try to maintain the pace of Senna and Mansell would have rooted my rear tyres, I think, so I sat back for a while, took it quite easy."

Prost, too, was concerned about tyre wear: "I started with less downforce than Mansell, which was obviously a mistake, because the car was sliding around too much. Also, I was worried about the brakes from quite early in the race."

Moreno had made the same set-up mistake as Prost – to the extent that, on lap 36, he needed new tyres for the Benetton. After that, he found the car much better, even setting fastest lap at one stage.

At the front they continued to circulate, crocodile-style, for a long time, Senna inching away from them all the while. But Ayrton, too, had his worries, although it didn't look that way: "I was on the limit all the way, because I couldn't use the brakes as I would have liked. To save the fronts, I adjusted the balance too much towards the rears." Later that was to have a crucial bearing on the race.

Senna, though, was in fine shape compared with his hapless team-mate, for Berger was suffering again with the problem – doubtless the legacy of being too tall for his car – which had afflicted him at Interlagos, back in March: "I had an incredible pain in my right foot when I braked hard, and sometimes it was so bad that I had to lift off on the straight to ease it. Near the end I was using the side of my foot for brake and throttle. And this is maybe the longest and hardest race of the season..."

On lap 43 Mansell spun into an escape road, without forfeiting his second place, but inevitably losing a bundle of time to Senna. Indeed, now Nigel had Piquet right with him, and when he had another wild moment, two laps later, Nelson went by the Ferrari.

"As soon as I'd had the spin, I knew I needed fresh tyres," said Nigel, "but they need a lap's notice that you're coming in – the tyres have to be heated – so I had to stay out longer than I wanted."

On lap 47 Mansell rushed in for a perfectly executed stop, from which he rejoined in fifth. This looked like the start of a charge, and so it proved.

"At that point in the race," Piquet said, "I began to relax a bit – which was probably a mistake, because I was only about 10 seconds up on the bunch behind me…"

By now Prost had got by Berger finally, when the McLaren man went off the road and over a high kerb, and briefly the Ferrari began to close on the Benetton. "I thought maybe I could catch Nelson," Alain said, "but by now my tyres and brakes were in bad shape, so I was making a lot of mistakes. As it turns out, a tyre change was the best solution for us in this race, as Nigel proved."

The race's complexion changed absolutely on lap 62, when suddenly there was no Senna. The McLaren-Honda had been close to half a minute in the lead when Ayrton arrived at a corner, tried vainly to get down to second gear and slid off into a tyre barrier. With the gearbox in neutral, those rear-biased brakes had been little use to him. Now the Australian Grand Prix was up for grabs, and, as at Suzuka, Piquet found himself at the front.

"I was happy enough," said Nelson, "until I got badly held up by backmarkers, so that I lost four seconds in two laps."

Another attempt by Prost to close the gap succeeded briefly, but then Piquet responded again, and it was clear that if anyone were seriously to threaten him, it was Mansell, fresher tyres and all.

"Nigel was going much quicker than I was," Prost said, "so when I saw him coming up, I moved over to let him through."

By lap 73, with eight to the flag, it was Piquet, Mansell, Prost, Berger, Boutsen and Patrese.

Mansell's victory quest had been hampered considerably by the dreaded Grouillard, who held him up disgracefully, causing Nigel to lose his cool temporarily, so that he zigzagged alongside the Osella down the main straight, shaking his fist, and – one would have thought – losing himself even more time than necessary. "It's the last race of the season," Mansell said, "and I don't want to name names, or make a big fuss. But it was ridiculous."

The closing laps were all Piquet and Mansell. Moreno did sterling work for his friend and team-mate, holding up both Mansell and Prost for a time. With five laps left, Nelson had 6.6 seconds over Nigel; with four laps left, they were nose-to-tail, and surely the race was Ferrari's.

Not so. Piquet had made a mistake, run wide at a corner and lost virtually all of his lead, but now he bent himself to the task of holding on. "All I could do was go for it," he said.

Nelson's increased pace in the dying laps rather shook Mansell, who frankly admitted as much afterwards: "I think he'd agree that those last four or five laps were like qualifying…"

On the last lap, coming to the end of the long Brabham Straight, Nigel tried one of his famous all-or-nothing moves. Piquet was coming up to lap Modena – and under braking for the corner Mansell tried to overtake both of them. The Ferrari j-u-s-t avoided contact, and Nigel lost time during the ensuing confusion as he ran very wide. At the chequered flag Piquet was three seconds ahead.

At Suzuka Nelson had won without much pressure, the race effectively handed to him by the antics of the McLaren and Ferrari representatives. This win, though, was reward for a real fight.

"I'm grateful to Benetton for giving me the chance again, after the two hard years I had," he said. It was an incongruously gracious remark with which to bring down the curtain on a singularly graceless Grand Prix season. ■

RESULTS

81 LAPS (190.251 MILES)

1	Nelson PIQUET	Benetton B190	1h49m44.570s
2	Nigel MANSELL	Ferrari 641/2	1h49m47.699s
3	Alain PROST	Ferrari 641/2	1h50m21.829s
4	Gerhard BERGER	McLaren MP4/5B	1h50m31.432s
5	Thierry BOUTSEN	Williams FW13B	1h51m35.730s
6	Riccardo PATRESE	Williams FW13B	80 laps

WINNING SPEED 104.017mph

FASTEST LAP MANSELL, 1m18.203s (108.124mph)

POLE POSITION Ayrton SENNA, 1m15.671s (111.742mph)

LAP LEADERS SENNA 1-61; PIQUET 62-81

Having fended off Mansell's charge on new rubber, Piquet takes an exuberantly waved chequered flag (above) – and celebrates in customary style (right)

WHAT HAPPENED NEXT...

Senna won the first four grands prix of 1991, and this was to be the basis of his third world title. By the season's end, however, it was clear that Mansell had got to grips with Williams's active suspension...

Hill rises to challenge as heavens open

Michael Schumacher and Benetton were usually a step ahead of Damon Hill and Williams, especially in the wet. But this time it was the doughty Brit who held all the aces – and his nerve

BY NIGEL ROEBUCK

DAMON HILL | 1994 JAPANESE GP | NOVEMBER 6 WILLIAMS FW16B

THERE SHOULD BE more like this. Appalling weather suggested anything but a classic race at Suzuka on Sunday, and when the rain worsened, bringing accidents, the safety car, and finally the red flag, there seemed a possibility that the Japanese Grand Prix would not be restarted. Had it not, we would have lost what proved to be far and away the most exciting race of the 1994 season. Best of all, it provided the result that anyone outside of Benetton wanted: Damon first, Michael second. The fat lady won't be singing until Adelaide.

The fight was truly absorbing, with the two World Championship contenders, as at Jerez, away on their own, battling the elements. Alesi and Mansell fought memorably over third place, but neither was ever in a position to worry Hill and Schumacher. On this occasion Benetton tactics probably lost, rather than won, the race for Michael, but this is to take nothing away from Damon. At Suzuka he had to deliver, and deliver he did. An unforgettable day.

QUALIFYING

Benetton's Michael Schumacher struck the first psychological blow by taking pole position with a lap of 1m37.2s. The only interloper in the Schumacher/Hill and Benetton/Williams battles was Heinz-Harald Frentzen's Sauber. The German knows Suzuka like the back of his hand from his days of Japanese F3000, and excelled himself with third-quickest time on Friday afternoon.

"Since the Belgian Grand Prix in August we have found more competitiveness in both the chassis and engine," said Frentzen, who was hoping for a wet race. "Physically the wet is less demanding. I used to know where all the grooves were and how the track drained, but it's all changed since it was resurfaced."

Nigel Mansell looked sharper in Suzuka than he did at Jerez, despite not testing between races. Indeed, it was Mansell who was closest to Schumacher on Friday morning, the margin being 0.60s. Hill then asserted himself when it mattered during the first qualifying session and lapped with a half-second of the championship leader. Frentzen was just five-hundredths adrift, himself only two-hundredths clear of Mansell's FW16B.

Johnny Herbert was another six-hundredths behind on his Benetton debut and enjoyed exactly the same margin over Eddie Irvine, who had all of two-hundredths' breathing space over Jean Alesi's Ferrari. Alesi was the man you felt sorry for. Normally, a qualifying time within 0.21s of the second-place man stands you in better stead than seventh.

Throughout the day a Williams man watched every move made in the Benetton pit. "It's nothing sinister," said Williams team boss Ian Harrison. "They watch us and we watch them. It's just being efficient, really." One thing not to be seen in the Williams garage, Mansell's at least, was one D Coulthard. Frank Williams refused to pass comment, but it appears that Mansell had requested Coulthard keep out of his pit, reportedly so as not to disturb the mechanics.

Enter Jochen Mass. The former McLaren GP driver-turned-TV commentator found a picture of the Scot, affixed it to the wall in Mansell's garage and bordered it with red tape. Another diagonal strip across David's features indicated a Coulthard-free zone.

On Saturday morning Mansell found time and was 0.35s below Schumacher's provisional pole. The world championship leader was not fazed: "Nigel was on new rubber whereas I was on old tyres and could easily do a low-1m36. The time Nigel has found is what the circuit naturally picks up on the second day."

In the event he didn't have to. With everything in place for a superb final hour on Saturday afternoon, leaden skies and rain meant Friday's grid was the definitive one. Nigel would have to start fourth.

MILD SEVEN
Bitburger

The safety car's headlights pierce the Suzuka gloom. Even at this slow speed the walls of spray are almost impenetrable. No wonder most of the drivers wanted the race to be stopped

RACE

On Saturday, the forecast had suggested a 10 per cent chance of rain, and for half the day it poured down. That being so, no one was too hopeful for race day, when the predicted figure was 60 per cent. From early morning on, it was 100 per cent. At least.

After qualifying, both Schumacher and Hill had said they were not too concerned about the prospect of a wet race. They would prefer a dry one, of course, but each felt his car was working well on a slippery track.

Some, though, had cause to hope for rain on Sunday, among them Brundle and Frentzen. In Saturday's wet session, Martin – on fine form throughout qualifying – was fastest of all, and in the damp race morning warm-up he maintained his position, expressing delight with his McLaren's handling, unlike team-mate Häkkinen, who found both his own and the spare car appalling.

Williams looked strong as race time approached, Mansell, as in practice, looking like Mansell again, and setting second-fastest time, ahead of Frentzen, Blundell, Hill, Alesi – and Schumacher, who did not have the trouble-free session for which he would have wished. Michael spun in his race car, and then had a minor gearbox problem,

'A helicopter in Ayrton's helmet colours completed a lap before disappearing into the mist'

which was fixed before the end of the session.

Later in the morning Viviane Lalli, the sister of Ayrton Senna, took part in a moving ceremony in memory of the great man: worshipped in Japan as nowhere else, save Brazil. A helicopter, in the colours of Ayrton's helmet, then completed a lap over the Suzuka circuit before disappearing away into the mist.

As race time neared, the rain continued to come down, not always hard, but with persistence. At one o'clock, 26 apprehensive drivers set off on the formation lap for the first wet race of the season, Schumacher and Hill playing mind games with each other, crawling along, then momentarily sprinting to get some heat into their tyres.

At the green flag, Schumacher's Benetton veered violently right in a welter of wheelspin, but Hill was not troubled by it: "He came across my side of the track, yes, but he was quite a way in front of me – I didn't make the greatest start."

Hill's second place was never threatened, however, and he duly followed Schumacher into the first turn, trailed by Frentzen, Herbert, Alesi and Mansell, who lost three places away from the grid. Out within a few corners of the start was the luckless Lehto, who parked his Sauber-Mercedes when the engine began to tighten. On the next lap his team-mate Frentzen slid off, but kept the engine running, and motored out through a gravel trap, dropping from third to sixth in the process.

This elevated Herbert to third, but after only two laps Johnny was nine seconds adrift of Hill, who sat a second or so behind Schumacher. Now, though, the rain severely worsened, and the accidents began. "In those conditions," Hill said, "the car was literally undriveable. I came down the pit straight in third gear, and even so the car was squirming all over the place."

Herbert, sadly, was among those who went off: "Just as I was coming into a quick corner, they radioed me to say the rain was getting harder. Then the car aquaplaned, and I spun."

Inoue's Formula 1 debut concluded against a barrier, and the crowd's hero, Katayama, hit the pit wall very hard, ending what had been a traumatic home Grand Prix weekend for him. "I was pushing hard," Ukyo said, "and when the really heavy rain arrived, I just lost control. There was so much water on the track that I couldn't do anything. The whole weekend has made me very unhappy – I was hoping for so much from this race."

The cars trailed round behind the safety car for seven laps, and during this time many drivers radioed their pits to say they wanted the race stopped. The powers-that-be thought otherwise, however. There was standing water at a couple of points on the circuit, but the rest of it they felt acceptable. At the end of lap nine, the safety car pulled into the pit lane, and the race was on again.

After the original start, Hill had somehow managed, despite the dead reckoning visibility behind Schumacher, to keep up with his rival, but on the restart Michael – who has clearly been studying Indycar procedure – broke clear. After slowing the field almost to

Schumacher's Benetton B194 set the pace for most of the weekend, but for once the team's strategy failed it: two stops to Hill's one was too much time to regain – even for Michael

a stop towards the end of the final lap behind the safety car, he suddenly accelerated very hard, towards the final chicane, and was moving very swiftly indeed by the time he reached the start-finish line. Damon seemed to be caught rather on the hop, and within two laps had fallen five seconds behind the Benetton.

If the rain had lost some of its ferocity, conditions remained truly awful. Lagorce's first Grand Prix ended in an accident at the first corner when he was hit by Martini's Minardi, with Alboreto's sister car spinning off in sympathy only a few seconds later. Matters turned serious, however, on lap 13, when Morbidelli had a big accident at the Degner Curve. Although the driver was unhurt, his Footwork was badly damaged, and beached in a gravel trap.

Near at hand was a caterpillar tractor, and while its function — to drag wrecked cars from the sand was obvious enough — the vehicle itself constituted a major hazard. "At the drivers' briefing in the morning," Brundle said, "I'd drawn attention to the caterpillar, and asked if it could be moved."

A lap after Morbidelli, Martin went off at the same point, and found himself heading straight for the object of his concern. "I really thought that was it," he said. "Somehow the car missed it, but I've no idea how." Instead, the McLaren hit a barrier, then skittered along between the barrier and Morbidelli's car, which was being attended by marshals. "I saw this bloke in front of me," Brundle said, "but I could do absolutely nothing to miss him." Miraculously, the corner worker suffered only a broken leg, but Martin, while intensely relieved, was in some shock afterwards.

At this, the officials decided to red flag the race. On the pit straight, the drivers stopped their cars, and some of them were for abandoning the race at that point. Mansell and others went off to Race Control, but Schumacher paced around on the grid, looking disconsolate, and Hill stayed resolutely in his car, helmet on.

The weather improved during the break, which is to say that rain eased to light drizzle, and it was announced that the race would be restarted. Three laps were to be deducted from the original 53, which meant that race two, given that 13 laps had already been run, would be over 37 laps. In light of the conditions, it was also sensibly decided that a rolling start should be employed.

The balance of the afternoon would now be complicated, of course, as 'aggregate' races invariably are, the cars' positions on the road not necessarily their true positions on time. Hill, for example, began the second part of the race with a seven-second deficit to Schumacher, while Alesi was six seconds adrift of Damon, and four ahead of Mansell.

Away they went again, behind the safety car, and this time, when Schumacher hung back prior to hooting it towards the end of the lap, Hill was ready for him. As they went through the chicane, and accelerated towards the start-finish line, the Benetton and the Williams were close together. Significantly, both men were at once lapping in the 1m57s bracket, while no other driver was under two minutes.

Only five laps into the restart, Schumacher was in for fuel and tyres, he and his team having decided on a two-stop strategy. The car was stationary for only eight seconds, but by the time Michael had rejoined, he was 17 seconds back of Hill. Although he was actually in second place, what complicated matters for the spectators was that Alesi and Mansell, scrapping furiously, were ahead on the road.

The battle between Jean and Nigel provided some of the best on-car camera work ever seen. The all-or-nothing characteristics of the Ferrari engine made the car very difficult to drive in the slippery conditions, but Alesi drove quite beautifully at Suzuka, and never made the slip which would have let Mansell past. Time and again the Williams driver experimented with different lines, seeking better traction out of the corners, so as to slingshot by the Ferrari on the following straight. The policy never quite worked, but Jean was impressed by Nigel's courage. "One metre behind my wing — completely mad!" he smiled afterwards. "For an old man, he was good..."

Indeed, fighting with Alesi, Mansell may not have run at the leaders' pace, but he looked his old combative self, and markedly more impressive than at Jerez.

Wheel of fortune: Hill (left and right) savours his win. One week later his title dream was wrecked by a ruthless rival

At the end of his 25th lap (the 12th since the restart), Hill was into the pits, taking on fuel and tyres in a fraction over nine seconds. Only three tyres, though, for his right-rear wheel obstinately refused to come off, so that particular tyre had to run the entire race distance, which was to be no help at all to him in the late, crucial stages of the race. Schumacher and Benetton, though, had of course no idea that this was to be Damon's only stop.

Hill rejoined immediately behind the Alesi/Mansell tussle, but was not delayed by it, for Nigel came in only a lap later, and Jean three laps after that. Schumacher had seemed to be losing time behind Häkkinen's McLaren, but later denied this was so: "'After my stop, the car was not so good for a while – more fuel on board, new tyres – and I couldn't lap any faster than Mika. When it started working better, he immediately moved over and let me by. No complaints there." Nice to hear a driver reject an apparent excuse.

After 30 laps, with 20 to go, Hill led Schumacher by 5.4 seconds, with Alesi third, then Mansell, a predictably impressive Irvine, Häkkinen and Frentzen. Accidents had accounted for eight retirements, and Berger's ill-handling Ferrari had gone out with electrical troubles, Barrichello's Jordan with a problem in the gearbox control unit, and Blundell's well-driven Tyrrell with engine failure.

Now Schumacher had the hammer down, and he fairly scythed into Hill's advantage. As he chased after the Williams, Michael was risking a lot on the treacherous track, and perhaps the thought went through his mind that it might be smart to settle for six safe points, and then resolve this thing in Australia. What he could not afford was a win for Hill, and an accident for himself: in those circumstances, Damon would take a five-point lead into the last race – where he could afford to settle for second place, and still take the world title by a point. But if Schumacher contemplated playing safe, however, there was no sign of it in his pace. What he really wanted was to secure his title here in Japan, and by lap 36 he was back in the lead – on time, if not on the road. At this stage of the game, it looked as if the championship was settled; what no one knew, though, was that Michael would he stopping again, and Damon would not.

RESULTS

50 LAPS (182.186 MILES)

1	Damon HILL	Williams FW16B	1h55m53.532s
2	Michael SCHUMACHER	Benetton 194	1h55m56.897s
3	Jean ALESI	Ferrari 412T1B	1h56m45.577s
4	Nigel MANSELL	Williams FW16B	1h56m49.606s
5	Eddie IRVINE	Jordan 194	1h57m35.639s
6	Heinz-Harald FRENTZEN	Sauber C13	1h57m53.395s

WINNING SPEED 94.322mph

FASTEST LAP HILL, 1m56.597s (112.502mph)

POLE POSITION SCHUMACHER, 1m37.209s (134.940mph)

LAP LEADERS SCHUMACHER 1-18, HILL 19-50

In five laps, the Benetton pulled out four seconds over the Williams, but then, on lap 40, Schumacher peeled off again into the pit lane. The stop was quick, at seven seconds even, but by the time he rejoined, Hill had a true lead of just under 15 seconds, with nine laps to go. And the rain, at last, had stopped.

Behind the leading pair, Mansell had again caught Alesi, whom he was engaging in vigorous fight, but once more Jean was proving equal to the task, and resolutely held his place, making no mistakes in the twitchy, but powerful, Ferrari. On time, from the first part of the race, he led Nigel by around five seconds, but well knew that if the Williams once got by, it would probably be capable of making that up. Mansell, for his part, had forgotten that this was an 'aggregate' race – a legacy of two years' Indycar racing, perhaps? – and believed himself in a straight fight for position.

Diverting as this battle was, everyone's concentration was on the one that truly mattered, for at issue between Schumacher and Hill was much more than a single championship point. In the Benetton pit, Flavio Briatore's expression was one of consternation: was Hill not going to make a second stop, after all?

He wasn't. Time after time, we waited for him to flick towards the pit lane, but the Williams stayed out. And now Schumacher, on fresh tyres, had to begin another charge. "I was on the radio every lap," Damon said, "to keep myself informed of Michael's progress, and that just spurred me on."

Even so, chunks of his lead disappeared every time around. On lap 43, the gap was 12 seconds, and then it came down like this: 10.1, 8.3, 7.0, 5.2, 4.2. With one lap to go, Hill led by just 2.4 seconds. Would it be enough?

It would. There had been the odd anxious moment – slow cars perhaps getting in the way, a locked wheel into the hairpin – but Damon had a clear road before him as he went into his last lap, whereas Michael had a couple of cars in front of him. They did not materially delay him, but put paid to any question of a banzai finish.

Hill drove his last lap as fast as possible, crossed the line – and then waited for information from his team. Had he done enough?

"I got down to the first corner on my slowing-down lap, and then suddenly about four people got on the radio. They were all yelling 'P1' to me, but there was so much interference that all I could hear was 'P-blah-bleagh'. I had to tell everyone to calm down, shut up, and tell me where I'd finished!"

At the press conference, Damon looked relaxed for the first time all weekend. In qualifying, he had not truly looked like a winner of this race; whereas Schumacher's Benetton had been quick from the instant it took to the track, getting the Williams to that sort of pitch had taken a lot of work. As David Coulthard has observed, though, the more you fling at Hill, the better he responds, and the point was never better illustrated than at this day in Suzuka.

"In the back of my mind, I kept thinking how nice it would be if I could win, and we could go to Adelaide with just one point in it, but I also had to tell myself to be realistic. Beating Michael is a tall order – this year, he's been the class of the field, and most times he has managed to beat us. But today we got things right."

Schumacher was gracious in defeat: "Damon drove a great race today, I must say. Of course I'd be happier if I'd won the championship today, but the important thing is that I can still win it next week – I finished, and I got six points. Today we had a risky pit stop strategy, and it didn't work out."

'Damon drove a great race today, I must say. We had a risky strategy and it didn't work'

As Hill pointed out, Formula 1 has waited too long for a race as exciting as this: "It was just a shame that we were racing against the clock, rather than fighting for the same piece of track."

To the end, Mansell believed he and Alesi were doing just that. Into the chicane, on the last lap, the Williams slipped by the Ferrari, and Nigel waved both arms as he took the flag, thinking he had made the podium. Jean, though, had not forgotten his time advantage: "I knew how much the gap was, so I braked quietly and let him pass."

So now everything will be decided in Adelaide. Schumacher and Hill, both magnificent here, are separated by a point, so a safe finish won't be enough for either. Only the podium's top step will do ■

WHAT HAPPENED NEXT...

Adelaide, that's what. Schumacher was leading, but Hill was chasing hard, when the Benetton man hit the wall. Damon saw his chance, dived into a gap – and had it unceremoniously slammed in his face. Both men were out. The title was Schumacher's.

SCHUMACHER **PIT-STOP STRATEGY** SINKS McLAREN

When overtaking was impossible, no team was better at manufacturing 'passes' than Ferrari. Its boffins were bright, regularly outsmarting rivals, but there was no doubt that they rode on the back of a superstar driver

RACE BY NIGEL ROEBUCK; QUALIFYING BY ANDREW BENSON

A blistering sequence of 'qualifying laps' by Schumacher during the race allows Ferrari to make work a three-stop strategy; McLaren's Mika Häkkinen (below right) might have fended this off but for a late-race handling imbalance

"YOU DREAM OF the ideal result," said Michael Schumacher on Sunday, "and this is it. Before the race, I had hoped I might win, with Mika second, but this is unbelievable. I think now we have a very good chance in the championship."

He had every reason to be exhilarated after the Hungarian Grand Prix. While a virtuoso drive brought him victory, Häkkinen, the championship leader from the first GP on, scraped but a single point. The Finn's McLaren-Mercedes, after starting from the pole and leading more than half the race, was hobbled by a mysterious handling problem and slid down the order.

Ferrari, emphatically back from the dead (after an abysmal performance at Hockenheim), won by virtue not only of its number one driver's skills but also of a superior strategy. "We could have gone for either two or three stops," said Schumacher, "and Ross Brawn [Ferrari's technical director] decided to go for three. At the time I was worried about it, but it turned out to be the right choice."

So it was – but, for success, it depended on the German being able to run for a long time at an extraordinary pace, so as to build up enough of a lead to permit the third stop. "For me it was like a qualifying race," he said.

'We had a problem today, and whenever we have a problem, Michael's there, ready to pounce.' There is no disputing that

The McLarens, which stopped only twice, ran one-two for the first 44 laps and looked like winning again, albeit narrowly, but Ferrari's revised strategy allowed Schumacher to move ahead of Häkkinen and David Coulthard at their second stops. When the Finn eventually began to fall back, the issue was settled. "We had a problem today," said McLaren team boss Ron Dennis crisply, "and whenever we have a problem, Michael's there, ready to pounce." There is no disputing that.

He was aided by having the right tyres for the job. Twelve months ago, Bridgestone had the upper hand here, but this time Goodyears were the thing to have. Although Coulthard finished second, he was never able to threaten Schumacher, and admitted he was all out of grip.

Third was Jacques Villeneuve, and a great third it was – the world champion lost his power steering after 10 of the 77 laps, and the Hungaroring is a tiring place. The Williams couldn't frighten Ferrari or McLaren, but the Canadian was pleased by its balance and grip at a track where expectations had not been high.

Fourth and fifth, ahead of the unfortunate Häkkinen, were Damon Hill, thereabouts all weekend for Jordan, and Heinz-Harald Frentzen, who was weakened by gastric flu. The Williams man deserved some kind of gallantry award simply for finishing what was a long, hot race.

QUALIFYING

The warning signs for Schumacher's victory were there after qualifying, but you had to look hard. McLaren drivers Häkkinen and Coulthard qualified ahead of him, but the German gave a hint on Saturday afternoon of what was to come the following day with what might have seemed an inconsequential comment.

"They have a gap in qualifying, but the race is a different story," he said. It would have been easy to dismiss that as the Ferrari man talking up his chances and putting pressure on McLaren, but Sunday afternoon proved he was deadly serious.

The Ferrari-Schumacher combo was quicker than the cars in front of him in Hungary, but that was disguised by the fact that the German chose the harder of Goodyear's two tyre compounds and McLaren the softer Bridgestone. The Ferrari man found little difference in lap times between the hard and soft tyres, so he selected the hard one because he knew it was better for the race.

Tributes to the greatest driver of his generation came in all sorts of shapes and sizes. A lot of 'work' has gone into this one – and they have still got the M, A, C, H, E and R to do. Keep drinking, fellas. Cheers!

McLaren, meanwhile, felt the softer Bridgestone was better in race *and* qualifying. However, its choice was coloured by an admission made after the event by Coulthard. "If we'd used the harder one," the Scot said, "I don't think we'd have been on pole. You have to say there's a bit of work to do on the tyre front."

That was not so obvious after qualifying, when the McLarens had the edge on Ferrari.

Schumacher always goes well in Hungary. The dusty, low-grip surface allows him to grab the car by the scruff of the neck and the slow average speed means the McLaren's advantage in aerodynamic efficiency cannot show itself to the same extent as at quicker tracks.

It was not enough. Schumacher was briefly fastest – because he had been baulked by Heinz-Harald Frentzen's Williams on his first run more rubber had been laid down by the time he set his first quick time – on his second run – than for the McLarens, which were out earlier.

Schumacher's first flying lap of 1m17.505s put him ahead of Häkkinen by 0.289s, but shortly afterwards Coulthard set a 1m17.131s, which was followed by a 1m16.973s for the Finn.

Neither McLaren was to improve, but they did not need to, for Schumacher set a 1m17.366s on his third run, and his last-ditch attempt in the dying minutes was wrecked when he ran wide at the penultimate corner.

Häkkinen had traffic on his third run. He tried again on a final set of tyres, but was 0.009s slower than his best. Coulthard, meanwhile, was heading for a faster time on his third run – which he thought might have sneaked him ahead of his team-mate – when he bounced over the kerbs at the last chicane. His fourth attempt was ruined by traffic.

'If we'd used the harder one I don't think we'd have been on pole. You have to say there's a bit of work to do on the tyre front'

Häkkinen said: "I could maybe have gone a little quicker on my last run by taking big risks. But there was no point. It was an unusual qualifying session for me. We made more changes to the car than we would usually do to try to improve it in certain areas, but if we managed to make it better at some places on the track, it was worse at others.

The Finn said he had hoped he could extend the margin over the second-placed Coulthard, but "with the speed David was going – he was very fast – it was difficult to make that gap any bigger."

Coulthard said: "It was extremely disappointing not to get the last run, but qualifying is all about getting a lap in. I started my last run, but there was just so much traffic. I was late getting out of the pits and I came up behind a Minardi at the last corner before starting my lap. I tried to leave a gap, but he was held up by a Jordan which was doing the same, and I had to overtake it in the first corner. There's a lot of dust off the line here, and after I'd done that, I was never going to get pole."

The McLaren drivers used the slightly wider tyre that Bridgestone brought to Hungary. "It gives a little more stability, on our car at least," said DC.

Schumacher, despite being third was not entirely unhappy. He knew that his position would give him the clean line off the start. "Starting third," he said, "I can have a good race…"

Barring this off during practice, David Coulthard was fast, feisty and flawless. But, as often proved to be the case, this was insufficient to beat Schumacher's Ferrari. Mika Häkkinen passes in the background

RACE

Häkkinen and Coulthard duplicated their qualifying performances in the warm-up, with the courageous Frentzen third, then the Schumachers (Michael ahead of Ralf), Villeneuve, Hill, Eddie Irvine, Giancarlo Fisichella and Johnny Herbert. Seven of the top 10 cars were on Goodyears.

The McLaren boys were happy enough, however, and had a trouble-free session. Häkkinen admitted to a touch of understeer. He said it could have been dialled out, but he preferred to live with it, so as to preclude any chance of tyre-destroying oversteer in the early part of the event.

If anyone had cause to worry before the race, it was the unfortunate Frentzen, who said he felt a little better than in practice but was still seriously debilitated, having eaten nothing for two days. He would take the start, it was decided, but there were doubts that he'd be able to make it to the end.

There had been predictions that it might rain, but there was no sign of any such thing as the cars went to the grid. In fact, it would stay dry, hot and sticky all afternoon.

The grid at the Hungaroring has always been tricky for those with even-numbered qualifying slots. They start on the right, where the cars rarely run, and thus the surface there is dusty, which is not what you need for good traction when the lights go out. The suspicion had been that Schumacher, starting third, directly behind poleman Häkkinen, would be able to get the better of Coulthard on the sprint down to the first turn. In fact, the Ferrari driver made a very middling start, not only failing to pass DC, but coming close to losing places.

This was bad news for Hill, who got away well, then had to back off for the German, which, in turn allowed Irvine to get by him. Into the opening corner, it was Häkkinen, Coulthard, Schumacher, Irvine, Hill and Villeneuve. This being the Hungaroring, where overtaking is an endangered species, that was also the order at the end of the first lap.

It was to stay that way for some considerable time. Actually, that's not strictly true: on lap five, Shinji Nakano and Tora Takagi passed Esteban Tuero. That apart, there was no movement whatever until lap 13, when Irvine brought his Ferrari into the pits — too early, one thought, for routine service, and so it proved. The Irishman was clearly in no hurry. His car was immediately pushed into its garage, its gearbox short of fourth and fifth. Astonishingly, it was his first mechanical failure of the year, and only the second Ferrari has suffered all season (the first being Schumacher's engine breakdown at the opening round in Melbourne). At the time his problem struck, Irvine had been running fourth, and actually gaining slightly on his team leader, who was now left to fight the McLarens on his own.

Not that Schumacher was showing signs of panic, mind you. If we had expected, from their qualifying and warm up performances, that Häkkinen and Coulthard would ultimately ease away from the rest, such was not the case. After 10 laps, the Finn had led the Scot by three seconds, with the lead Ferrari a second or so further back. Fifteen laps in, and the McLarens were only two seconds apart, and Schumacher continued to keep a close watching brief.

From the outset it had been clear that this was to be another contest exclusively between McLaren-Mercedes and Ferrari; after 15 laps, Hill, running fourth, was 14 seconds behind Schumacher and consistently dropping a second a lap to him.

Nor were the McLarens stroking. "The early

part of the race was fine for me," Häkkinen said. "I had David in my mirrors all the time, so I was driving more or less flat-out, but I felt quite comfortable about that. Then I decided to push even harder, as my first stop was approaching, and I built up a small gap."

The significant pit stops began with Hill, who was running the softer Goodyears, and came in on lap 24. Next time round it was Schumacher's turn, then Coulthard's (lap 26), and finally Häkkinen's two laps after that. No significant problems were encountered by any of them. However, while the McLaren pair kept their first and second places, Schumacher came out behind Villeneuve's Williams, which was not to pit until lap 31.

"We'd gone into the race with the possibility of making either two or three stops," Schumacher said, "and when Ross Brawn decided to make it three, I was worried that it was the wrong choice, because at that point I was stuck behind Jacques. I'd made my stop earlier than the McLarens, hoping that it would get me ahead of them, but they both rejoined in front of me. Fortunately, the race then developed in a way that allowed me not to lose hope. There was a long way to go, and I just told myself to keep pushing."

Villeneuve's stop finally left the Ferrari driver with a clear road, and he responded immediately with a new fastest lap, the first under 1m20s. Within three laps he was back on the tail of Coulthard, but DC was equal to the situation, and proceeded calmly to keep the Ferrari at bay.

'We had the possibility of making two or three stops, and when Ross made it three, I was worried that it was the wrong choice'

On lap 43, Schumacher was in for his second stop, and the time — a mere 6.8s — told you that it would not be his last. For all that, McLaren seemed to be responding to the German's every move. On the very next lap, one of the silver cars peeled off into the pit lane.

In the circumstances, it might have appeared more logical to have brought Häkkinen in first. He had a lead of almost four seconds, whereas Schumacher had been right on Coulthard's gearbox when he made his stop, and there was every chance of his making up a place here. Nevertheless, it was DC who came in — and DC who indeed came out too late to keep the Ferrari from taking over second place.

Two laps later, Häkkinen pitted — and the same happened again. Now Schumacher, on fresh tyres and with a light fuel load, was really able to get the hammer down. "Ross told me, 'You have 19 laps to build up a 25-second lead,'" he recounted. "I said, 'Thank you very much!'"

In fact, his task was to prove easier than he might have expected. Not all was well with the McLarens. It was not merely that they had made their last stops, and were now very fuel-heavy, with a long stint for their tyres ahead of them, but also that both cars were in some trouble.

"Just before my second stop," Häkkinen said, "I started to experience what felt like oversteer, but I wasn't 100 per cent sure what the problem

Searing speed and stealthy strategy: this win is the epitome of Schuey's fecund partnership with Ross Brawn

WHAT HAPPENED NEXT...

Leading the Belgian GP by a mile, Schumacher ran into the back of Coulthard's McLaren in the mist. He won in Italy, but Häkkinen beat him at the Nürburgring, and a puncture for the Ferrari man at Suzuka ensured that the Finn won the world title.

was. After the stop it became almost impossible to drive, especially over the bumps and through the corners."

His lap times immediately dropped off by a couple of seconds or so. At which point his team-mate should have been given orders to go by, to take up the chase of Schumacher. Even that wasn't the simple matter it should have been, however. There was a problem with Häkkinen's radio and it was some time before his crew was able to understand what he was saying.

After four frustrating laps behind his team-mate, Coulthard finally went past, but by now the Ferrari was 14 seconds up the road, and apparently beyond reach. "Michael had a lot less fuel," DC explained, "and I simply couldn't stay with his pace." It didn't help that the Scot's car was not handling as it should, one of the rear tyres on his final set being incorrectly pressured.

Schumacher, of course, knew nothing of these dramas at the time. Indeed, he did not even know he was in the lead!

"On lap 52," he said, "I went off the road at the last corner, simply because I was pushing so hard." The Ferrari got sideways, and slithered briefly off, but rejoined without problem.

The German made his third, and final, stop on lap 62, coming in with a lead of 29 seconds – rather more than he needed. Prior to pitting, he put in an amazing sequence of four sub-1m20s laps. On his way again after just 7.7 seconds stationary, he now led Coulthard by five. Given the latter's predicament, he swiftly extended this by a couple of seconds a lap or so.

For Häkkinen the closing stages were heart-breaking. As his car became progressively more difficult, so he fell into the successive clutches of Villeneuve, Hill and Frentzen. By the end of the race he was glad to come away with a point.

Hill, fourth for the second time in a fortnight, maintained Jordan's recently acquired points-scoring habit, and was pleased with his day. The Williams folk had every reason to applaud Villeneuve for a fighting drive (without power steering, remember) and the tormented Frentzen for simply taking part in the race, never mind scoring.

Four races to go, seven points only between Häkkinen and Schumacher, Spa the next port of call. "I love Spa," Michael said. "It's near where I was born, and I think of it as my home circuit." He has won there four times already. ■

RESULTS

77 LAPS (190.498 MILES)

1	Michael SCHUMACHER	FERRARI F300	1h45m25.550s
2	David COULTHARD	McLaren MP4-13	1h45m34.983s
3	Jacques VILLENEUVE	Williams FW20	1h46m09.994s
4	Damon HILL	Jordan 198	1h46m20.626s
5	Heinz-Harald FRENTZEN	Williams FW20	1h46m22.060s
6	Mika HAKKINEN	McLaren MP4-13	76 laps

WINNING SPEED 108.157mph

FASTEST LAP SCHUMACHER, 1m19.286s (112.064mph)

POLE POSITION HAKKINEN, 1m16.973s (115.432mph)

LAP LEADERS HAKKINEN 1-46, SCHUMACHER 47-77

Spinner takes all

Mika Häkkinen was a match for Michael Schumacher in terms of pure speed, but it was rare that he overtook him. On the occasions he did, however, they were spectacular in the extreme

RACE BY NIGEL ROEBUCK; QUALIFYING BY ANDREW BENSON

West
Schweppes
KENWOOD
KENWOOD
West
1
Mobil
1

FOR THE NEXT few nights Ricardo Zonta may sleep with the lights on. This can happen to you if you're minding your own business, proceeding up the hill from Eau Rouge at something over 180mph and then two cars simultaneously come by you, one on either side.

It really was as well that Zonta kept a cool head in this situation, for if he'd moved left, he would have collected Michael Schumacher's Ferrari: if right, Mika Häkkinen's McLaren-Mercedes. Fortunately, he kept his BAR arrow straight, and they all made it into Les Combes.

This was the defining moment of the Belgian Grand Prix – and quite possibly of the entire 2000 season, for Häkkinen took the lead from Schumacher, and within four laps of the flag. If Mika ultimately beats Michael to the title by fewer than four points – the gap between first and second – it will be sweet indeed to reflect that this one move decided the world championship in his favour.

There was an unfamiliar look about the grid as they lined up on Sunday. Häkkinen was on pole position, but those nearest him were not the usual suspects, but Jarno Trulli's Jordan-Mugen Honda and Jenson Button's Williams-BMW, the two youngsters having excelled in qualifying on this driver's circuit *sans pareil.* Schumacher was only fourth, and many suspected that even that position flattered his car; team-mate Rubens Barrichello was 10th.

Clearly, Ferrari's best hope was for a wet race, and Maranello prayers were answered – to a point. There was rain for much of the morning, and although it abated by noon, the track was still damp when the race began – behind the safety car, unfortunately.

Häkkinen led from the outset and, following a coming-together between Trulli and Button, Schumacher was soon into second place. So quickly did the track begin to dry out that after five and six laps the leaders pitted for dry tyres.

On lap 13, Häkkinen had a colossal slide at Stavelot which ultimately became a spin and allowed Schumacher into the lead, which at one point grew to nearly 12 seconds.

After their second stops, Mika began hunting Michael down and in the closing laps was looking for a way by. After being… rebuffed, let's say, at the top of the hill on lap 40, he made it stick next time round when the pair encountered the aforementioned Zonta.

Häkkinen will never score a greater victory than this.

Third was Ralf Schumacher, followed by David Coulthard, Button and Heinz-Harald Frentzen. It is too early to discount DC from the championship, but, with four races to go, he is seven points behind Schumacher and 13 adrift of Häkkinen. Increasingly, this looks to be coming down to the usual two-horse race, and the momentum is indisputably with Mika, a world champion back to his very best.

Häkkinen celebrates pole position. His advantage is great, but Michael Schumacher's Ferrari (left) will give him a run for his money in the race

QUALIFYING

One way and another there was plenty to talk about after qualifying. While it wasn't exactly a surprise that Häkkinen took pole position, not too many would have anticipated a margin of close to a second over anyone else – and fewer still that the only man to threaten Mika would be Trulli.

Häkkinen and McLaren-Mercedes were in a class of their own as they made the world's most demanding motor racing circuit bend to their will. They were 0.773s faster than the impressive Trulli. That same margin separated Jarno from Johnny Herbert in ninth.

Spa's sweeping bends were always likely to give the McLaren MP4-15 a stage upon which to parade its superiority – but the margin still took the breath away. It was a demonstration of the all-round class of the silver car, which blends the characteristics needed in a Formula 1 car better than anything else on the grid.

As the top three drivers pointed out, the challenge of Spa is to find a set-up that allows a car to be quick down the straight, in fast corners – including the daunting Eau Rouge, Pouhon and Blanchimont – and in the slow and medium-speed corners. Häkkinen was not particularly superior to his rivals in the first sector of the lap, which includes the slow La Source hairpin, Eau Rouge and two long straights, or in the second, which includes all the medium-speed corners. But he was able to combine that with superb speed in the last sector – incorporating the flat-out Blanchimont sweep and the clumsy Bus Stop chicane, two areas very different in their demands.

Out in the forest, watching the cars through so many of those famous corners, the McLaren's ability was plain to see. It was not only faster than anything else, it also looked it. To paraphrase Mario Andretti talking about the Lotus 79, the car that really started the age when aerodynamics became key in F1, it cornered like it was painted to the road – at least in Häkkinen's hands, anyway. Coulthard was only fifth, nearly a second away. "The balance was fine," DC said. "I just couldn't seem to generate enough grip."

> *'The sweeping bends of Spa were always likely to give the McLaren a stage upon which to demonstrate its superiority'*

Häkkinen played down his qualifying advantage, pointing out that Schumacher had been quick in the first and second sectors on his last run but had to slow down at the Bus Stop because Jean Alesi's spun Prost was stranded in the middle of the road. The fact was, though, that the Ferrari simply was not quick enough.

Trulli, too, was on a quicker lap at the end of the session, only to lose it because of Alesi. The major aerodynamic changes Jordan introduced three races ago were working well, and Jarno was expecting a place in the top five, if not the front row. The Italian was quickest of all in the first sector, which includes Eau Rouge.

Button, though, was the real sensation of Saturday afternoon. He may have raced here before in Formula 3 but, as he said on Friday:

> ***'It's amazing how different it is to run in an F1 car on this track. The right word for it is outrageous. It's a bit of a shock'***

"It is simply amazing how different it is to run in an F1 car on this track. The right word for it is outrageous."

Like Trulli, Button was expecting to be on the third row, not at the front. "It's a bit of a shock," he said. Team-mate Ralf Schumacher, sixth and 0.3s behind, was not impressed. The thoughts of team owner Frank Williams, who has released Button to a Benetton team with a works Renault engine to make way for Juan Pablo Montoya, were not revealed. But Patrick Head, not a man given to hyperbole, could barely contain his enthusiasm for Jenson's performance: "He drives this circuit like Prost used to drive it." Praise indeed.

Schumacher wasn't far away. At the very end of the session, he set his fastest lap, and that scraped him onto the second row alongside Button, and ahead of Coulthard. It took all his genius to do it, though, for Ferrari was in pretty poor shape: a new low-downforce aero package tested successfully at Mugello proved far less efficacious at Spa, and Barrichello never got the car remotely to his liking.

RACE

Spa was at its most majestic throughout the practice days, hot and cloudless, but the teams' highly paid weather forecasters gloomily suggested that everything would change for Sunday, and they were right. The morning dawned misty and wet. Spa's dreaded *mini-clime* had struck again.

It was on the assumption of poor weather that everyone had opted for Bridgestone's softest compound: it would be of help to them in qualifying – and the choice of a dry compound might not be a factor in the race. So long as it was wet, anyway, and it was certainly that during the warm-up, in which Button was again mighty impressive, setting third-best time and infiltrating McLaren-Ferrari territory once more. Häkkinen was fastest, followed by Schumacher, with Barrichello fourth, Coulthard fifth.

There were quite a few incidents in the warm-up, the most serious of which was a sizeable accident to Giancarlo Fisichella who put his left-rear wheel on the white line at the exit of Blanchimont, then overcorrected the consequent slide. The Benetton hit the tyre barrier very hard, bounced off, then tipped over. Giancarlo was quickly out, quite unhurt apart from a bruised knee, but he looked a touch shaky as he walked to the medical car, and no wonder. A check-up revealed nothing awry and he was able to start the race in the spare car.

Villeneuve went off, too, sliding backwards into a barrier which substantially damaged the rear of his BAR. "Any incidents?" someone asked. "Not really," JV said. "Oh, I had a little spin…"

The start at Spa is always frantic, for the first corner – not very far away – is La Source, a hairpin. Häkkinen admitted he was a touch concerned by his unfamiliar neighbours: "It's a different situation this time. I've got new guys around me, and I don't know what they'll do – I mean, I know what Michael does when we get to the first corner! But these guys… they're good and smart, I'm sure they'll be all right."

In the end, the question was academic, for although by two o'clock there had been no rain for a couple of hours, it was announced that there would be a 'safety car start'. Not surprisingly, this news was received with great disappointment, but it was apparently at the request of the drivers, so that was that.

After a single lap of the damp track they were given the signal to

Ralf Schumacher during his lonely race to third for Williams (left); meanwhile, his brother is involved in a do-or-die battle with Häkkinen for the win (right)

FedEx
FedEx

Häkkinen's crew welcomes its hero. It's Häkkinen's most emotional win since his debut success, at Jerez 1997

WHAT HAPPENED NEXT...

Schumacher won the next four GPs – Italy, USA, Japan and Malaysia – to end Ferrari's 21-year-old title drought in the drivers' championship. This was the first of five consecutive titles for the German. Häkkinen, in contrast, would retire after 2001.

go and at once Häkkinen set about capitalising on his pole position, pulling quickly away from Trulli, who soon came under pressure from the eager Button. Schumacher, in fourth, seemed unable to keep with Jenson at this stage.

He was soon back with him, however, for Trulli's third lap was very slow, and caused those following to bunch up behind the Jordan. At the Bus Stop chicane, Michael was able to nip by Button, and then, into La Source, he got by Trulli, too. Jenson thought to do the same, but Jarno came out of the hairpin on a tight line, and the Williams hit the Jordan, knocking it into a spin.

"I think he was too aggressive," Trulli said. "I was struggling with my rear tyres under a heavy fuel load and he'd probably have got past me soon, anyway."

The Jordan was out on the spot, but Button's car was able to continue, albeit not in perfect condition. "It took me too much time to overtake," he said. "And after the contact my steering was heavier than it had been."

Ultimately, Jenson would finish fifth and admitted that, after qualifying third, he was a bit disappointed: "I could have achieved more, but… it's good to have scored some points."

Whatever, in the eyes of most onlookers, his speed at this greatest of GP circuits raised his stock by a considerable amount: if you're quick at Spa, you're a real racing driver.

At the end of lap four, Alesi decided the time was right for dry tyres, and he was in before anyone else. At once Jean began setting new fastest laps and vaulting up the order, so the message was clear. Half the field, including Schumacher, stopped at the end of lap six. Next time round most of the rest, including Häkkinen, were in.

The unfortunate Coulthard had to stay out until the end of lap eight, and one thought that McLaren might have been better to bring him in behind Häkkinen, even if a little queueing were necessary. The lap at Spa is a long one and by the time DC's car had been serviced, it was back in ninth place, behind Frentzen's Jordan. It was to stay there a very long time.

Running dry tyres, on a not completely dry track, Schumacher was quicker than Häkkinen and he began to close in at the rate of 0.5s a lap, sometimes more. On lap 13, Mika spun at Stavelot. For a long time the McLaren slid sideways, almost like a rally car, and it looked as if Häkkinen might save it, but eventually it swapped ends, and by the time it was back on the track, Schumacher was past and gone. Once in front the Ferrari began to go away, sometimes by a second a lap, and the outcome of the Belgian GP looked settled.

On lap 22 – precisely half-distance – Michael came in for his second and final stop, and Mika went back into the lead until lap 27, when he, too, came in. It was now a race to the finish between the pair of them, and the gap was six seconds.

"We made a change to the car on the second stop," Häkkinen said, "and it made the car much faster." He declined to go into detail about the change, but it is thought to have been to the McLaren's electronic differential. Now there were 17 laps to go, and Häkkinen was on a mission. Every time round he took another chunk out of Schumacher's lead, and within 10 laps had cut it from six seconds to a few yards.

Ferrari's day was beginning to unravel, for Barrichello, after setting some blistering lap times, including the fastest of the day on a light fuel load, had retired on lap 33. Rubens had come to a halt in the pit lane entry road, and the team's official explanation was his engine had cut because of a drop in fuel pressure. Fuel pressure tends to drop when there is no fuel left.

As Barrichello disappeared for the day, so, sadly, did Alesi after a magnificent showing at a circuit where sheer driving ability can compensate to some degree for middling machinery. Jean had the Prost-Peugeot as high as fourth, lapping as quickly as Schumacher Jr's Williams, but now he pulled off. Fuel pressure again, apparently.

All eyes were necessarily on Schumacher and Häkkinen, but behind them Ralf ran a solitary third ahead of Coulthard, who had powered by Button's Williams up the hill to Les Combes. Jenson held on to fifth without a problem, for Frentzen's surviving Jordan was too far behind to be a threat.

'Mmm, Michael's car was… too wide on that lap. It was hectic. Not a pleasant moment. I wasn't sure if we'd touched…'

On lap 40 Häkkinen took a run at Schumacher as they headed towards the braking area at the top of the hill, into Les Combes. Michael held to the middle of the road, but still Mika was looking to go by on the inside – at which point the Ferrari chopped him. At 190mph, the two cars almost touched. Häkkinen wasn't impressed.

He does not, however, get into public spats, and never has. "Mmmm, Michael's car was… too wide on that lap. It was hectic. Not a pleasant moment.

"When something like that happens," Mika went on, "you tend to lose concentration briefly. I wasn't sure if we'd touched or not and wondered if maybe my front wing was damaged. For a few corners I didn't run at the maximum, just making sure the car was okay."

It was, and a lap later he again took yards out of Schumacher through Eau Rouge, then stalked him up the long hill – at which point they came upon Zonta, who was in the middle of the track. Ricardo looked in his mirrors, but all he could see was the scarlet of Schumacher, for Häkkinen's McLaren was directly behind the Ferrari. As they neared Les Combes, Michael flicked left to pass the BAR, and a fraction later Mika went right, passing both of them in the process. Later Zonta admitted he had no idea the McLaren was in the vicinity; that being so, it was good he stayed where he was.

Mika's was a move of stunning audacity, perfectly executed. As he followed Häkkinen into the corner, Schumacher knew the race was lost. "Mika did an outstanding manoeuvre," he said. "I really didn't expect it. But if he hadn't passed me then, he'd have done it a lap or two later. I mean, you're allowed to make one move, but even so…"

The pair of them completed the last three laps, Häkkinen taking it comparatively easily now, knowing he was safe. As he took the flag, Ron Dennis showed more emotion than anyone could remember; there were tears in his eyes as he embraced his daughter before walking back from the pit wall to greet his driver.

"I'm sure," he said, "Mika's overtaking manoeuvre will go down as one of the greatest in Formula 1 history."

No one could reasonably argue with that. As Häkkinen laid further bricks in the foundations of a third world championship, we reflected that Spa had been everything that the Hungaroring was not: Grand Prix racing, rather than merely Formula 1. ■

RESULTS

44 LAPS (190.507 MILES)

1	Mika HAKKINEN	McLaren MP4-15	1h28m14.494s
2	Michael SCHUMACHER	Ferrari F12000	1h28m15.598s
3	Ralf SCHUMACHER	Williams FW22	1h28m52.590s
4	David COULTHARD	McLaren MP4-15	1h28m57.775s
5	Jenson BUTTON	Williams FW22	1h29m04.408s
6	Heinz-Harald FRENTZEN	Jordan EJ10	1h29m10.478s

WINNING SPEED 129.536mph

FASTEST LAP Rubens BARRICHELLO, 1m53.803s (136.965mph)

POLE POSITION HAKKINEN, 1m50.646 (140.872mph)

LAP LEADERS HAKKINEN 1-12, 23-27, 41-44; SCHUMACHER 13-22, 28-40

RAIKKONEN WINS a Race of Champions

With the drivers' title already decided, and the grid muddled by a rain-hit qualifying, F1's two hottest shoes knew they could afford to – and must – take risks if they wanted to win this one. Cue a flurry of brilliant moves

BY MARK HUGHES

KIMI RAIKKONEN | 2005 JAPANESE GP | OCTOBER 9
McLAREN MP4-20

Giancarlo Fisichella looks set to win for Renault (below), but he underestimates the speed of his team-mate Fernando Alonso and eventual winner Räikkönen as they charge from mid-grid (below)

QUALIFYING

WITH JUST THE teams' world title left to battle over, fate heavily favoured Renault over McLaren on Saturday. But for many at the track the battle of the giants was not between the two title contenders but Honda and Toyota. As such, the rainfall lottery played out a beautifully poetic ending.

Held on a wet track but with no rain initially falling, it was intermediate tyre territory for most of the session, the track becoming gradually quicker, though still over 15s away from a dry time. But the dark clouds hovered and dropped their load before the hour was up. As such, it turned out that 13th and 14th slots were the ones to have – those of Ralf Schumacher's Toyota and Jenson Button's BAR-Honda.

Ralf had been happy all weekend with the revised TF105B, revelling in a stronger front end, especially on a track he knows so well. Furthermore, the team had opted for a light three-stopping fuel load in contrast to almost everyone else, the weight advantage bringing more time in these conditions than in the dry. Team-mate Jarno Trulli was not as keen on the new car, feeling that its heavier steering compromised his ability to make rapid corrections over a single-lap. That may have been a contributory factor in him dropping the car into the gravel trap at Turn 8 where adverse camber conspired with standing water. Ralf had no such adventure, kept things tidy and his 1m46.106s was 0.3s beneath Christian Klien's earlier benchmark.

On a harder tyre and heavier fuel load than Ralf, Button understeered heavily through the first sector. He went quickest of all in sectors two and three but it wasn't quite enough to overcome his deficit. "I thought it was a slow lap," he said. "I was surprised it put me where it did."

Giancarlo Fisichella was out two cars later than Button but by now the rain was beginning to fall quite hard. Nonetheless he was still fastest of all through the first sector, but thereafter he was fighting a losing battle, the car aquaplaning so badly down the straight between Spoon and 130R that he couldn't even maintain full throttle. It left him third, bumping Klien down a place. It looked and sounded a very committed effort towards the end, apparently flat through 130R in heavy rain on intermediates. "To do that in worsening conditions was an exceptional effort," said Pat Symonds. Fisi was looking very good for the race – as the only truly quick car in a decent grid position.

The other three – team-mate Fernando Alonso and the two McLarens – were punished badly for their Brazilian top-three finishes, which put them out right at the end when the rain was heaviest. Alonso was 16th after trudging around 8s off pole. Räikkönen – penalised for yet another engine failure on Friday – trailed slowly around only to get ahead of those drivers (Trulli and Monteiro) who hadn't recorded a lap. McLaren told Montoya to pit at the end of his lap for fuel strategy reasons.

So we had a topsy-turvy grid. Making the most of a near-ideal running slot, Klien's fourth place came from a sharp, aggressive run in the Red Bull

that included a stunning reaction save into the treacherous Turn 8. Team-mate David Coulthard was first man out and recorded his most impressive qualifying lap of the year. It stood as sixth-fastest, repelling the challenge of many on better running slots. The understeery balance the intermediates gave the car filled him with confidence and he was particularly ballsy through 130R.

Takuma Sato, like team-mate Button, found the BAR-Honda more understeery than he was expecting and was very satisfied with his fifth-fastest time, though frustrated at not being able to take fuller advantage of his Suzuka-special Honda.

Both Williams-BMWs proved an oversteering handful during their early slots. (The FW27s were running their 11th new front wing of the season.) Mark Webber did well in the circumstances to go seventh-fastest, with Antonio Pizzonia 12th after spinning during his out-lap but keeping it running.

Jacques Villeneuve ran a very heavy fuel load in the Sauber and was forced to be conservative through Turn 8 for Trulli's yellow flags (the session should really have been halted while the Toyota was cleared). Nonetheless, using unconventional wet-weather lines, he took the wildly oversteering machine round to eighth-fastest time. Team-mate Felipe Massa, running directly after him, went for a conservative set-up and harder tyres, a combination that gave him excessive understeer, leaving him 0.8s and two places behind.

Had the session required full wets throughout, we probably would have seen Michael Schumacher's Ferrari on a dominant pole. That was the impression given by the very wet morning practice when he'd completed only one lap before spinning out and damaging the car at Turn 3, but that lap nonetheless stood as fastest of the session by over 2s.

Courtesy of his fourth place in Brazil, his slot after Fisichella coincided with the onset of heavy rain, leaving Michael stuck on intermediates. Even so he was still 0.5s up on team-mate Rubens Barrichello in sector one alone despite a much wetter track. Thereafter the heavens opened, leaving him to gingerly complete the lap 14th-quickest, meaning Ayrton Senna's record pole tally is still intact. Barrichello was ninth, appearing to just not get with the programme, and unhappy with the balance. His running slot was between Button's and Fisi's and the analysis from the team suggested that if Schuey had been able to run from that slot he'd have been on the front row.

Narain Karthikeyan, who had been second-fastest in the full wet-tyred morning practice, enjoyed using the conditions to showcase his spectacular car control in the Jordan and was 11th-quickest. Team-mate Monteiro lost it at Turn 8 and would start from the back.

Of the Minardis, Christijan Albers, in 13th, was a couple of places ahead of Robert Doornbos.

RACE

Rev-limiter in seventh as the two cars go side-by-side, tyre sidewalls virtually kissing, into the last lap. And that was only the icing on the cake, the climactic end to 90 minutes of some of the most stunning racing narrative the sport has produced,

SERENGETI® EYEWEAR
www.serengeti-eyewear.com
Stockist enquiry line 020 8391 4700
Serengeti.
The ultimate driving sunglasses.
"INTELLIGENT" PHOTOCHROMIC POLARIZED lenses with a SPECTRAL CONTROL® FILTER for unparalleled glare free vision, high definition contrast and superior colour enhancement. Complete with a BLUE LIGHT FILTER to reduce the eye fatigue caused by driving. Available in PRESCRIPTION.
THE CHOICE OF PATRICK DEMPSEY
Model: Dante
SERENGETI

littered with totems of greatness. That freeze-frame moment in time as Kimi Räikkönen's McLaren-Mercedes sat a few millimetres to the left of Giancarlo Fisichella's Renault at 200mph, a grand prix win on the line, will go down as one of the sport's iconic images.

How the race arrived at this decisive moment was a complex and thrilling roller-coaster story of red raw tests of steely nerve, of racing desire purple intense, of two very, very great drivers triggered into performances beyond even their norm by a particular set of circumstances. Kimi Räikkönen won and Fernando Alonso finished third from 17th and 16th respectively with drives that alternated between heart-in-the-mouth commitment, occasional grudging patience and pure up-for-it desire. They were separated only by an FIA penalty imposed upon Alonso. Between them they put a total of three passing moves on Michael Schumacher driving at the top of his own form albeit in a Ferrari that was never in the same league and in which he ultimately struggled to finish seventh. But if the successors wanted his place, they would have to earn it and he was defensively perfect. Thus on two occasions, the world's three greatest drivers formed a high-speed snake with a red head.

The future overtook the past on lap 20 at 130R, one of only three corners on the F1 calendar worthy of hosting such a moment. The Renault's aerodynamic efficiency and traction gifted Alonso a straight-line advantage of 6mph over Schuey's Ferrari as they approached this moment of truth, blue nose tracking the red car's gearbox as if guided by a heat-seeker as Michael feinted this way and that trying to discourage the move. Engine screaming at 18,000rpm in seventh and still climbing, Michael finally staked his claim to the inside, daring Fernando to try for the long way round. As the Ferrari darted left, Alonso just kept on coming, moving alongside and grinding ahead – but not by enough to cleanly cut across.

He could have backed out of the move. It would have been the act of a reasonable man. This is one of the few situations where a current-day F1 driver can know that the stakes are so high, he's not risking just a wrecked car if it goes wrong. This is a genuine 200mph corner. An interlocking accident here would probably be fatal. It's one of the few places where the sport's raw essence still pokes its head above the parapet. So Alonso turns in from a shallow angle a long way back, thereby giving Schuey maximum notice that he's coming across. He makes for an apex a couple of metres right of the inside kerb and that two metres – the width of an F1 car plus a fag paper – is his survival space. If the Ferrari had begun to run wide, Alonso would have felt the bump and nothing more… ever again.

He was through, in fifth place, and in clean air for the first time. He'd have to do it all over again some laps later. But then he had not expected a straightforward race from where Saturday's rain had dumped him. Same went for Räikkönen, next on Schuey's tail.

At this point the trio were only around 10s adrift of the leader. Which wasn't much 20 laps in after starting from near the back – and that was a product of bold, incisive racecraft on the opening lap, each of them finding gaps in the places supposedly strictly off-limits to feasibility. Fifteenth, 16th and 17th thus became seventh, eighth and 12th within a few corners. Even that wouldn't have been enough to keep them in touch with the lead had it not been for a safety car that kept the field bunched for five laps.

That was triggered by first-lap low tyre pressures, the fact that 130R leads into the chicane (one of the track's few passing places), that the cars bottom out on their low pressures and heavy loads over 130R's bumps, and the usual unreasonable

'This is a genuine 200mph corner. It's one of the few places where the sport's raw essence still pokes its head above the parapet'

racer's ambition. The factors funnelled to a point of conflict behind Schuey at the chicane. Jacques Villeneuve is uncompromising in defence, Alonso irresistible in attack. The heavily fuelled Sauber couldn't be hustled quickly enough through 130R – and Fernando sniffed his next scalp on the run to the chicane. JV refused to accede, and they each outbraked themselves. Alonso went clean over the AstroTurf, Villeneuve bounced across the kerb and onto the grass on the exit.

Jacques was looking to his right at Alonso as he rejoined, irritated that the Renault had got by in this way. Juan Pablo Montoya – who had clipped team-mate Räikkönen as he passed him through the first couple of turns – was moving to pass the momentum-checked Sauber on the left, going for a gap that was likely to be closed by the time he got there. JPM hit the tyre wall hard enough to rip both left-hand wheels off, JV kept going and out came the safety car. Lined up behind it were Ralf, Fisi, Button, DC, Webber, Klien and Michael.

The heady adrenaline-fuelled runs of Alonso and Räikkönen were the brilliant hues of this race and all else rather fell into background detail, just a canvas on which they imprinted themselves. Its structure can be summarised as follows: the safety car made victory feasible for Alonso and Räikkönen by keeping the field bunched at a critical time. Thereby Montoya's accident paved the way for his team-mate's victory. It also rendered junk Ralf's three-stop strategy, preventing him from streaking away in the early laps, dropping him into traffic after he pitted. He'd cease to be a factor after stops on laps 12 and 28, and eventually finish eighth, leaving Fisichella to build a comfortable lead over Button. The BAR again had no race pace, Jenson complaining of entry understeer, exit oversteer. Team-mate Taku Sato went off at the start but rejoined and took out Trulli in a ridiculous passing attempt at the chicane.

Webber passed Coulthard in the pitlane as they each stopped on lap 23, then did the same to Button when they stopped on lap 40. Only a pass by Alonso in the final stint kept Webber off the

podium. By which time everyone but Fisichella had been either passed or leapfrogged by Kimi. Klien slipped out of the picture with a lack of grip, his Red Bull not working as well on hard tyres as Coulthard's on softs, DC going on to finish sixth, hard on Button's tail.

Klien, though, played a decisive role in the destiny of this race. As the safety car pulled in, Schuey got a run on the Red Bull for sixth, passing it around the outside as they approached Turn 1, this giving Michael some brief breathing space from Alonso. Fernando now tracked the Red Bull through the lap and made a move into the chicane that foundered on Klien being super-late on the brakes, obliging Alonso to again cut across the chicane to avoid contact. He backed off, surrendering the place he'd gained illegitimately, before then slipstreaming Klien down to Turn 1 and slipping down the inside. Through the ninth lap, Alonso closed down fast on Schuey, stayed flat through 130R and looked for all the world like he was going to put a move on the Ferrari into the chicane. But then suddenly backed off.

A message had appeared on Renault's pitlane screen from race director Charlie Whiting to the effect that Alonso must surrender his place to Klien – again. Alonso was three seconds down the road from the Red Bull by this time, so far from trying to pass Schuey, he instead had to wait for Christian and let him by. The team had protested that Alonso had already surrendered the place – and back came the message cancelling the previous instruction, saying that it was okay for him to stay ahead. By which time he'd allowed Klien past! So Alonso had to repass again, going into lap 13, after spending a lap at Red Bull speeds.

"The incident in itself cost us 8.8s," said Pat Symonds. But that was only the beginning of it. Alonso was fuelled to run only until the end of lap 22. He'd made that stunning 130R pass on Schuey a couple of laps earlier but the Ferrari was fuelled to run four laps longer, enabling Schuey to leapfrog back ahead. Were it not for the messing about with the phantom penalty, Fernando would have cleared the Ferrari. In fact, the slower traffic he dropped into after his stop – that he would otherwise have avoided – cost him around nine seconds in the five laps after rejoining. It was this that allowed not only Schumacher back in front but also for Räikkönen to get ahead of the Renault for the first time. These three were soon line astern again.

"I felt for the first time this year that I was faster than Kimi," rued Alonso later. In fact their fastest laps were virtually identical – a full second faster than the best of the rest – and if the Renault wasn't faster than the McLaren, these times would suggest it was certainly closer than at any time since the very early season. However, the pace of Kimi early in his last stint, when carrying around 30kg of fuel, suggests that the McLaren's ultimate low-fuel lap time could have been around 0.5s quicker. It looks therefore like the McLaren did have a small but significant speed advantage, but that Alonso's quickest lap was closer to his car's limit than Räikkönen's. The McLaren advantage was perhaps smaller than usual and partly that was down to a strong tailwind down the pit straight that left the McLaren short-geared, Kimi routinely hitting the limiter (in top gear past 200mph) whereas Fernando wasn't.

Räikkönen had not so far managed to pass Schumacher, but in his climb through the field had made up five places on the opening lap before picking off Massa, Pizzonia and Villeneuve. As others pitted ahead of him, so he thrust himself onto Schuey's tail, but could not pass either on track or at the stops and rejoined still on the Ferrari's gearbox. The Ferrari was about 1.2s per lap slower and Kimi was all over it like a bad smell, with Fernando snapping at the McLaren's tail. Schumacher's defence was faultless, and by being able to take a lot of momentum into Turn 1 made himself difficult to pass at the end of the straight. But that's where Räikkönen eventually nailed him, making Michael go defensive down the inside on lap 30 and then simply slicing past around the other side. With 23 laps to go, that put Kimi fourth, 17.5s off the lead and closing down fast on Button and Webber.

Alonso couldn't afford to hang around too long behind the Ferrari and so set about passing Schuey for the second time. He did it beautifully, dummying Michael into thinking he was trying to pass at the chicane, forcing Schuey to run wide there, making the Ferrari slow onto the straight as they began lap 33. It was then relatively simple for Alonso to cut around the outside on the approach to Turn 1. He began setting Räikkönen-matching times, inwardly fuming still at that earlier delay. He'd said after clinching the title in Brazil that he looked forward to being able to drive more aggressively now – and here he was delivering on that promise. But Alonso was fuelled for only three more laps. Although Räikkönen went on for a further nine, it wasn't too costly for Renault as Kimi spent most of those nine laps trapped at Button/Webber pace, costing him around 12s. He got four laps in clean air after they pitted.

Fernando meanwhile passed Button on lap 43 and quickly closed down on Webber. The Williams was performing quite well in the aero sections of

There's no doubting who the crowd's favourite driver is (top), but the pressure rather gets to local hero Takuma Sato (above)

the track but was losing chunks of time out of the traction territories – the hairpin and chicane. On lap 49 Alonso got Webber lined up as they raced down to Turn 1, and made a dive for the inside. Still flat in top, Webber moved right to discourage him, leaving him not quite a car's width. It was a hard, no-compromising move and most anyone but Alonso would have capitulated. Instead, with not enough asphalt to get through, he simply took some grass as well – and as the wheels spun in seventh, he briefly felt the rev-limiter cut in. But he was through, with yet another breathtaking pass.

Through all the red-zone excitement, Fisi continued to run apparently untroubled at the front. He'd come into this race thinking that all he had to do was beat the two slower cars of Ralf and Button – that Alonso and the two McLarens had too many slow cars between them and him to offer a threat. The safety car period, and the time it bought Alonso and Räikkönen, should have triggered him to change his approach. When Ralf pitted from the lead on lap 12, Giancarlo needed now to start building up a margin while he still could. But he didn't. He just continued at a comfortable pace – around 0.6s off the car's fuel-corrected potential.

He made his final stop on lap 38, two after Alonso, seven before Räikkönen, and rejoined in fourth, directly behind the McLaren on the road, though effectively around 20s in front with 15 laps to go. Enough, surely? As it turned out, no.

Upon rejoining and sensing a possible rout, Kimi began lapping at an extraordinary rate. Given that he was carrying around 50kg of fuel, you'd expect times of around 1m32.6s, getting faster by a 0.15s each lap. In fact his two post-stop flying laps were 1m31.8s and 1m31.9s. Even allowing for a tweak in power on the fuel mapping, this was a stunning effort that appeared to blow Fisi's resolve.

"Honestly, I was pushing 100 per cent as he was catching me," a crestfallen Fisichella insisted. "He was just much quicker. I was struggling with the rear end in slow-speed corners and with traction. He seemed to have better traction out of the hairpin and chicane. He was just quicker, as usual. What can I do?"

Yes, the McLaren was probably quicker. But that wouldn't have mattered had Fisichella pushed harder earlier. The fact that he hadn't was reflected in a fastest lap that was almost a second shy of Alonso's. With three laps to go, Fisi's mirrors were full of Räikkönen and he began defending into the chicane, even when the McLaren wasn't really 'there'. It was this that was his final undoing. Going in too deep on the chicane's defensive line as they approached the start of the final lap, Fisi ran out wide and was slow onto the straight.

Kimi could barely contain himself. Catching, catching all the way down that straight, so we pick up at that iconic freeze-frame moment. Let the tape run and the McLaren goes around the outside, takes the lead. This can be a magnificent sport. ■

RESULTS

53 LAPS (191.117 MILES)

1	Kimi RAIKKONEN	McLaren MP4-20	1h29m02.212s
2	Giancarlo FISICHELLA	Renault R25	1h29m03.845s
3	Fernando ALONSO	Renault R25	1h29m19.668s
4	Mark WEBBER	Williams FW27	1h29m24.486s
5	Jenson BUTTON	BAR 007	1h29m31.719s
6	David COULTHARD	Red Bull RB1	1h29m33.813s
7	Michael SCHUMACHER	Ferrari F2005	1h29m36.091s
8	Ralf SCHUMACHER	Toyota TF105B	1h29m51.760s

WINNING SPEED 128.790mph

FASTEST LAP RAIKKONEN, 1m31.540s (141.904mph)

POLE POSITION R SCHUMACHER, 1m46.106s (122.424mph)

LAP LEADERS R SCHUMACHER 1-12; FISICHELLA 13-20, 27-38, 46-52; BUTTON 21-22, 39-40; COULTHARD 23; M SCHUMACHER 24-26; RAIKKONEN 41-45, 53

McLaren team boss can't wait to praise Räikkönen (above); Michael Schumacher drives brilliantly, but is completely overshadowed (top left)

WHAT HAPPENED NEXT...

Räikkonen and Alonso went head-to-head again, this time in China – and with the manufacturers' championship still at stake (see the next page).

ALONSO SEALS TEAM DREAM

It's a necessarily selfish business: F1 driver. But it's a team sport, too. These factors can be uncomfortable bedfellows, as Spain's star has proved. But this victory was definitely 'one for the guys'

BY MARK HUGHES

FERNANDO ALONSO | 2005 CHINESE GP | 16 OCTOBER RENAULT R25

The spectacular architecture of Shanghai is the epitome of the new-era Formula One circuits

QUALIFYING

IF McLAREN LOOKS back this year on the different points at which the team lost the championship, its car's inability to use its tyres hard enough over a qualifying lap in the first three events will be right up there. Although it was a problem largely corrected by Imola, the ghost of that characteristic reappeared whenever the track surface wasn't offering up much in the way of grip. Just like at Shanghai on Saturday. Result: a Renault one-two on the grid.

"Yeah," admitted Kimi Räikkönen after a lap that included two moments wrestling a recalcitrant front end into a slow-corner apex, "we had difficulty getting our tyres to work straight away, even though I'm confident they'll be good in the race."

One year in, this is still an unusual track surface. Last year it was put down to its newness, to bitumen that hadn't quite sunk through the stones. This year that didn't apply. It was a bit dusty from the preceding Porsche session, but that's often the case at other tracks, too. No one offered a convincing explanation for the anomalous surface.

Whatever, it meant Räikkönen had no front-end grip, and the Renaults did. Fernando Alonso – his every move saying that, since Brazil, he's felt released, able to do anything, confidence surfing a massive wave – made full use of the opportunity to take pole with a flawless-looking lap. Team-mate Giancarlo Fisichella admitted to being too conservative into Turn 1 and making a follow-on error into 2. That accounted for the 0.4sec difference between the two Renaults but, critically, it was still enough to give the first all-Renault front row since Malaysia 2003.

Juan Pablo Montoya was the second man out on account of his early bath in Japan, and so McLaren loaded him up slightly heavier on fuel and made his the only car in the field on the harder of the two Michelin choices. He coped well in the circumstances to be just 0.6sec off Räikkönen, but it wasn't enough to put him on the second row. Fourth was snatched off him by Jenson Button.

With a graceful lap of flowing momentum, Button wrung all there was from the BAR-Honda. "I was very pleased with that," he said. "There was a bit of understeer, but generally we got everything out of the car on that lap."

It certainly looked that way. Team-mate Takuma Sato was first man out and, anticipating the time penalty of this, he was loaded with a lot of fuel, a combination that left him 17th, despite his new-spec 965bhp Honda with revised camshaft and new inlet port.

Michael Schumacher made a good recovery from an overcommitment into the first turn that took him out wide. Not only did he somehow retain the Ferrari's momentum, but he was very quick in the final sector, making good use of his soft Bridgestones to go sixth. Team-mate Rubens Barrichello, on the same-spec tyres, ended his final qualifying session for Ferrari around where he's spent most of the others – 0.3sec and a couple of places behind.

Splitting the red cars was David Coulthard's quite fuel-light Red Bull, which had proved very well balanced all weekend. Christian Klien spoiled his lap with a big oversteering moment at Turn 3 when he hooked his front wheel inside the kerb, throwing it wildly off line. It left him back in 14th.

Ralf Schumacher, struggling with an understeering Toyota, was forced to lift twice through Turns 12 and 13, the long entry onto the critically long back straight. This had been the TF105B's limiting factor all weekend, and even final set-up changes that were expected to give strong oversteer failed to change the characteristic. It all left the Suzuka pole-sitter 1.6sec adrift in ninth. Team-mate Jarno Trulli had also had to contend with an early running slot, and was 12th.

Mark Webber rounded out the top 10 in his Williams-BMW, but

it could've been significantly better had he not run too deep into the heavy braking zone of Turn 14. Up until that point, his busy, hustling style – a lightning fast oversteer save through Turn 8 – had the FW27 looking good for around sixth-fastest. Antonio Pizzonia – 13th, 0.7sec slower than even Webber's error-spoiled lap – perhaps suffered because of his early running slot. But it wasn't the sort of lap designed to save his Formula 1 career, either.

Felipe Massa managed to get some sense out of a Sauber for the first time all weekend during his qualifying lap. Up until then its balance had been inconsistent on new tyres, and both drivers were struggling. Key set-up changes on the eve of the session paid off, enabling him to record a respectable 11th-best time. By contrast team-mate Jacques Villeneuve, despite quite radical set-up changes, found his car no better than it had been through the practices. He was a full 0.9sec slower and languishing way down in 16th.

Narain Karthikeyan went fast enough in a Jordan filled with an extremely light load of fuel to sneak ahead of Villeneuve for 15th. This was despite choosing the harder of the Bridgestone compounds, in common with his team-mate and the Minardis, but in contrast to the Ferraris. Running around 50kg heavier (around two seconds-worth of the 2.5sec difference), Tiago Monteiro was 19th in the other Jordan.

Christijan Albers was the quicker of the Minardis in 18th, with Robert Doornbos bringing up the rear.

RACE

Maybe, just maybe, Narain Karthikeyan's lap 30 accident cost McLaren the constructors' championship. But it's doubtful. Maybe, just maybe, McLaren had the legs of Renault here like it usually has. We didn't get to find out for sure, the timing of the two safety cars meaning the race never really got to play out, the McLaren didn't get to stretch its legs. But again it's doubtful. No, the best evidence suggests that Renault came here for a constructors' title-decider with a genuinely faster car than its rival – for perhaps the first time all year. The team attacked its task and won in style.

Fernando Alonso pulled into the prized centre spot of the post-race collecting area and hung his revised V10 – 15bhp up on what he had in Japan thanks to an upgrade based on having to last only one event – on the rev-limiter for more than 10 celebratory seconds, a climax of a stunning season. Engine overheated, mixture leaned out, there was even a small post-coital fire at the Renault's rear.

> ***'Yes, the car was very fast at the end, but it was very difficult to drive at the beginning. It became fast about 40 laps too late'***

The general assumption was that McLaren was fuelled heavier, doing its usual thing of converting a raw pace advantage into a better race strategy. That remained the assumption after the race because the first safety car – triggered on lap 18 after a drain cover was dislodged from the Turn 10 kerbing – came out before either car had made its first stop, and because both then used that safety car as an opportunity to pit early. But actually Alonso had been fuelled to run until lap 23, exactly the same as Räikkönen. Renault had sewn up the front row, in other words, on the same weight as McLaren.

Although Räikkönen set the race's fastest lap on the final time around in his forlorn late chase of Alonso, it was only 0.3sec faster than that set by Alonso when he still had 11 laps of fuel on board. Eleven laps-worth of fuel around Shanghai would account for around 0.5sec. Even allowing for a bit of tyre degradation, the Renault was every bit as fast as the McLaren at their respective peaks – and seemed genuinely faster most of the time. "Yes, the car was fast at the end," said Räikkönen, "but it was very difficult to drive at the beginning. It became fast about 40 laps too late."

McLaren boss Ron Dennis, understandably feeling the pain of losing, suggested that the safety cars had prevented McLaren from demonstrating its superior strategy. But he was assuming that Alonso had been coming in on the very lap the first safety car was deployed, and that was a false assumption.

Besides which, Räikkönen was almost 20sec behind Alonso by that time. If anyone was robbed by that first safety car, it was Alonso. All the cushion that team-mate Giancarlo Fisichella had bought him by apparently holding back the pack was wiped out by its deployment. Furthermore, the fact that Alonso stopped first allowed McLaren to measure how long the Renault rig was attached – and then to fuel Räikkönen longer. An estimated 15kg extra went into the McLaren's tank, five extra laps. *Now* it was on a better strategy.

That being the case, all Räikkönen had to do was wait for Alonso and Fisichella to make their second stops, then let rip for those five laps. That would have bought him around eight seconds. So, as long as he was less than eight seconds behind Alonso when the Spaniard made his second stop, he'd jump him. But that was to reckon without Fisichella, Alonso's prized buffer.

Had it not been for the second safety car – deployed on lap 30 after Karthikeyan's Jordan had a huge shunt – Alonso would have made his second stop around lap 46. You can bet that Fisichella would have ensured Kimi was more than eight seconds behind Alonso at the critical time.

Fisichella played his part for Renault perfectly. From second on the grid he robustly forced Räikkönen out wide at the start and set Alonso free. For most of the first stint he lapped around a second per lap off his potential. His team-mate disappeared into the distance, the two silver cars sat on his tail. But not that closely. The McLarens had nowhere near enough straight-line speed to put a pass on the Renault and nor were they balanced enough through the turns to get a run going on the exits.

They may have been running a little more wing, but the main reason for the McLarens' straight-line deficit was almost certainly engine performance. Räikkönen's was a two-race-spec unit that had been through an extremely tough Japanese Grand Prix. Those in the Renaults were not only fresh but had been developed specifically for one-race duration only. "Yes, there were parts on it that would not have lasted two races," confirmed engine tech director Rob White. "During qualifying we were able to use more revs than I think has ever been seen in Formula 1 [19,250rpm] and, yes, I'm pretty sure we had an engine performance advantage here."

Given that an F1 engine typically loses around 15bhp over the course of a race weekend, and that the one-race-spec had found Renault a 15bhp boost, it's quite conceivable that Renault was running with 30bhp over McLaren-Mercedes throughout the weekend, a net swing of around 0.3sec of lap time. That engine performance was also worth its weight in gold when defending on race day.

Then there was the fact that the McLaren didn't seem as balanced. Although Alonso felt his Renault oversteery through the first stint (necessitating an increase in front tyre pressures at his first stop), he could still get more of a tune from it than could Räikkönen from his car. There was still some of the reluctant front end that had been evident in qualifying. The track never really did rubber-in as expected, and this seemed to hurt the McLaren more than the Renault.

In fact Montoya, despite his harder compound rubber, looked for all the world as if he could've gone quicker than Räikkönen. Running all the first 18 laps tight in his team-mate's slipstream, he didn't spot the upturned drain cover on the exit kerbs of Turn 10 until it was too late. The car took a heavy whack, punching a hole in the chassis and damaging the right-front tyre. As he pitted to replace the damaged tyre, the safety car was scrambled and almost everyone took the opportunity of making their first stop.

Which was bad news for those – notably Jenson Button and David Coulthard – who had been running not far behind the two

Narain Karthikeyan's huge accident wrecked his Jordan and closed up the field (above); even so, Kimi Räikkönen (below) could do nothing about Alonso

Alonso and Renault team boss Flavio Briatore celebrate (below and right); Alonso signals that this is his seventh win of a successful campaign (bottom)

WHAT HAPPENED NEXT...

Alonso made the shock announcement that he would be a McLaren driver in 2007. Despite this, he and Renault kept their eye on the ball in 2006 to beat Michael Schumacher and Ferrari to the titles.

on the exit of Turn 13, in fourth gear and at 135mph. The Bridgestones were taking a long time to come back up to temperature and pressure after the safety car – the same reason Barrichello was holding up those behind him – and Narain was still struggling with them. "I was following [Jarno] Trulli," he said. "I got onto the artificial grass and that just sucked me into the wall." It was a big impact, bits of Jordan spread across the width of the track.

Not everyone pitted this time. Ralf Schumacher's Toyota, Felipe Massa's Sauber and Christian Klien's Red Bull stayed out. Which meant they were between Alonso and Räikkönen upon the resumption of racing. Kimi had leapfrogged 'Fisi' through not needing as much fuel on account of having fuelled longer at the first stops, but any realistic prospect of catching Alonso was now effectively over. "We turned the revs right down at this point," said Alonso, "and just chilled out."

Fisichella vaguely tracked Räikkönen at this point but his work for the day was effectively over. He'd performed his role to perfection,

'Michael Schumacher's day started badly when on his drive to the grid he was taken out by Albers' Minardi, a bizarre crash'

including stacking the field up behind him at the first stops. The FIA had issued a warning after Räikkönen did a similar thing at Spa, to the effect that unreasonable obstruction under these circumstances would be penalised in future, but it was vaguely worded. It was decreed that Fisi had transgressed this vague rule and he was issued with a stop/go late in the race. This dropped him behind Ralf Schumacher and ensured the Toyota got a podium.

"We got a lucky break with the safety car," said Ralf, "just as we were unlucky with it last time." It was luck, but Toyota reacted well, like a seasoned, savvy race team. "After the first stops we had lost a lot of time stuck behind Barrichello," explained Mike Gascoyne, "and we wanted to avoid a repeat of that."

Sure enough, Barrichello's tyres were again slow to come back up to temperature after pitting under the safety car thereby delaying the closely following Webber, Button and Coulthard. In the four laps between the resumption of racing and Ralf's stop, the German was able to build up the cushion necessary to clear them. As were Klien and Massa.

Klien was running spectacularly quickly on low fuel, setting a best lap just 0.5sec off Räikkönen's. Running a lap longer even than Massa, he was able to leapfrog the Sauber for fifth.

Massa was left fending off a charging Webber through the race's closing stages but the Williams' lack of straight-line speed meant Felipe held onto sixth.

"We lost so much time behind Barrichello," rued Webber, a sentiment echoed by eighth- and ninth-place finishers Button and Coulthard, whose races never really recovered from having stopped just before the first safety car. Rubens defended hard but eventually the pressure and the high tyre wear led him to lock up both his font wheels into Turn 14, obliging him to stop for a replacement tyre, thereby dropping him to 12th.

But that was a much better performance than that of the other Ferrari driver. Michael Schumacher's day started badly when on his drive to the grid he was taken out by Albers' Minardi, a bizarre crash that wrecked both cars and for which Schumacher was held to blame. Starting in the spare from the pitlane, and on worn tyres used during practice, he made no progress, unable even to pass Tiago Monteiro's Jordan. Then, just to bring his perfect day and perfect year to an end, he spun out under the safety car while trying to warm his brakes. What a difference a year makes. ■

McLarens who had already pitted. The Renaults got out still running one-two from Kimi, with Rubens Barrichello now up to fourth and having to defend heavily from Ralf Schumacher's Toyota and Mark Webber's Williams upon the resumption of racing five laps later.

After falling out of the running, Montoya then fell out of the race with an engine failure that was unrelated to the drain cover incident, but may be not unrelated to running in the hot air of a slipstream for so many laps, followed immediately by two pitstops.

This of course put a very different complexion on the battle for the constructors' championship. Renault's two-point cushion going into this race meant it could even afford now to let Räikkönen win, so long as Alonso and Fisichella filled the podium.

So it almost didn't matter when the second safety car came out just five laps after the first one had come in. Karthikeyan had lost it

RESULTS

56 LAPS (189.559 MILES)

1	Fernando ALONSO	Renault R25	1h39m53.618s
2	Kimi RAIKKONEN	McLaren MP4-20	1h39m57.633s
3	Ralf SCHUMACHER	Toyota TF105B	1h40m18.994s
4	Giancarlo FISICHELLA	Renault R25	1h40m19.732s
5	Christian KLIEN	Red Bull RB1	1h40m25.457s
6	Felipe MASSA	Sauber C24	1h40m30.018s
7	Mark WEBBER	Williams FW27	1h40m30.460s
8	Jenson BUTTON	BAR 007	1h40m34.867s

WINNING SPEED 113.857mph

FASTEST LAP RAIKKONEN, 1m33.242s (130.773mph)

POLE POSITION ALONSO, 1m34.080s (129.608mph)

LAP LEADERS ALONSO 1-56

INDEX

Editor Paul Fearnley
Art Editor Emily Canino
Managing Editor Peter Hodges
Sub Editors Marcus Simmons, Henry Hope-Frost
Executive Editor Andrew van de Burgt

Display sales Tina Vyas, Michael Gooch, Nyan Amer, Karen McCarthy
Ad sales Manager Pierre Clements
Ad Director Matthew Witham

Production Saba Bonser

Publishing Manager Sam Jempson
Publisher Rob Aherne
Publishing Director Peter Higham

Photography LAT, DPPI
Origination Colour Systems
Printed by Wyndeham Heron Ltd
Distributed by Frontline Ltd

Published by Haymarket Consumer Media, Teddington Studios, Broom Road, Teddington, Middlesex TW11 9BE

haymarket
Haymarket is certified by BSI to environmental standard ISO14001